# JOHN MIL1
# AND THE TRANSFORMATION
# OF ANCIENT EPIC

For a list of other titles in the BCPaperback series
see the end of the book.

# JOHN MILTON

## AND THE
## TRANSFORMATION OF
## ANCIENT EPIC

*Charles Martindale*

Second Edition

Bristol Classical Press

This edition published in 2002 by
Bristol Classical Press
and imprint of
Gerald Duckworth & Co. Ltd.
61 Frith Street, London W1D 3JL
Tel: 020 7434 4242
Fax: 020 7434 4420
inquiries@duckworth-publishers.co.uk
www.ducknet.co.uk

First published in 1986 by
Croom Helm Ltd

A catalogue record for this book is available
from the British Library

ISBN 1 85399 650 5

Cover illustration: 'The Expulsion' by Nicholas Chapron, after Raphael.
Whitworth Art Gallery, Manchester.

Printed and bound in Great Britain by
Booksprint

# CONTENTS

In Memoriam
Vivienne Levy (1922–1985)

                          sad task, yet argument
Not less but more heroic than the wrath
Of stern Achilles on his foe pursued
Thrice fugitive about Troy wall, or rage
Of Turnus for Lavinia disespoused,
Or Neptune's ire, or Juno's, that so long
Perplexed the Greek and Cytherea's son.

*Paradise Lost* IX. 13–19

# ACKNOWLEDGEMENTS

I have re-used some material from my previous writing on Milton. In particular Chapters 4 and 5 are based on earlier articles: 'Paradise Metamorphosed: Ovid in Milton', which appeared in *Comparative Literature*, vol. 37 (1985), pp. 301-33, and 'The Epic of Ideas: Lucan's *De bello civili* and *Paradise Lost*', *Comparative Criticism*, vol. 3 (1981), pp. 133-56, published by Cambridge University Press. Fuller documentation on certain points will be found in the original articles. I have also included material from 'A Homeric Formula in Milton', *Notes and Queries*, vol. 24 (1977), pp. 545-7; 'Milton and the Heroic Simile', *Comparative Literature*, vol. 33 (1981), pp. 224-38 (the basis of the second section of Chapter 3); 'Unlocking the Word-hoard: in Praise of Metaphrase', *Comparative Criticism*, vol. 6 (1984), pp. 47-72; and the Introduction to *Virgil and his Influence*, Bristol Classical Press, 1984, pp. 1-24. I am grateful to the various editors and publishers for permission to republish. The quotation from David Jones appears by kind permission of Agenda Publications.

# PREFACE

There are many things that one can do in a preface; one of the best is to try to pre-empt one's critics.

The Bible teaches us that 'of making many books there is no end'. Certainly what has been called the Milton industry continues without visible sign of abatement. Why then another book on *Paradise Lost*? A lofty justification would be that one is extending the frontiers of knowledge. This book, however, makes no claim to novelty, though I hope that in the course of it I have adduced some fresh illustrative material and offered new readings of some passages in *Paradise Lost*. The essential aim is rather a conservative one: to re-assert old truths that are in danger of neglect. A mountain of innovative scholarship — one might be tempted to call it a mausoleum — has been piled over *Paradise Lost*; if no more I hope to have pulled down some part of it again. If Milton had read all that has been claimed for him, it is doubtful whether he would have found time to write many words.

In this regard I have found as much illumination in earlier critics as in those most fashionable today. It is curious that in this relativist age literary criticism is so often viewed teleologically. Yet the opinions of Dr Johnson or Keats or Coleridge are quite as worth pondering as those of C.S. Lewis or Christopher Ricks or Stanley Fish, three whom I name *honoris causa* as the authors of what are perhaps the finest book-length studies of *Paradise Lost* written in this century. The best short introduction to the poem probably remains the collection of papers by Addison first published in *The Spectator* in 1712. Addison brought to Milton an easy familiarity with classical texts. If I share nothing else with Milton's earliest readers,I share the experience of coming to Milton only after years of living with the epics of Homer and Virgil. At any rate this brings a difference of perspective from that of most of Milton's modern readers.

I have treated each of the four classical poets concerned in separate chapters. This has some disadvantages. In particular Homer and Virgil came to Milton not independently but in intricate combination, so that separate treatment involves some artificiality.

Likewise at times repetition of the argument is necessary in a way that might have been avoided with a different arrangement. The advantage is that each chapter largely stands on its own, and can be read separately by readers interested in only part of the subject.

I have tried to keep annotations within bounds; exhaustive bibliography can too easily become a scholarly self-indulgence. As my old tutor Ian Crombie wrote, 'books exist to be learnt from'. Much in these pages I learned from the writings of others, and though, where I am able, I normally try to record my debts, often I can no longer remember where I first encountered a particular view or piece of information. The experienced scholar will know better than I where I am in agreement or disagreement with others; to most readers it scarcely matters. The literature on the five great poets treated in this book is vast; I make little apology for having read only a fraction of it.[1] Doubtless had I read more I would have avoided errors, but equally I might never have found the time to write this book.

I owe much to many: to those who at Oxford persuaded me to enter, light-heartedly, for the Passmore Edwards Prize (on classics and English literature) which launched me on a voyage of discovery of which this book is part of the fruit; to my mother, whose dislike of Milton encouraged me to try to prove her wrong; to the University of Sussex for compelling me to move outside my original specialisms. Other debts are more conventional. I have learned from students at Sussex whom I have taught various courses that treat the classical influence on later poetry. It was with the needs of them, and of those like them, in mind that this book was conceived: the needs, that is, of those whose classical education is circumscribed through no fault of their own but who are prepared to read the ancients in translation to gain fuller understanding of what the European tradition means. A. D. Nuttall first suggested the idea of this book to me — he would himself have been the ideal author of it — and has helped me at many stages thereafter. My sister Dr Joanna Parker lent me her Oxford D.Phil. thesis on the influence of Horace in the seventeenth century (scandalously unpublished) and advised me on several points. I am also grateful to Dr Robert Parker for reading my manuscript, to the members of the Renaissance Seminar of the University of Sussex, in particular Stephen Medcalf, for listening to parts of it and offering their comments, and to Kay Smith for typing it. But my greatest debt is to my wife Michelle. Her assistance goes far beyond that encouragement given with fortitude by a loyal wife of which so many prefaces speak; I have discussed every point with her, and she deserves to be regarded as joint author. Thus, in presenting the book to her, of her own do I give her. The mistakes which the various readers of my manuscript did not spot are of course my own.

C.A.M.

Shoreham-by-Sea

## Notes

In citations spelling and punctuation are modernised throughout (I give page numbers to standard modern editions for ease of reference). Translations are also my own unless otherwise stated.

1. New books and articles on Milton appear constantly (*Milton Quarterly* provides information on recent publications). In particular Claes Schaar's important and learned study *The full Voic'd Quire Below* came into my hands only after this book was finished, and its argument thus could not be taken into direct account in the text (I have incorporated references to Schaar's discussions in the notes). In general Schaar's concept of 'infracontext' seems to me to evade, not solve, the problem of what constitutes an allusion, and I am consequently unpersuaded of the relevance of much of the learning deployed. Moreover his highly iconographic reading receives little real support from Milton's earliest commentators and critics. Nevertheless, the book remains a useful guide to possible sources, parallels and analogues. Richard J. Du Rocher's interesting *Milton and Ovid* (Cornell University Press, 1985) appeared when this book was already in proof; it includes a useful appendix of verbal echoes.

# PREFACE
# TO THE SECOND EDITION

There is a special magic about the publication of one's first book, as about the birth of one's first child. I am therefore grateful to Bristol Classical Press for the opportunity to republish. If I were writing this book today, it would necessarily be rather different – more postmodernist in both style and doctrine. Piecemeal alteration, however, would serve no useful purpose. I have accordingly included a list of minor errors and misprints on p. xiv, but left the text as it was. I find that I am not unduly ashamed of what I have written; fashions in criticism change, but great literature abides.

Much valuable work on Milton has appeared since this book was first published. Among studies of particular relevance to the subject I would cite in particular:

Richard J. DuRocher, *Milton and Ovid* (Ithaca NY & London, 1985) – but see my review in *Comparative Literature* 39 (1987) 181-3.

William M. Porter, *Reading the Classics and 'Paradise Lost'* (Lincoln NB, 1993).

Colin Burrow, *Epic Romance: Homer to Milton* (Oxford, 1993).

John K. Hale, *Milton's Languages: The Impact of Multilingualism on Style* (Cambridge UK & New York, 1997).

David Norbrook, *Writing the English Republic: Poetry, Rhetoric and Politics, 1627-1660* (Cambridge, 1999), ch. 10 on Milton and Lucan.

Clifton                                                                                    C.A.M.
July 2002

# Corrigenda

p. 1 line 6: *for* any way *read* anyway

p. 18 line 2 from foot; p. 71 line 7 from foot, p. 108 lines 17 & 11 from foot; p. 109 lines 2, 11 & 16: *for* La Cerda *read* de la Cerda

p. 19 line 6: *for* aid *read* end

p. 20 lines 24-5: *for* common sense and judgement *read* the exercise of judgement

p. 23 line 1: *for* 'tis *read* 'tis

p. 27 line 3 from foot: *for* o'erfraught *read* o'erfraught

p. 29 line 12: *for* the climax of the action *read* the account of the Fall

p. 57 lines 11-12: *for* Chapman ... notes *read* Chapman used the Latin translation and notes in Spondanus' edition

p. 58 line 12: *after* Gabriel *insert* (Gabriel in Hebrew means 'might of God')

p. 62 last line; p. 115 line 21: *for* O'er *read* O'er

p. 66 line 21: *for* much *read* some

p. 77 line 9: *for* 'Twere *read* 'Twere

p. 82 line 18; p. 189 line 4: *for* one-dimensional *read* two-dimensional

p. 90 line 26: *for* new fallen *read* new fall'n

p. 100 line 18: *for* comprison *read* comparison

p. 107 line 5 from foot: *for* republican *read* historian

p. 108 lines 8 & 6 from foot: *for* La Cerda *read* De la Cerda

p. 116 line 6: *for* such writing *read* writing like this

p. 116 line 6 from foot: *for* 'Advancing' *read* 'advancing'

p. 134 line 8: *for* 'twas *read* 'twas

p. 148 line 15: *for* lautus *read* 'lautus'

p. 151 n. 50 line 7: *for* Atro lumine *read* 'atro lumine'

p. 224 line 22: *for* fortitude O *read* fortitude / O

p. 226 n. 23: *add at end* This preface may derive from material left by Rowe.

# 1

# INTRODUCTION

## The Limits of Allusion

Milton was a formidably learned man, capable of correcting classical texts and of writing accomplished poetry in Latin and Italian. But it would be wrong to conclude that *Paradise Lost* is a recherché poem, designed for the scholarly only ('the last reward of consummated scholarship' in Mark Pattison's discouraging phrase), or to take too literal-mindedly Milton's claim (any way a commonplace) that he wrote it for 'fit audience . . . though few' (VII.31). Addison concedes — and, perhaps rightly, regards as a fault — Milton's occasional ostentation of learning in technical matters such as astronomy, geography and theology.[1] But in *Spectator* 70, in a discussion of ballads, he treats *Paradise Lost* as having like them a universal appeal: 'Homer, Virgil or Milton, so far as the language of their poems is understood, will please a reader of plain common sense, who would neither relish nor comprehend an epigram of Martial or a poem of Cowley.'[2] Modern scholars have something of a vested interest in exaggerating the learning of *Paradise Lost* and in multiplying sources and allusions. Milton certainly expects his readers to have a thorough familiarity with the Bible and a decent working knowledge of classical poetry, in particular the epics of Homer and Virgil and the *Metamorphoses* of Ovid, but in a seventeenth-century context that is far from being a learned requirement, since these were works which, in the most literal sense, every schoolboy knew.

In general the number of allusions in *Paradise Lost* has been overestimated. It is not sufficient to show a vague general similarity with some other text, nor is allusion the same as 'influence', about which, given the mysterious alchemy of poetic creation, there must always be a large measure of uncertainty. Allusion implies conscious design by the writer, and, if the writer is playing fair, should be to something which a properly informed reader has a reasonable chance of recalling. It is thus important to consider whether the original passage is celebrated or memorable; in other

1

words how likely it is to be in a competent reader's repertoire. In general the eighteenth-century critics who had the classics in their blood are better guides than many moderns to whom one passage in Homer or Virgil is as foreign as another, and who in consequence are inclined to be overawed by Milton's classical learning and thus to exaggerate it.

Where a passage from classical poetry was widely familiar Milton could allude to it with confidence. For instance one of the most celebrated statements in the *Metamorphoses* is Medea's notorious 'video meliora proboque, / deteriora sequor' (VII. 20–1, I see and approve the better, but follow the worse). Milton wittily makes Adam invert the sentiment in VIII. 610–11 'yet still free / Approve the best, and follow what I approve'. The allusion may be ironic in view of the sequel, for Adam is eventually to follow the worse course when he eats the forbidden fruit.[3] Again no one who has read it in Latin is likely to forget the grim response of the Sibyl to Aeneas' request to descend to the Underworld (*Aen.* VI. 126–9):

> Tros Anchisiade, facilis descensus Averni (Averno in modern editions)
> noctes atque dies patet atri ianua Ditis;
> sed revocare gradum superasque evadere ad auras,
> hoc opus, hic labor est.

> (Trojan son of Anchises, easy is the descent to Avernus — night and day the door of black Dis is open. But to recall one's step and get out to the air above, this is the task, this the toil.)

In the Renaissance the lines were as hackneyed as the opening of Hamlet's soliloquy 'To be or not to be' is today. For example Spenser had cleverly fused them with Christ's doctrine of the two ways (Matthew 7: 13–14) in *Faerie Queene* II. 3. 41. 7–9:

> But easy is the way and passage plain
> To pleasure's palace; it may soon be spied,
> And day and night her doors to all stand open wide.

Accordingly Milton can perform ingenious variations on the familiar Virgilian theme. In II. 81 Moloch inverts the Sibyl's sentiments, arguing that, since for angels the natural motion is upwards, they can readily return to heaven: 'The ascent is easy then.' The ironic presence of the allusion mocks Moloch's arrogant certainties. Later in the same book (432–3) the Sibyl's words are again recalled when Satan makes his offer to journey to earth: 'long is the way / And hard that out of hell leads up to light.' Satan, as often, here indulges in self-dramatising heroics as he seeks to present himself as the worthy hero of his own story. It is only Milton who in III. 19ff can use the Sibyl's words with integrity:

> Taught by the heavenly Muse to venture down
> The dark descent, and up to reascend,
> Though hard and rare.

It is not Satan but Milton who, like Aeneas, guided by heaven goes down to hell to emerge again unscathed.

Similarly Milton three times recalls another celebrated and resonant Virgilian line. In *Aeneid* I. 11 Virgil tells the Muse to explain why the good Aeneas underwent such suffering, and asks whether gods can be so angry: 'tantaene animis caelestibus irae?' While the immediate reference is to Juno's anger with Aeneas, the question strikes at the heart of belief in divine justice, and the doubts which it raises ramify throughout the whole poem and are never quite laid to rest. La Cerda, whose edition as we shall see might have been consulted by Milton, rightly observes that Virgil is implying a criticism of the gods: 'as though he said: are even the gods angry? It is not fitting.' Milton imitates the line straightforwardly in VI. 788 as the devils take the field against the armies of God: 'In heavenly spirits could such perverseness dwell?' Satan's role in *Paradise Lost* to some extent corresponds to Juno's in the *Aeneid* as the main heavenly opponent of the human protagonist. In IX. 729–30 Satan produces a variant in his attempt to persuade Eve to eat the apple; God could have no good reason, he argues, to object if man gained knowledge: 'Or is it envy, and can envy dwell / In heavenly breasts?' The obvious irony is that, whereas God could feel no envy, Satan both can and does. Virgil's anguished question, which raises the issue of theodicy and points to a pessimism that lies near the heart of the *Aeneid*, could for Milton have only one answer, as the third, most oblique allusion to it makes clear. In III. 216 the Father asks if anyone could pay the price of man's sin: 'Dwells in all heaven charity so dear?' This is a very different question from Virgil's and one that admits of a very different answer. The Son then makes his saving offer of the Atonement, and we know that in the end, in the Father's words, 'So heavenly love shall outdo hellish hate' (298). In effect the threefold Miltonic allusion not only recalls the Virgilian line but operates cunningly as a kind of extended commentary upon it. Miltonic imitation can be dynamic in this way, rather than decorative or inert.

Such allusions are beyond dispute. However, inevitably there will be occasions when an allusion must be accounted probable rather than certain. Satan's first speech in the poem is followed by Milton's abrasive comment (I. 125–6):

> So spake the apostate angel, though in pain,
> Vaunting aloud, but racked with deep despair.

Such probing psychological comments are rare in Homer, but Virgil is particularly good at them.[4] Aeneas' speech of encouragement to his men in *Aeneid* I, to which Satan's speech to some extent corresponds structurally, is followed by the observation (208–9):

> Talia voce refert, curisque ingentibus aeger
> spem vultu simulat, premit altum corde dolorem.

> (Such things he says aloud, and while sick with great cares pretends hope in his face and stifles his deep grief within his heart.)

The allusion in Milton, if it is such, may be ironic, underlining the perverse heroism of Satan. Aeneas is a true leader who conceals his private emotions in the interest of his public duties; Satan by contrast speaks out of mere bravado, and his concealment serves his own evil desires, not the true interests of those he has misled. Alternatively the allusion may be less focused, simply giving a Virgilian or epic colour. Anyway a proper understanding of Milton's lines in no way depends on a recognition of its probable Virgilian basis; the allusion rather supports that understanding, or adds an enhancing resonance.

Many supposed allusions, both verbal and structural, turn out, on careful inspection, to be mere will-o'-the-wisps that have led the amazed interpreter from his way into bogs and mires. In particular there is a tendency to confuse allusion with aspects of genre or with the use of traditional material, including the so-called commonplaces or *topoi*. For example Francis Blessington supposes that the 'great consult' of devils in *Paradise Lost* II alludes to the council of

4

war held by Agamemnon at the beginning of *Iliad* II, and offers an elaborate reading on that basis.[5] But such councils are a conventional feature of epic, and the reader would be just as likely to think of (say) Latinus' council of war in *Aeneid* XI at which Turnus and Drances contend in a heightened rhetorical manner not unlike Milton's. The infernal debate is Milton's version of a typical epic feature, and alludes to no one particular source within a rich tradition. Even where a specific verbal reminiscence is likely we must beware of drawing the wrong inferences. Blessington notes that certain details in the description of Pandaemonium recall Dido's palace in *Aeneid* I, and argues that we are invited to contrast the sympathetic Dido with the perverse Satan.[6] Part of the problem here is that there is such a surplus of possible sources for Pandaemonium that no one of them comes into anything like sharp focus or dominance. This may discourage us from making any kind of detailed comparison with any of the possible analogues. There is no irresistible reason to think specifically of Dido at this point, and in any event we could hardly be sure that Milton took the sympathetic view of her assumed by Blessington. It would be more plausible to argue that Milton is associating the devils with the Carthaginians who resisted the rise of Rome and thus the will of Jupiter. It is certainly true that the sequence of Aeneas' arrival in Carthage and his sight of the newly rising city has helped to shape this whole section of *Paradise Lost* both as regards some of the details and, more significantly, in terms of the overall structure. In both cases crucial epic business is afoot. But comparisons of Satan and Dido are probably beside the mark.

In such cases we may say that Milton evokes a whole tradition as much as any particular passage or author. A famous simile is perhaps the most familiar example of this phenomenon (I. 301–4):

> angel forms, who lay entranced,
> Thick as autumnal leaves that strew the brooks
> In Vallombrosa, where the Etrurian shades
> High overarched imbower.

Behind this passage lies Glaucon's famous comparison of men and leaves in *Iliad* VI. 146ff, together with similes in Virgil (*Aen.* VI. 309–10) and Dante (*Inferno* III. 112–17) comparing the dead with falling leaves, and one could cite other relevant parallels from the Bible and from classical poetry. Milton characteristically gives a strongly individual stamp to the traditional comparison. Certainly the reference to autumn leaves exploits the feeling of transience, melancholy, loss and waste that is the accumulated legacy of previous treatments of the topic, but that is only one — and not necessarily the most important — element in the complex mood. We are taken away from the immediate setting, the 'inflamed sea' (there is surely a hint here about the colour of the leaves) to a romantic Tuscan landscape, one that is dark and mysterious, and, like the immediately preceding simile about the moon and Galileo, full of Milton's feelings about Italy. The precision about the location is a characteristic Miltonic touch, not present in Virgil or the classical analogues known to Milton.[7] The passage conveys the utter helplessness of the fallen angels; in particular 'entranced' gives a sense of mysterious stillness but also, a characteristic shared by a number of other passages in the first two books, imparts a magical flavour. The mood shifts again in line 302. Milton doubtless means us to reflect on the etymology of Vallombrosa — 'the valley of shadow' — while the final phrase 'high overarched imbower' combines vast space with a feeling of claustrophobia to connect with Milton's general presentation of hell. The amazing complexity of timbre concentrated into just a few lines — lyrical, magical, melancholy, weird and fearful — shows that Milton is far from letting the tradition do all his work for him.

Similarly the satiric attack on riches in *Paradise Lost* I. 685ff, when Mammon teaches men to rifle the earth for hidden treasure, is not best described as an allusion to Ovid. Rather it is an example of the ancient *locus in divitias*, the stock critique of wealth, of which the most familiar instance occurs in Ovid's *Metamorphoses* I. 130ff in the account of the Iron Age. Ovid presumably suggested to Milton the image of the 'bowels' of the earth (cf. *viscera terrae*, 138), but the phrase 'for treasures better hid' recalls rather Horace, *Odes* III. 3. 49, 'aurum irrepertum et sic melius situm' (gold undiscovered and thus better placed). Once again a whole tradition is being evoked; an earlier example in English is Spenser's *Faerie Queene* II. 7. 17.

The reader thus needs to be sensitive to accumulated resonances, but without confusing a commonplace with an allusion. What can happen if the distinction is neglected is well illustrated by a passage about Eve where Milton's careful contrivance has been often reduced to chaos by his interpreters (VIII. 59–63):

With goddess-like demeanour forth she went,
Not unattended, for on her as queen
A pomp of winning Graces waited still,
And from about her shot darts of desire
Into all eyes to wish her still in sight.

On a number of occasions in Homer a character is described as
going 'not alone' but accompanied, usually by two maidservants in
the case of a woman or two attendants in the case of a man (for
example *Iliad* III. 143; XXIV. 573; *Odyssey* I. 331, VI. 84, XVIII.
207). The Homeric basis of *Paradise Lost* VIII. 59ff has long been
recognised by commentators. Some have supposed that Milton
intends an explicit allusion to *Iliad* III. 143, where the formula is
used in connection with Helen, and that Eve is thus being compared
to Helen. Since the same motif is used about Nausicaa and Penelope
it could be concluded that Eve is being compared to those figures
too.[8] However in view of the differences between the three women
and in particular between Helen and Penelope (one in the
Renaissance a type of dangerous sensuality, the other of chastity),
the triple comparison would be confusing, and in truth Milton is not
alluding to any one Homeric passage — the formula is simply too
common for that — but rather producing a witty mannered
variation of a Homeric motif. Unlike some of his interpreters
Milton also understood the significance of the motif. Recent
Homeric scholarship has made us more aware both of the ubiquity
of traditional motifs in the *Iliad* and *Odyssey* and, more
importantly, of their connotations for Homer's original auditors.
Thus for a woman to go accompanied is a mark of her respectability,
as Penelope makes clear in *Odyssey* XVIII. 182–4:

> but tell Antonoë and Hippodameia
> to come, so that they can stand at my side in the great hall.
> I will not go alone among men. I think that immodest.
>
> (Lattimore[9])

Similarly the presence of an escort is a sign of a man's status within
his society. Thus the adolescent Telemachus, whose authority is
insecure in his father's absence, goes accompanied only by two dogs
(*Odyssey* II. 11, etc.) instead of the usual servants or squires. The
significance of the formula would be more readily perceived by
Milton than by modern readers of the Homeric poems. Milton

needed no commentator to point out that a man's retinue constituted an external mark of his status (one could compare the question of Lear's knights).

Milton cleverly adapts the topos to the solitary conditions of Paradise. Eve literally goes unaccompanied, but this does not imply any diminution of her status. She has in fact a train, although only a metaphorical one, 'a pomp of winning Graces'. The presence of 'attendants' is fitting, since her respectability and chastity are not at this stage in doubt. However, this does not prevent her from shooting darts of desire, just as Penelope 'loosens the knees' of the suitors when she appears in the hall (*Odyssey* XVIII. 206ff). Thus the tension between Eve's as yet unimpaired chastity and her beauty and desirability — the latter with ominous implications for the future — is presented in this passage in a very subtle manner. Christopher Ricks rightly points out the delicacy with which the sexual provocativeness of Eve is evoked and then defused, since the phrase 'darts of desire' appears at first sight to stand on its own but is then immediately qualified by 'to wish her still in sight'.[10] Earlier in V. 350–7 there had been a balancing description of Adam:

Meanwhile our primitive great sire, to meet
His godlike guest, walks forth, without more train
Accompanied than with his own complete
Perfections; in himself was all his state
More solemn than the tedious pomp that waits
On princes, when their rich retinue long
Of horses led and grooms besmeared with gold
Dazzles the crowd, and sets them all agape.

The basic similarity between the two passages is one of context — both describe 'our grand parents' going forth and both deal with the question, in the circumstances clearly an artificial one, of whether they went alone or were accompanied — but there are also a number of verbal similarities. *Paradise Lost* V. 350ff is a brilliant inversion of the Homeric formula of accompaniment. Adam's status depends not on 'tedious pomp' but on his 'virtue', yet like Eve he has a metaphorical train, 'his own complete perfections'.

Milton here advances the traditional view, as much Stoic as Christian, that there is no connection between virtue and the external trappings of rank. He uses an ingenious variation of the common Homeric formula as a peg on which to hang his moralising attack on 'the tedious pomp that waits on princes'. It might be objected that the actual terms of the attack suggest not so much Homeric society, which was relatively austere, as, for example, the greater glamour of the world depicted by Virgil in the *Aeneid*. Thus when in the fourth book (129ff) Dido and Aeneas ride out for the hunt, they are surrounded by a throng of attendants ('magna stipante caterva', 136) and there is much stress on gold. Such an objection carries little weight, since the lines describing Eve's 'attendants', whose Homeric basis is not in doubt, are also anything but Homeric in atmosphere. In both cases Milton's starting point was the same Homeric formula, with the connection between the presence of an escort and the character of the person accompanied that the formula implies. *Paradise Lost* V. 350ff is perfectly intelligible to someone unaware of its Homeric basis. The main point is a moral one of general application. Nevertheless it is likely that Milton is also criticising, if in this case only by implication, what he regarded as the moral shortcomings of classical epic, and adapting a Homeric formula to indicate as much to the reader. The lines thus have their full resonance only when it is recognised that Milton is adapting a Homeric motif with a particular set of connotations.

Not dissimilar is Milton's witty use of a formula in favour with a number of ancient writers.[11] In *Georgics* IV. 176 Virgil compares his bees with the giant Cyclopes 'si parva licet componere magnis' (if one may compare great things with small). Three times in *Paradise Lost* and once in *Paradise Regained* Milton uses the *topos*, and in each case the wit derives from the fact that Milton's 'small things' are in ordinary human terms far from being small at all but of very considerable grandeur: they are the storming of a great city (*PL* II. 921–4); the clash of two planets (VI. 310–15); Xerxes' building of the bridge over the Hellespont (X. 306–11); the wrestling match between Hercules and Antaeus (*PR* IV. 563–8). Milton thus cleverly overgoes his predecessors, showing that their 'great things' are trivialities in comparison with the subject-matter of his epics. Again the reader has to recognise the formula and understand the normal way in which it is used to appreciate Milton's perversion of it, but again allusion is hardly the best way to describe Milton's procedure.

In such cases Milton uses the standard building-blocks of epic. A further example will show the skill with which he does so. The formal description of a place in Latin narrative poetry is regularly introduced by a variant of the phrase *est locus* (there is a place . . .). Milton gives us such an *ecphrasis* (as it is called) in *Paradise Lost* VI. 4ff:

> There is a cave
> Within the mount of God, fast by his throne,
> Where light and darkness in perpetual round
> Lodge and dislodge by turns, which makes through heaven
> Grateful vicissitude, like day and night;
> Light issues forth, and at the other door
> Obsequious darkness enters, till her hour
> To veil the heaven, though darkness there might well
> Seem twilight here; and now went forth the morn
> Such as in highest heaven arrayed in gold
> Empyreal; from before her vanished night,
> Shot through with orient beams . . .

Since this ecphrasis deals not only with place but with time, Milton is also drawing on the rich tradition of descriptions, often with personification, of night and day in ancient poetry. Milton moves effortlessly among the conventions involved; one could cite innumerable parallels from Virgil and Ovid, but there is no question of any allusion. Milton is not adapting a particular passage but recreating in English a *manner* of writing. Yet, as often, the effect is not quite that of his classical models: the apparent descriptive clarity of the ecphrasis dissolves when the details are inspected. First, Milton seems to be exploiting the ambiguities of the word 'heaven', sometimes the empyreal heaven the home of God, at others the skies and what we would call space. Part but only part of the sense of this passage can be seen in astronomical terms as we are shown how matters might appear from the perspective of the heavens, 'though darkness there might well / Seem twilight here'. Furthermore, while Milton gives us a notion of night and day as on earth, he will not allow us any certainties: the vicissitude of light and darkness is only like the change between night and day, not identical with it, so that it does not have to represent the human sense of time passing (cf. VI. 685: 'Two days, as we compute the days of heaven'). The ecphrasis is perfectly adapted to its context. Ovid in *Metamorphoses* II had used military metaphors in connection with the motions of the stars (*agmina cogit, statione*, 114–15), and Milton here does

10

likewise ('dislodge', 'issues forth', 'obsequious'). The language prepares us smoothly for the view of Satan's armies described in an increasingly dazzling portrayal of flashing light: 'bright', 'flaming', 'fiery', 'reflecting blaze on blaze'. Though Milton employs commonplaces, there is nothing commonplace about the way that he employs them.

In all these passages we can trace Milton's easy mastery of the craft of epic writing, his understanding of the manner and subject-matter traditionally considered appropriate in epic, his observance of decorum. As important as an alertness for allusion is a feeling for the fluctuating stylistic qualities of the writing and the levels of style involved. For example the phrase 'horrent arms' (II. 513) would not necessarily evoke, even in a learned reader, the Virgilian parallel regularly cited ('horrentibus hastis', *Aen.* X. 178); what is important is to observe the special flavour imparted by the Latinate diction. Similarly the words of the Son when he makes the offer of the Atonement (III. 236–7):

> Behold me then, me for him, life for life
> I offer; on me let thine anger fall

and its later echo by Adam when he at last recognises his guilt (X. 831–3):

> first and last
> On me, me only, as the source and spring
> Of all corruption, all the blame lights due

are both instances of a rhetorical patterning that owes much to classical example. Editors rightly quote Nisus' words in *Aeneid* IX. 427 when he tries to save his friend Euryalus from death at the hands of the Latins: 'me, me, adsum, qui feci, in me convertite ferrum' (me, me — I who did it am present — on me turn your weapons), but this should be seen as a close parallel rather than as an allusion, since thoughts of Nisus and Euryalus would distract the reader from the issue to no clear purpose. What should be recognised is the excitedly rhetorical tone.

If Milton is a master of decorum, in this as in other matters he is unusually imperious. His epic style can incorporate elements of pastoral, of satire, of elegy and of non-classical Biblical modes (there are many passages best described as psalmic). In effect there are two concepts of decorum. The first, and most familiar, is the idea that each genre has its own appropriate style. Thus epic requires the grand style, while satire, for example, employs a more casual style closer to urbane conversation. But a poet may break the rules of the genre (*lex operis*) to preserve the essential underlying principle of decorum, the matching of manner and matter. For example, the satirist Juvenal deliberately raised the stylistic level of satire; the justification was that the grand scale of vice could not be adequately treated by the colloquial insinuations of a Horace — a declamatory sub-epic style was required, though one continually punctuated by debasing detail and a spicing of low words.[12] This second concept of decorum is as relevant to *Paradise Lost* as the first. Milton constantly adapts style to matter in a way that overleaps what could be felt to be the proper limits of the epic genre.

An example is 'the Paradise of Fools' (III. 440ff), an excursion into satire, for which Milton took the material not from the tradition of Homeric epic, but from the *Orlando Furioso* of Ariosto and from medieval anti-clerical writing (there are parallels in Dante for lines 474ff). The neoclassical critics were quick to condemn. Addison thought that the passage lacked 'probability enough for an epic poem' and that it savoured of 'the spirit of Spenser and Ariosto',[13] a judgement echoed by Dr Johnson: 'his desire of imitating Ariosto's levity has disgraced his work with the "Paradise of Fools", a fiction not in itself ill-imagined, but too ludicrous for its place.'[14] Addison's further complaint that such passages are 'the description of dreams and shadows, not of things or persons'[15] ignores the obvious point that 'dreams and shadows', vanities, are precisely what Milton is treating in the Paradise of Fools, particularly in the lines that describe light objects jumbled together flying in the wind (445ff; 486ff). Satan has been wandering long 'bent on his prey' (440), and the sense of aimlessness in the Paradise of Fools mirrors the elaborate futility of his workings. Since the tradition on which Milton draws belongs clearly to the realms of fiction and has no historical or Biblical authority, his comment, rather pedantic in tone, about the proper location of the place may be curiously tongue-in-cheek (459ff). Stylistically the whole passage is something of a *tour de force*, modulating between a sense of insubstantiality and withering scorn. There are word plays ('dissolved' things waiting for 'final dissolution', 457–8; 'devious air', 489) and heavy puns ('in vain', 457; 'pass', 480ff); 'wicket' (484) is a 'low' word, while the phrase 'the backside of the world' (494) allows for a coarse reading. There is a long Christian tradition of such writing which, while it would be incongruous in Virgil, finds a place within the wider spectrum of tones, Biblical and Christian as well as classical, in *Paradise Lost*. The reader must be flexible, alert to such changes of manner and aware of their different literary ancestry.

The stylistic flexibility of *Paradise Lost* may indeed owe something to the example of the Bible, which was difficult to categorise in terms of the genres of classical antiquity. Another Biblical poet, George Wither, in *A Preparation to the Psalter* (1619) observes that the psalms contain elements of heroic poetry, tragedy, pastoral and satire, and that these shifts in register are justified by the variety of the subject-matter:

> Note also that these holy hymns are not written all in one kind of poesy, but the prophet hath made use almost of all sorts . . . Sometimes his odes are heroical, sometime tragical, sometime pastoral, sometime satirical, and this is by reason of the necessity of the matter. For one while he introduceth Adam and his posterity bewailing their miserable condition . . . and then his odes are tragical. Other while he takes occasion to set forth the malicious conditions of the enemies of the Messias and his kingdom; then he is satirical. Another while he sings the sweet contentments of that shepherd with his flock; there he maketh pastorals. But when he intends either to set forth the wondrous works of the eternal God or the glorious magnificence of our redeemer's empire, then his divine muse mounts the height of heroical poesy.[16]

\* \* \*

The confusion of an allusion and a commonplace is not the only danger to confront the student of *Paradise Lost*. Much modern criticism simply assumes, without argument, that an allusion necessarily brings in its train the whole context of the original. It is certainly the case that Virgil often uses his Homeric material like this, so that we can perceive behind Virgil's words the continual ghostly presence of the plot of the *Iliad* and *Odyssey*, and may be encouraged to reflect on both differences and similarities. Milton's allusions sometimes work in this way, but it is doubtful whether this is so with the majority. Indeed there are occasions on which we need positively to repress any knowledge of the original context. Thus Milton ends his Latin elegy (no. 3) for Bishop Lancelot Andrewes with the words 'Talia contingant somnia saepe mihi' (may such dreams always fall to my lot). The phrasing is Ovidian; in the last line of *Amores* I. 5, in which Ovid describes an amorous encounter with his mistress, he wishes for many more such successful middays: 'proveniant medii sic mihi saepe dies' (26). The echo is justified, despite the embarrassing difference of context, because Milton is writing an elegy in Ovidian style. Similarly the moving words of Aeneas to Dido in the Underworld 'invitus, regina, tuo de litore cessi' (VI. 460; unwillingly, queen, I left your shore) recall a line in a frivolous poem of Catullus, the translation of Callimachus' 'Lock of Berenice' (66); the lock, leaving the queen's hair to become a star, says 'Invita, o regina, tuo de vertice cessi' (39; unwillingly, o queen, I left your head). The reader who recognises the source is not invited to reflect long on the context in Catullus. Virgil has given a new and far worthier setting for a memorable line from one of his favourite poets, who moreover had been constantly in his mind when writing of the love affair between Dido and Aeneas.

The interpreter of *Paradise Lost* has thus to decide in the case of each allusion whether the context of the original is likely to be of significance. A particularly difficult example occurs near the beginning of *Paradise Lost* with the opening words of Satan's address to Beelzebub (I. 84–7):

> If thou beest he — but o how fallen, how changed
> From him, who in the happy realms of light
> Clothed with transcendent brightness didst outshine
> Myriads though bright!

In *Aeneid* II the ghost of Hector appears to the sleeping Aeneas to tell him to leave the now burning city of Troy and rescue the household gods. Hector is covered with blood as when Achilles dragged him round the walls of Troy (274–6):

> ei mihi, qualis erat! quantum mutatus ab illo
> Hectore, qui redit exuvias indutus Achilli
> vel Danaum Phrygias iaculatus puppibus ignes!

(Alas how he looked! how changed from that Hector who returned having put on the spoils of Achilles or thrown Trojan fire on the Greeks' ships.)

It would be possible to argue that what we have in Milton is not really a Virgilian allusion, but rather a rhetorical formula of which the most famous example happens to occur in the *Aeneid*. La Cerda's edition of Virgil lists a large number of parallels for the rhetorical contrast between past and present condition.[17] One of the closest is in Ovid's *Metamorphoses*, where, perhaps in imitation of Virgil, the almost identical formula is used of Niobe (VI. 273–4):

> Heu quantum haec Niobe Niobe distabat ab illa
> quae modo Latois populum submoverat aris.

(Alas, how this Niobe differed from that Niobe who had just removed the people from Leto's altar.)

La Cerda observes — and we shall see that this is important — that the figure is designed to arouse pathos. However, granted that Satan's words allude directly to Virgil, the question still remains whether it is relevant to recall the full context in the *Aeneid*. Blessington has no doubts that this is so:

> The whole situation of Troy burning and Aeneas hastening into exile should be recalled. The parallel between the defeat of the Trojans and the defeat of Satan's forces shows how Milton has extended the conception of the epic from the earthly to the spiritual realm, how hopeless the plight of the rebel angels is, how pagan and un-Christian their behavior, and how ignoble their subsequent action when compared to Aeneas' and Hector's, heroes who served as models for Christian behavior during the Renaissance. By looking at Hector, Aeneas has a vision of death and must learn to accept defeat at the hands of the Trojans [*sic*]. The same vision appears to Satan but it is now the look of spiritual, not physical, death on the face of his companion; yet Satan, unlike Aeneas, does not heed the message. Parallels to the major classical epics ripple out like this one in such a significant manner that to follow them out is almost never an unprofitable exercise.[18]

There are mistakes here and details which one might query; in particular *Paradise Lost* hardly encourages us to treat the heroes of classical epic as models of Christian behaviour. But, more importantly, this whole highly schematic analysis smacks of the study and not of the direct experience of reading, while it assumes an alertness to context in allusion which we shall see reason to believe may not have been general in the seventeenth century. Also it accords Virgil a primacy in this passage which he does not have. The Virgilian echo, if it is that, quickly gives place to one more important. Isaiah 14 contains a satiric attack on the king of Babylon which includes the famous verse (12): 'How art thou fallen from heaven, O Lucifer, son of the morning! How art thou cut down to the ground, which didst weaken the nations!' The Hebrew writer here exploits a myth of the overthrow of a lesser god by a greater; the verse was later interpreted by Christian exegetes as referring to Satan and the fall of the angels. As so often when Milton fuses classical and Biblical material it is the latter which is richer in significance and implication. Thus, while the Virgilian motto should be noted, it must not be accorded a disproportionate importance. I would suggest that Milton has two main purposes in alluding briefly to Virgil, if that is what he is doing: first, to establish a classical epic timbre so that the passage is enriched, for those who recall them, by memory of the Virgilian lines, and secondly to give Satan a pathetic manner that is designed to arouse our sympathies. However, since we already know that Satan is the father of lies, we must, to some extent, be on our guard against the seductive rhetorical tones adopted both by him and, in connection with him, by the poet.

It is important to consider Satan's opening words in the context of his speech as a whole. The syntax of the first sentence is strikingly incoherent, mirroring the wavering of Satan's thought and the ambiguity of mood, in contrast to the more straightforward plangency of Aeneas' words. The broken phrasing seems an expression of spontaneous pity, though, since Satan sees in Beelzebub a mirror of his own pain, pity may be in large part self-pity (it is also noticeable that Satan's first thought involves the unqualified assumption of the superiority of heaven to hell). But soon Satan modulates into a clearly calculated or semi-calculated rhetoric for the remainder. Most of the speech has an odd lack of intimacy, with Beelzebub addressed as though he were a public meeting. In the opening sentence there is a strong metrical emphasis on 'changed' and 'fallen', the latter in this poem of particular resonance, with — although only for the reader — a double sense; the fall is moral as well as physical.

The chapter in Isaiah sets two styles of writing against each other: the glamorous mode of verse 12 and the homely and abrasive manner of Hebrew satire which places and judges the glittering mythological moment. Harold Fisch notes that a kind of demythologising is at work and argues that verse 12 should be seen as 'an ironic figure', not as an endorsement of the myth.[19] However, at least in the Authorised Version, the beauty of what is rejected is acknowledged.

Milton appears to adopt a similar approach; the pathos of Satan intoxicates the reader but will eventually be set in true perspective by the poem as a whole, a point to which I shall be returning more than once. Later Pope was to use the Miltonic-Virgilian figure, in a clearly satiric context, of the Duke of Buckingham (*Epistle to Bathurst*, 299ff); yet even here it retains some at least of its original power:

> In the worst inn's worst room, with mat half hung,
> The floors of plaster and the walls of dung,
> On once a flock-bed but repaired with straw,
> With tape-tied curtains never meant to draw,
> The George and Garter dangling from that bed
> Where tawdry yellow strove with dirty red,
> Great Villers lies — alas, how changed from him,
> That life of pleasure and that soul of whim! . . .

Milton's lines seem delicately balanced between Virgilian pathos and Popean mockery — other passages in *Paradise Lost* are poised on the brink of the mock-heroic — in a way that might have been suggested by Isaiah 14.

Certain doubts may be raised against the general validity of Blessington's whole approach illustrated by his comments on this passage, an approach which is characteristic of much modern criticism. First, the method is dangerously open-ended, lacking sufficient checks to subjectivity; as one context is played, with ever increasing ingenuity, against another, almost anything may — and in practice does — result. More importantly, the approach does not seem to be grounded in a sufficient sense of what imitation as a poetic procedure meant to Renaissance writers. Indeed it probably hides an unconscious unease about the legitimacy of this aspect of Renaissance poetics which may be a partly unacknowledged legacy of Romanticism, with its stress on originality; hence the desire of post-Romantic critics to discover implausible layers of allusive subtlety to justify the practice. It was the habit of Renaissance poets, Ben Jonson for example, to incorporate in their works what are in effect passages of free translation of appropriate classical poetry (or even on occasion prose).[20] In so doing they were carrying over into adult life what they had been taught to do as schoolboys by way of translation and imitation of the classics. The prudent defence is the greatness of the poetry that resulted. Thus in *The Tempest* Shakespeare translates a passage from Ovid's *Metamorphoses*, with some help from Arthur Golding's version, for the opening of Prospero's great speech of renunciation 'Ye elves of hills' (V. i. 33ff).[21] This is not really an allusion to Ovid, although the more learned members of the audience will have recognised the 'source', which was a *locus classicus* for the treatment of magic in ancient poetry; rather it is a characteristic if superb instance of this habit of adaptation with results which in this case certainly justify the procedure.

Renaissance theorists, like the critics of antiquity, laid considerable stress on the imitation of earlier poetry. It was grounded in ancient precedent; thus Virgil had imitated Homer and Cicero Demosthenes. Rightly conducted it was not plagiarism, partly because there was normally no attempt to conceal the source of the borrowing, and partly because the process was not one of stale copying but of a creative adaptation of old material to a new context and purpose.[22] Imitation naturally encouraged the critic to set a passage of poetry against its source for careful comparison. But such comparisons were limited in scope; factual differences were noted and observations made on whether the adaptation had been skilfully and decorously performed and whether the details fitted the new context. Again it was the ancient critics who showed the way.[23] In the *Noctes Atticae* of the second-century antiquarian Aulus Gellius we find comparisons of passages in Virgil and their Greek originals. For example in XVII. 10 a description of Etna in *Aeneid* III. 570ff is compared with Pindar, *Pythian* I. 21ff, and Virgil's language is condemned as being in comparison with Pindar's imprecise and hyperbolical. Similarly in IX. 9 Gellius gives the grammarian Probus' view that the simile in *Aeneid* I. 498ff comparing Dido with Diana is less apt to its context than its source in *Odyssey* VI. 102ff where Nausicaa is likened to Artemis. (It is noteworthy that there is no suggestion that Virgil is associating Dido with Nausicaa.) Such comparisons feature in the *Saturnalia* of the fifth-century scholar Macrobius, and were continued in the notes of Renaissance editions like La Cerda's Virgil. Frequently it was shown how Virgil had made good deficiencies in passages of Homer by fresh details. Roger Ascham in *The Schoolmaster* (1570) explains how such an exercise should be conducted (he is talking about Cicero's debt to Demosthenes):

(i) Tully [i.e. Cicero] retaineth this much of the matter, these sentences, these words.
(ii) This and that he leaveth out, which he doth wittily to this aid and purpose.
(iii) This he addeth here.
(iv) This he diminisheth there.
(v) This he ordereth thus, with placing that here, not there.
(vi) This he altereth and changeth either in property of words, in form of sentence, in substance of the matter or in one or other convenient circumstance of the author's present purpose.[24]

Some difference of emphasis between Ascham's method and that of Blessington and other modern scholars is obvious. Ascham is much more concerned with the craft aspect of imitation and with the verbal texture, much less inclined to look beyond the immediate context to larger questions of meaning and interpretation. It is often felt that the ancient comparisons are disappointing; even so sympathetic a writer on ancient literary criticism as Donald Russell finds the results 'superficial and unhelpful'.[25] Nevertheless it may be better to refine on the method employed by the critics of antiquity and their Renaissance followers rather than to abandon it altogether. *Paradise Lost* is not in general allusive in quite the manner of *The Waste Land*, but Milton's use of his predecessors displays, in terms that Ascham would have understood, remarkable artistry and imagination.

Finally we should notice certain Renaissance reading habits and educational practices that positively encouraged the ignoring of context. Many Renaissance readers made, like Hamlet, their own collections of favourite passages in commonplace books — Ben Jonson's *Discoveries* is an extended example — and most of Milton's own commonplace book survives with sections for ethics, 'economics' and politics.[26] Furthermore *florilegia*, assemblages of passages from classical works, were in widespread use both inside and outside the classroom. For example Octavianus Mirandula's ever popular *Poetarum Illustrium Flores* arranged appropriate passages from Latin works under headings like *De Abstinentia, De Adolescentia, De Adversitate* (I give the first three entries — about abstinence, youth, adversity). Authors and works but not line numbers are given. The *flores* must have encouraged a kind of piecemeal reading, and meant that readers might be familiar with a passage without having read the whole work from which it came. Similarly Renaissance writers and readers often obtained their information, not directly from the original Latin works, but from handbooks and dictionaries of various kinds. It has been shown that even a writer as learned as Milton probably made considerable use of these short cuts to knowledge. A likely instance of this is Milton's reference (IX. 505ff) to the story of the transformation of Cadmus and his wife into snakes, which is told by Ovid in *Metamorphoses* IV. 563ff. Cadmus' wife, unnamed in Ovid, is properly called Harmonia; in Milton, as in Sandys's translation, she is Hermione. The intermediate source in Milton's case may well be Charles Stephanus's popular encyclopedia *Dictionarium Historicum Geographicum Poeticum* which gives the form Hermione.[27] Milton of course knew the *Metamorphoses* well, but when reminding himself of the details of a particular myth must often have consulted Stephanus's convenient summaries.

The reader of *Paradise Lost* must bear these various points in mind when considering Milton's use of classical poetry. In the last resort, however, there is no magic key to Milton's practice in imitation and allusion. Every case must be considered on its own merits; there can be no substitute for common sense and judgement.

### The Two Ways (i)

Milton's poetry, like that of most of his contemporaries, derives from two primary sources, the classics and the Christian tradition, the latter firmly rooted, in Milton's case at least, in the text of the Bible. Of these there is no doubt which is the more important. As Coleridge wrote to a friend, 'there is not perhaps *one* page in Milton's Paradise Lost, in which he has not borrowed his imagery from the *Scriptures*'.[28] It is often argued that, while Milton regarded the Bible as the spring of truth, he found classical poetry more alluring aesthetically. Thus John Carey claims that there are no ' "Christian" moments' in *Paradise Lost* to set beside such evocations of classical myth as the lines on Mulciber, Proserpine or Orpheus.[29] However, we are not obliged to agree with him. For example the psalm-like hymns of Adam and Eve to their creator or the exuberant account of the Creation, passages of Biblical origin, are of outstanding quality, while the lines on Jacob's ladder, discussed in detail in Chapter 3, are as perfect in their way as anything in the poem. It is also interesting that perhaps the least evocative lines in the catalogue of devils, the material of which was largely supplied by the Old Testament, are those dealing with the Greek gods (I. 507ff). It is probably true that there are no purely New Testament moments of the greatest poetic intensity, but that is a different point from Carey's. The Bible, and in particular the Old Testament, influenced Milton towards both a greater simplicity of diction (as in the Jacob passage) and a greater boldness of imagery (for example God and the compasses in VII. 225ff) in a way that immeasurably strengthens the poem. It was Coleridge who in the same letter noted the *tameness* of Homer and Virgil in comparison with the more unbuttoned passages of Scripture.

What little evidence we have suggests that Milton, a student of Hebrew as well as Latin and Greek, shared Coleridge's view of the literary superiority of the Bible to pagan literature, at any rate as regards lyric poetry. In *Paradise Regained* IV, Christ, who has already rejected the political grandeur that was Rome, is offered by Satan the literary glories of Greece. The Saviour spurns these no less abrasively, and argues for the higher merit of Hebrew poetry (331ff):

> Or if I would delight my private hours
>  With music or with poem, where so soon
> As in our native language can I find
> That solace? All our Law and story strewed
> With hymns, our psalms with artful terms inscribed,
> Our Hebrew songs and harps in Babylon
> That pleased so well our victor's ear declare
> That rather Greece from us these arts derived,
> Ill-imitated, while they loudest sing
> The vices of their deities and their own
> In fable, hymn or song, so personating
> Their gods ridiculous and themselves past shame.
> Remove their swelling epithets thick-laid
> As varnish on a harlot's cheek, the rest,
> Thin-sown with ought of profit or delight,
> Will far be found unworthy to compare

With Sion's songs, to all true tastes excelling,
Where God is praised aright and godlike men . . .

We may be tempted to regard this merely as rhetorical excess, or as
evidence of growing intolerance in the ageing poet, but Milton had
in fact said much the same, though more quietly, in *The Reason of
Church Government* published in 1642:

> Or if occasion shall lead to imitate those magnific odes and
> hymns wherein Pindarus and Callimachus are in most things
> worthy, some others in their frame judicious, in their matter
> most an end faulty; but those frequent songs throughout the law
> and prophets beyond all these, not in their divine argument
> alone, but in the very critical art of composition may be easily
> made appear over all the kinds of lyric poesy to be
> incomparable.[30]

Such views were in no way eccentric; thus Donne regarded David
(as author of the Psalms) as 'a better poet than Virgil'.[31] The
apparent reluctance of critics to accept these statements may reflect
their own comparative indifference to the literary splendours of the
Bible.

The balance in Milton's poetry between Christian and classical
varies from work to work. It is customary to see a development in
three stages from the more or less relaxed humanist inclusiveness of
the early works, through the tenser conjunctions of *Paradise Lost*,
to the obscurantist rejection of classicism in *Paradise Regained*, and
moreover to take this as evidence of Milton's own changing
attitudes. There is doubtless some truth in such a picture. It is
instructive, for example, to compare Milton's treatment, first in
*Comus* and then in *Paradise Regained*, of the standard way that
pagan literature had been accommodated to the needs of a Christian
culture; pagan writers were regarded as having glimpsed through a
glass darkly what were later to be the revealed truths of Christianity.
For example Virgil was commonly taken to have foretold the
Incarnation in *Eclogue* IV, though naturally without full under-
standing, so that, in Dante's words, 'he was like him that goes by
night and carries the light behind him and does not help himself but
makes wise those that follow' (Sinclair's translation of *Purgatorio*
XXII. 67–9). In *Comus* Milton refers to the doctrine, with a notable
generosity of interpretation, when the Attendant Spirit observes
(512–18):

'tis not vain or fabulous
(Though so esteemed by shallow ignorance)
What the sage poets, taught by the heavenly Muse,
Storied of old in high immortal verse
Of dire chimeras and enchanted isles
And rifted rocks whose entrance leads to hell,
For such there be, but unbelief is blind.

The romantic glow of the lines shows that Milton's imagination was caught by the idea. (This attitude may reappear in *Paradise Lost* IX. 439–43 if 'mystic' there means 'containing a concealed truth', though normally in *Paradise Lost* Milton is more antagonistic towards such a view.)[32] By contrast in *Paradise Regained* IV Christ makes of it only the most grudging of concessions when he talks of pagan writings 'where moral virtue is expressed / By light of nature not in all quite lost' (351–2).[33] Doubtless this difference reflects growing austerity in Milton's religious outlook. But distinction of genre is also an important determining factor: on the one hand a Biblical short epic, perhaps modelled on the book of Job; on the other, masque, naturally receptive of allegory and classical embellishment.

Certainly it would be wrong to think in terms of a straightforward linear development from receptivity to exclusion, straightforwardly reflecting Milton's own developing outlook. The tension between classical and Christian — or the relative absence of it — is not to be taken as naively confessional, but as at least in part tactical and rhetorical. Thus the passage in *Comus* authorises allegorical understandings necessary to the masque structure; by contrast the obscurantism of *Paradise Regained* suits the temper of a poem that presents Jesus' saving work in terms of his rejection of the world, the flesh and the devil, even if the view that sees the redemption primarily in terms of denial reflects Milton's own Puritan temper. Yet even in *Paradise Regained* not all can be reduced to order. The climactic moment of the contest between Christ and Satan — 'Tempt not the Lord thy God, he said and stood. / But Satan smitten with amazement fell' (IV. 561–2) — is compared with the wrestling match between Hercules and Antaeus (traditionally allegorised as the victory of spirit over body), and with the discomfiture of the Sphinx by Oedipus. Each of Milton's major poems reveals a conscious strategy in this regard, though one that is perhaps incompletely controlled by the poet. Possibly it is in *Samson*

*Agonistes* that Milton comes nearest to achieving consistency. Here allusions to paganism are either covert, like the hint of Circe's cup in 934, or brief and unevocative. Thus the story of Atlas is mentioned dismissively in 150 'like whom the Gentiles feign to bear up heaven', but its poetic power is not exploited. Similarly in 499–500 reference is made to Tantalus' punishment in Hades, but only as a gentile 'parable' and again without directly naming the classical figure involved or making the pagan myth live poetically. Yet even in *Samson* Johnson could find the reference to the phoenix, an image of rebirth with a long history in Christian literature, offensive as being 'so evidently contrary to reason and nature that it ought never to be mentioned but as a fable in any serious poem'.[34] Coming at the climax of the story (1699ff) the phoenix simile shows that not even in this most austerely scriptural work could Milton quite manage with the Bible alone.

The notion that with Milton early necessarily implies fusion and late tension or rejection is unsatisfactory. Milton's first important English poem the 'Nativity Ode', written when the poet was 21, offers no easy fusion of pagan and Christian, but rather sets the two at each other's throats. Admittedly Christ can be called the 'mighty Pan' (89) — because the name of the god, by means of a false etymology that went back to antiquity, was connected with the Greek word for 'all' — and that without embarrassment, at least on the poet's part. But the Incarnation is presented not so much in terms of a fleshly birth as of a victory over paganism (Milton took this idea from an ode on the Nativity by Tasso). What is perhaps the finest section of the Ode (stanza 18ff) details the various religions that are put to rout at Christ's birth; Milton here displays a fascination with what would today be called comparative religion, as he does later in the catalogue of fallen angels in *Paradise Lost* I. The stanza on the flight of the nymphs is, as we shall see, curiously indulgent, while even where Milton clearly rejects he acknowledges the full power of what is rejected (stanza 21):

> In consecrated earth,
> And on the holy hearth,
>   The lars and lemures moan with midnight plaint,
> In urns and altars round
> A drear and dying sound
>   Affrights the flamens at their service quaint;
> And the chill marble seems to sweat,

While each peculiar power forgoes his wonted seat.

Both the rejection and the fascination look forward to *Paradise Lost*, and that in a poem which is still profoundly Spenserian in style and diction. At the other extreme from the ode is a sonnet written in the 1650s, not long before Milton started work on *Paradise Lost*. The poem perfectly recreates — and gives religious authority to — the Horatian *carpe diem* philosophy of life which warns against excessive worries for the future and urges a measured enjoyment of the present. The poem well illustrates the Erasmian ideal of a Christian classicism, and shows Milton at his most relaxedly humanist:

> Lawrence, of virtuous father virtuous son,
>     Now that the fields are dark and ways are mire,
>     Where shall we sometimes meet, and by the fire
>     Help waste a sullen day, what may be won
> From the hard season gaining? Time will run
>     On smoother, till Favonius reinspire
>     The frozen earth, and clothe in fresh attire
>     The lily and rose that neither sowed nor spun.
> What neat repast shall feast us, light and choice,
>     Of Attic taste, with wine, whence we may rise
>     To hear the lute well touched or artful voice
> Warble immortal notes and Tuscan air?
>     He who of those delights can judge, and spare
>     To interpose them oft, is not unwise.

The first line serves as a sort of Horatian motto to alert the reader to the poem's literary ancestry; the shape of the phrase recalls the opening of *Odes* I. 16, 'O matre pulchra filia pulchrior' (O daughter more beautiful than a beautiful mother). Favonius (6), the Latin equivalent of the Greek Zephyr which was the normal name of the West Wind in Latin and neo-Latin poetry, comes from the Sestius Ode (I. 4), a poem which opposes the joys of spring and youth to the certainty of death. The picture of the West Wind unlocking the frozen ground, where the Latinate 'reinspire' is gracefully set off against plainer diction, recalls the opening stanza of the Sestius Ode. The argument of the sonnet as a whole, however, is closer to that of the Soracte Ode (I. 9); like the sonnet this ode is an invitation

25

poem, Horace inviting a friend, Thaliarchus, to share a fire and wine while all outside is in the grip of winter (music, while not mentioned in the Soracte Ode, is a regular feature of Horatian invitations). Stylistically too the sonnet is an exercise in the Horatian manner; the vocabulary is on the whole plain, even prosaic, exuberant metaphor and poetic embroidery is avoided, and the poem makes its quiet impact through the powerful control of syntax and careful placement of words, an art that is the more impressive through being concealed, not obtruded. There is only one Biblical allusion, but it is of the utmost importance. 'The lily and rose that neither sowed nor spun' alludes to Christ's teaching in the Sermon on the Mount (Matthew 6: 28–9): 'Consider the lilies of the field, how they grow; they toil not, neither do they spin. And yet I say unto you that even Solomon in all his glory was not arrayed like one of these.' Christ's teaching in this section is summarised in verse 34: 'Take therefore no thought for the morrow, for the morrow shall take thought for the things of itself. Sufficient unto the day is the evil thereof.' Milton thus insinuates, reasonably enough, that Horace's philosophy of life, and the views of Epicurus that lie largely behind it, are consistent with the words of Christ himself. The poem may be Milton's contribution to a Puritan debate about leisure, and shows him in this as in other matters liberal rather than repressive.[35] The argument thus demands not a disjunction, but a most delicate combination of pagan and Christian. The piece is of singular perfection, marred only by the uncertain meaning of the final lines. The ambiguity about the meaning of 'spares' (either 'refrain' or 'spare time for'), and thus the doubts about whether the pleasures Milton recommends are to be savoured seldom or often, is not enhancing but mere obfuscation, or the result of a carelessness which, Milton, like Horace, would normally have disdained.

*Comus* (1634) displays neither quite the effortless accommodations of the sonnet nor yet the disjunctions of the ode. Much of the work is relaxed and delightful, but some tensions exist which could to an extent relate to the clash which I am examining between Christianity and classicism. In large part, however, these tensions derive rather from Milton's 'habit of testing authority to destruction' in J.B.Broadbent's excellent phrase.[36] In *Comus* Milton overloads the delicate masque conventions with drama and argument in a way that puts the form under considerable pressure. Generations of schoolchildren have laughed at the strangely painstaking approximation to *stichomythia* (that curious formal

26

dialogue of Greek tragedy in which each speaker is allotted only one line at a time) in the interchange between Comus and the Lady (276ff). Few of their teachers point out how odd it is to find Greek tragic dialogue in a masque. Such extremism is characteristic of Milton. It can be argued that the tensions in *Comus* are also connected with the development of the conflict between virtue and vice. A.D. Nuttall no doubt speaks for many when he remarks that Milton entered masque in order to depose its ancient king, but was unable entirely to accomplish this reformation.[37] In particular the Lady is redeemed in the end not by virtue and reason alone but rather by a magic superior to Comus', while the seductive rhetoric of Comus himself steals the show, demonstrating yet again that the devil gets the best tunes or even that Milton was, at some deep level, of the devil's party. Since the figure of Comus is closely associated with the story of Circe and with Homeric myth, this could suggest that Milton is again showing an ambivalence about classical poetry and story.

These familiar points are not entirely convincing. First, it is not magic but grace that rescues the Lady, admittedly presented in mythological dress according to the masque conventions, with Sabrina as its main embodiment. As the Attendant Spirit puts it: 'if Virtue feeble were, / Heaven itself would stoop to her' (1021–2). The Lady by her chastity gains heavenly intervention. Secondly, while Comus' language certainly glitters and allures, we should be alert to the elements within it of decadence and excess (719–36):

> if all the world
> Should in a pet of temperance feed on pulse,
> Drink the clear stream and nothing wear but frieze,
> The all-giver would be unthanked, would be unpraised,
> Not half his riches known, and yet despised,
> And we should serve him as a grudging master,
> As a penurious niggard of his wealth,
> And live like Nature's bastards, not her sons,
> Who would be quite surcharged with her own weight,
> And strangled with her waste fertility;
> The earth cumbered, and the winged air darked with plumes,
> The herds would over-multitude their lords,
> The sea o'erfraught would swell, and the unsought diamonds
> Would so emblaze the forehead of the deep,
> And so bestud with stars, that they below

Would grow inured to light and come at last
To gaze upon the sun with shameless brows.

In terms of the stylistic progression of *Comus* both this
overnourished rhetoric — the Lady calls it 'gay' (89) — and the
stiffer, less sensuous language of the Lady and Elder Brother give
place to a fresher, purer, more lyrical mode for the closing episodes.
The epilogue genuinely overtops in loveliness all that has gone
before, making even Comus' finest speeches seem a trifle
meretricious by comparison. Moreover — and this is the most
significant point — the epilogue, though Christian in overall
content, is full of classical references (the gardens of the
Hesperides, Venus and Adonis, Cupid and Psyche) in the relaxed
decorative-allegorical mode of the *Faerie Queene*. In general the
Attendant Spirit is associated with a Platonist willingness to see the
world as an ascending chain of analogies rather than as disunified.
In *Comus* there is thus no clear disjunction of Christian and
classical, partly because of the nature of masque itself, and
mythological language is used by and about good and bad characters
alike. Admittedly both the scale and elaboration of *Comus* and its
complex literary ancestry mean that some sutures reveal themselves
to close analysis in a way that does not happen in the sonnet. But
Milton does not in general point to the gulf that in reality separates
the worlds of paganism and Christianity, but rather employs the
traditional accommodations, many of them symbolic or allegorical
in character, developed during the Middle Ages and Renaissance to
bridge that gulf. In a masque that could be done; in a Biblical epic,
in which the two elements are seen more closely for what they are, it
was not so easy.

### The Two Ways (ii)

In his great book *European Literature and the Latin Middle Ages*
E.R.Curtius draws attention to the paradox inherent in the notion
of a Christian epic:

> Throughout its existence — from Juvencus to Klopstock — the
> Biblical epic was a hybrid with an inner lack of truth, a *genre
> faux*. The Christian story of salvation, as the Bible presents it,
> admits no transformation into pseudo-antique form. Not only

does it thereby lose its powerful, unique, authoritative expression, but it is falsified by the genre borrowed from antique Classicism and by the concomitant linguistic and metrical conventions. That the Biblical epic could nevertheless enjoy such great popularity is explained only by the need for an ecclesiastical literature which could be matched with and opposed to antique literature.[38]

Unlike many of the writers of Christian epics Milton was alive to these contradictions, and built the tensions between pagan and Christian, epic and Bible, into the fabric of his work. The strategy reaches its climax at the beginning of *Paradise Lost* IX when, before the climax of the action, Milton openly denounces the matter and manner of previous epic.

The measure of Milton's success, and some of the reasons for it, can be gauged by a comparison of *Paradise Lost* with two other Christian epics with which Milton was familiar, Marco Girolamo Vida's *Christiad* (1535) — referred to in Milton's uncompleted poem on the Passion (26) — and Cowley's *Davideis*. The *Christiad* was designed to give Christ's life the dignity of Virgilian epic dress. Pope Leo X thought Vida the best man to celebrate in verse Christ's marvellous achievements (*res gestae mirae*), which before had been described inadequately, in 'a sublime and elegant style'.[39] It is relevant to recall that many Christians, from Augustine onwards, had doubted the stylistic adequacy of the Bible when tested against the tenets of classical rhetoric. In the *Christiad* the style, a skilful pastiche of Virgil, becomes a barrier between the reader and the story that is being told. The classical tropes seem in this context merely inappropriate mannerisms, as when of the miracle of water turned into wine Vida writes (III. 982): 'fontis aquam latices Bacchi convertit in atros' (he turns water of the spring into the dark liquid of Bacchus). The authentic sublimities of the Gospels are in this way submerged under the false sublimities of style valued for its own sake alone, as a comparison of Matthew's account of the Institution of the Eucharist with Vida's shows:

Jesus took bread, and blessed it, and brake it, and gave it to the disciples, and said 'Take, eat; this is my body'. And he took the cup, and gave thanks, and gave it to them, saying 'Drink ye all of it . . .' (26: 26–7)

Iamque heros puras fruges properataque liba
Accipiens, frangensque manu partitur in omnes;
Inde mero implevit pateram lymphaque recenti,
Et laticis mixti dium sacravit honorem,
Spumantemque dedit sociis, mox talia fatur:
Corporis haec nostri, haec vera cruoris imago,
Unus pro cunctis quem fundam sacra parenti
Hostia, ut antiquae noxae contagia tollam.
Vos ideo, quoties positas accedere mensas
Contigerit sacrasque dapes libamina iussa,
Funeris his nostri maestum referetis honorem,
Et numquam istius abolescet gloria facti.    (II. 651–62)

(And now the hero taking pure grain and sacrificial cake prepared in haste, and breaking it with his hand distributes it among them all. Then he filled a cup with unmixed wine and fresh water and consecrated the divine honour of the mixed liquid, and gave it foaming to his comrades. Then he speaks thus, 'This is a true image of my body and blood which one alone for all I shall pour out to my father, a holy victim, to remove the stain of ancient sin. You then, whenever it befalls that you approach prepared tables and sacred feasts, the ordered libations, will reenact with them the sad honour of my death, and never will the glory of this deed fade.)

This is bad in exactly the same way as Pope's *Messiah*, where, for example, Christ's healing of the blind is described thus (39–40):

He from thick films shall purge the visual ray,
And on the sightless eyeball pour the day.

Virgil in the *Aeneid* had often sought to dignify simple things by periphrasis (for example he never uses 'panis', the standard Latin word for bread), and had been praised for this by Servius and others;[40] Vida obediently follows suit in a context where simplicity is demanded (unqualified grandeur in Biblical paraphrase is often damaging). It is also inappropriate for Christ to be described, in such a non-allegorical passage, as 'heros' (elsewhere he is 'dux', leader); the writing blandly assimilates Jesus to Aeneas. The complete absence of any stylistic pressure from the Bible is stultifying.

Even more instructive, because it is written in English by a poet
held in high regard by Milton and on an Old Testament subject, is
Cowley's epic about the life of David. Cowley eventually
abandoned the project, but he published the four completed books,
together with an extensive commentary and a Latin translation of
the first book. The English version is in rhyming couplets, and looks
forward to the heroic manner of Dryden. Part of the trouble is
simply that Cowley is too small a poet for the magnitude of the task
he has set himself; whereas there can be successful minor lyrics, a
good minor epic is almost a contradiction in terms — the epic must
be great or fail. The traditional, grandiose epic claims of originality
and stature (I. 27–8; 33–4) sound in this poem hollow, or even
absurd, and Cowley himself seems to have been embarrassed by
them: 'I hope this kind of boast, which I have been taught by almost
all the old poets, will not seem immodest' (I, note 3). The notes
reveal an almost abject preoccupation with precedent. For example
Cowley is prepared to imitate Virgil's unfinished half-lines, not out
of some inner compulsion, but simply as an available rhetorical
device: 'Though none of the English poets, nor indeed of the
ancient Latin, have imitated Virgil in leaving sometimes half verses
. . . yet his authority alone is sufficient' (I, note 14). Sometimes the
results are almost ludicrous, as when the Hebrew name David is
replaced by a Greek patronymic, Jessides, son of Jesse (III, note
10). Too often Cowley leaves the tradition to work for him. For
example his jejune use of a traditional epic simile for Goliath's
spear, 'His spear the trunk was of a lofty tree, / Which nature meant
some tall ship's mast should be' (III. 393–4), is worth comparing
with Milton's dizzying treatment of the same motif (I. 292–5).

Johnson thought that it was the metaphysical conceits which
spoiled the poem, instancing the detailed account of Gabriel's
accoutrements as he descends to earth (II. 795ff):

He took for skin a cloud most soft and bright,
That e'er the midday sun pierced through with light;
Upon his cheeks a lively blush he spread,
Washed from the morning beauties' deepest red;
An harmless flaming meteor shone for hair,
And fell adown his shoulders with loose care;
He cuts out a silk mantle from the skies,
Where the most sprightly azure pleased the eyes;
This he with starry vapours spangles all,

31

Took in their prime ere they grow ripe and fall;
Of a new rainbow, ere it fret or fade,
The choicest piece took out, a scarf is made.

Johnson comments:

> That Gabriel was invested with the softest or brightest colours of
> the sky we might have been told, and been dismissed to improve
> the idea in our different proportions of conception; but Cowley
> could not let us go till he had related where Gabriel first got his
> skin, and then his mantle, then his lace, and then his scarf, and
> related it in the terms of the mercer and tailor.[41]

In fact, however, this pert, 'rococo' set-piece is one of the few
passages of the poem that lodges itself in the memory; elsewhere
Cowley's verse is merely dull, smoother than Milton's, but wholly
lacking energy and daring. One could directly compare Cowley's
pretty but enervate account of the Creation (I. 783ff) with Milton's.
For example:

> He smoothed the rough-cast moon's imperfect mould,
> And combed her beaming locks with sacred gold.
> Be thou (said he) queen of this mournful night,
> And as he spake, she arose clad o'er in light,
> With thousand stars attending on her train;
> With her they rise, with her they set again    (I. 811–16)

with

> then formed the moon
> Globose, and every magnitude of stars,
> And sowed with stars the heaven thick as a field.    (*PL* VII.
> 356–8)

Cowley is unhappy too in his subject. Where Milton chose what
we should today call a Biblical myth, Cowley was faced with the
complex meanderings of the historical books of Samuel, Kings and
Chronicles. As a result he fails to give the poem any unity of action,
falling into the same trap as the bad epic poets censured by Aristotle
who thought that a single hero was enough to confer such unity. The
historical nature of the material also created problems when Cowley

sought to elaborate the original with additional 'fictions', and his notes seem indeed to display considerable anxiety about the status and authority of these embellishments; on occasion the reader is told that some detail must be taken 'in a poetical sense' (I, note 11). For example, Asahel, said in II Samuel 2:18 to be 'as light of foot as a wild roe', becomes a veritable Camilla (*Aen.* VII. 803ff):

> Oft o'er the lawns and meadows would he pass,
> His weight unknown and harmless to the grass;
> Oft o'er the sands and hollow dust would trace,
> Yet no one atom trouble or displace.    (III. 83–6)

Cowley's note (9) shows his embarrassment and reliance on classical authority, in his words 'to excuse me in this place'; but such fantasy does not belong in the sober world of authentic history. The same problem was to confront Milton when he turned from Old Testament myth to the Gospels in *Paradise Regained*. Few readers are worried by Satan's journey through the abyss, although it has no Biblical authority, but it is much less convincing when Christ is presented by Satan with a *Tempest*-like magic banquet in *Paradise Regained* II. 337ff. It is true that Milton has in fact selected one of the episodes in the Gospels which has most the flavour of myth, but even so inventions of this kind sit awkwardly there. The historical subject-matter also made it difficult for Cowley to supply an appropriate divine apparatus. In *Paradise Lost* Milton selected a subject in which the divine action could play a natural role. By contrast Satan and his ministers in the *Davideis* are too evidently mere 'machines', behaving in exactly the manner of the gods of classical epic, and having little integral function in the plot.

Vida and Cowley are both, in their different ways, accomplished writers, and their failure highlights Milton's success in squaring the circle and also shows just what a knife-edged thing that success is. One could express the difference by saying that, whereas Vida and Cowley offer epicised Bible, Milton, rather, took the epic and Biblicised it. In Milton the tension between two styles and two sorts of content is acknowledged and its power exploited. There is no question of Milton trying to improve on the Bible stylistically since, as we have seen, he believed in the superiority of Hebrew to Greek poetry on literary as well as on moral grounds. Rather the Bible provides its own stylistic impulse in *Paradise Lost*, an impulse which often pushes against the classicising epic manner. An obvious example occurs in Book X where Milton follows quite closely the scriptural words of God's judgement on Adam and Eve and the Serpent so that, in Addison's words, 'he has rather chosen to neglect the numerousness of his verse [i.e. the regularity of metre] than to deviate from those speeches which are recorded on this great occasion'.[42] The opening of the poem contains a more subtle instance (I. 6–10):

> . . . heavenly Muse, that on the secret top
> Of Oreb or of Sinai didst inspire
> That shepherd who first taught the chosen seed
> In the beginning how the heavens and earth
> Rose out of chaos . . .

It is not just that the names and their associations are Biblical. In line 9 the stately epic movement momentarily flickers and gives place to the familiar prose rhythm of the opening of the English Bible: 'In the beginning God created the heaven and the earth.' Our sense of the verse falters briefly with the change of register. This Biblical impulse is, as I have already suggested, to an extent an impulse towards stylistic humility and simplicity. In Fisch's words, 'Critics have not always done justice to the importance of the "low" style — the *genus humile* — in *Paradise Lost*. This style is most evident where Milton most closely follows the narrative parts of the Hebrew Scripture' (Fisch cites VIII. 494–9 as an example).[43]

While the classical and the Biblical are intertwined throughout the poem, there is some overall movement from classical to Biblical, which is in part connected with the displacement of Satan as the poem's centre of interest, and which constitutes an increasing Biblicising of the epic mode. It is curious how reluctant some critics are to acknowledge this shift. For example, Blessington regards Book VII, the account of the Creation, as the expansion into a major structural unit of Iopas' song of creation in *Aeneid* I. 40–76.[44] In reality the book's source is simply the opening of Genesis and its progeny in Christian literature, and it is largely superfluous to invoke Virgil at all in this connection.

The tension between Christian and classical relates to another of the main tensions of *Paradise Lost*, that between external and internal, inner and outer. We normally think of the epic as being characteristically concerned with the public and the external, whereas Christian literature revolves around the individual soul's encounter with God. Many have felt like Johnson that, simple devotional works apart, Christianity does not afford a proper subject for literature: 'The ideas of Christian theology are too simple for eloquence, too sacred for fiction and too majestic for ornament; to recommend them by tropes and figures is to magnify by a concave mirror the sidereal hemisphere.'[45] It is for such reasons that C.S. Lewis concludes that *Paradise Lost* is not properly speaking a religious poem at all:

> If a Christian reader has found his devotion quickened by reading the medieval hymns or Dante or Herbert or Traherne . . . and then turns to *Paradise Lost*, he will be disappointed. How cold, how heavy and external it will all seem! How many blankets seem to be interposed between us and our object! But I am not sure that *Paradise Lost* was intended to be a religious poem in the sense suggested . . . It is a poem depicting the objective pattern of things, the attempted destruction of that pattern by rebellious self love, and the triumphant absorption of that rebellion into a yet more complex pattern. The cosmic story — the ultimate *plot* in which all other stories are episodes — is set before us. We are invited, for the time being, to look at it from outside. And that is not, in itself, a religious exercise. When we remember that we also have our places in this plot, that we also, at any given moment, are moving either towards the Messianic or towards the Satanic position, then we are entering the world of religion. But when we do that, our epic holiday is over: we rightly shut up our Milton. In the religious life man faces God and God faces man. But in the epic it is feigned, for the moment, that we, as readers, can step aside and see the faces both of God and man in profile.[46]

Certainly *Paradise Lost* is not as obviously a religious poem as the *Divine Comedy* or *Piers Plowman*, so that to an extent Lewis is right; but only to an extent, since *Paradise Lost* is not as consistently external and objective as he implies. We may take as an example the moment when the Son returns to heaven after the expulsion of the rebel angels, an event that anticipates the final triumph of the Last Judgement and is couched in the language of apocalypse (VI. 880–92):

> Sole victor from the expulsion of his foes
> Messiah his triumphal chariot turned;

To meet him all his saints, who silent stood
Eye witnesses of his almighty acts,
With jubilee advanced, and as they went,
Shaded with branching palm, each order bright,
Sung triumph and him sung victorious king,
Son, heir and lord, to him dominion given
Worthiest to reign; he celebrated rode
Triumphant through mid heaven into the courts
And temple of his mighty Father throned
On high, who into glory him received,
Where now he sits at the right hand of bliss.

The passage is complexly typological. The palm branches prefigure those of Revelation 7: 9, which in turn reflect the palms carried by Christ's followers at the entry to Jerusalem. The image of Christ received 'at the right hand of bliss' looks forward to the Ascension; the cosmic time-scale injects a strongly religious intensity. The last line is of especial significance. The present tense ostensibly refers to the time when Raphael is speaking, but, in view of its liturgical overtones, it is easily applied to any present time, whether Milton's or the reader's. Parts of the creed may be recalled: 'Thou that *sittest* at the right hand of God the Father', 'and ascended into heaven, and *sitteth* on the right hand of the Father, and he shall come again with glory'. The poet seems to employ familiar Biblical and liturgical phrases almost as an act of prayer; narrative has been tempered by meditation, time takes on the accents of eternity. It is with something of a shock that the reader is then reminded that it is Raphael, not Milton, who speaks. There is a similar shift in perspective in III. 410–17:

O unexampled love,
Love nowhere to be found less than divine!
Hail, Son of God, saviour of men, thy name
Shall be the copious matter of my song
Henceforth, and never shall my harp thy praise
Forget, nor from thy Father's praise disjoin.
    Thus they in heaven, above the starry sphere,
Their happy hours in joy and hymning spent.

Milton is reporting the psalm-like hymn that the angels sing in heaven to praise the Son after his offer of the Atonement. As the hymn proceeds, Milton seems to be engaging in a personal act of worship. 'Hail, Son of God' echoes the invocation 'Hail, holy light' at the beginning of Book III, and the words seem the direct utterance of the poet. It comes as a sharp switch when we read immediately afterwards that 'Thus they in heaven' were singing. In general one could say that the poem fluctuates between two poles. On the one hand there is all that is external, objective, solid — embracing, in Milton's scheme, all time and all space; the epic world, traditionally grand and impressive. The magniloquent epic claims become in Milton's hands the sober truth: his events are literally more momentous than any others, his characters literally larger. On the other hand there is the internal world of spiritual values. The huge epic structure, with its proliferation of vivid detail, its ordered universe, its gigantic figures — all that tends towards the concrete, the externally presented — this is the paradoxical vehicle in which abstract, internal conditions are recognised as ultimate truth. The external Hell is vividly evoked, but we soon learn that Satan is in hell wherever he is: 'Which way I fly is Hell, myself am Hell' (IV. 75).[47] Milton gorgeously describes the Earthly Paradise, but Michael later tells Adam that the crucial matter was the state of mind of its inhabitants. Eden is lost forever, destined to become a desert (XI. 829ff), but what remains is more valuable, the spiritual Paradise within, 'happier far' (XII. 587). It is the same with Milton's universe; he constructs a consistent model which he uses to dazzling effect, yet in VIII. 159ff Raphael, after expounding a geocentric system, hints that this model may be incorrect, concluding that for man the matter is of little significance — Milton thus lets the bottom fall out of the poem's apparently solid universe with characteristic insouciance. Most importantly, the figure of God in the poem is mainly presented in solid and concrete terms, disagreeable to many readers, though with both Biblical and classical precedent; yet in the end the need for such externality will cease, for after the Last Judgement 'Then thou thy regal sceptre shall lay by, / For regal sceptre then no more shall need; / God shall be all in all' (III. 339–41).

In general the poem moves from outer to inner, from the external Hell to the inner hell of Satan's mind, from the Earthly Paradise to the paradise within. Furthermore it has the characteristic movement of most religious poetry, a movement into pre-existing knowledge. As *Little Gidding* puts it: 'We shall not cease from exploration / And the end of all our exploring / Will be to arrive where we started / And know the place for the first time'. Adam learns at the end of the poem that 'to obey is best / And love with fear the only God' (XII. 561–2). This conclusion is circular, for this is what Adam always knew and had been content to express, but the shattering developments have given the old meaning a new dimension.

All this has a bearing on a long-standing problem. The presentation of Satan takes us into a critical quagmire. Early in the field was Blake with his celebrated dictum that Milton was of the Devil's party without knowing it.[48] Some versions of the 'Satanist heresy' ignore too many elements in the poem to be tenable. For example the view that Satan is the heroic opponent of tyranny ignores the fact that Satan's democratic rhetoric is specious and Stalinist; at the end of the infernal council the devils prostrate themselves before their new monarch, whose 'heroic' offer to journey to earth, which parodies the Son's self-offering in the Atonement, is designed to aggrandise himself and pre-empts potential rivals in supremacy (II. 466ff). In general a Satan who leers malignly in jealous loathing of the happiness of others (IV. 502ff) or who squats ignobly at Eve's ear (IV. 800) is not especially likeable. Yet we have what is in certain respects a glittering portrayal, and one that is bound up, in complex ways, with Milton's whole attitude to pagan epic. Satan comes enmeshed in echoes of some of the finest passages in Homer and Virgil, and he is more closely associated with epic values and activities than any other of the poem's major characters. For example in I. 133 Satan presents God's supremacy in terms of 'strength, or chance or fate', a pagan trinity (cf. II. 558ff), while in VI. 422 he appeals to the devils' desire for 'honour, dominion, glory and renown', an appeal that Achilles would have warmed to. By contrast Raphael in VI. 373ff refuses to 'eternise' the names of those who fought in heaven; the good are indifferent to men's praise, while the bad deserve only oblivion (admittedly he does not strictly carry out this programme). In IV. 82 Satan reveals his 'dread of shame', something he shares with Hector and other Homeric heroes. One might argue accordingly that Milton is teaching us to regard the world of classical epic as one among Satan's works. However Satan's relationship with classical epic heroism is more complex than this, since, as Blessington rightly insists, he is unsatisfactory also by Homeric or Virgilian standards; we are far from the deserving Odysseus whom Zeus commends for his piety, let alone the dutiful Aeneas labouring under the decrees of heaven to bring to pass a future he will never see at the cost of his own earthly happiness. Furthermore the good angels are also associated with classical epic, for example holding, like the devils, heroic games (IV. 551ff; cf. II.528ff). Indeed it has been shown that Milton's Satan is in certain ways *less* heroic that his counterparts in some of the continental poems about war in heaven.[49]

Why then did Milton allow a sense of Satan's glamour to persist? A famous interpretation, most fully formulated by Stanley Fish, sees as rhetorical strategy what before had been treated as unconscious or semi-conscious impulse. We are to be surprised by sin, caught out in our own fallenness, as we readily slip into a Satanic viewpoint. From such a position the poet and poem will, if we co-operate with them, gradually free us. There is, I think, deliberate strategy here, though perhaps Milton has not mastered it as fully as Fish believes. The approach works well with Satan's speeches, where the enveloping rhetoric is frequently rebuffed by the stern authorial voice, less so with those parts of the narrative where nothing theological or moral is at issue. Here the problem is that Milton writes more delicately and with more intensity about (say) Satan's flight than he does about the flight of the good angels, as if something in Satan released his imagination to a quite abnormal degree:

> . . . then soars
> Up to the fiery concave towering high;
> As when far off at sea a fleet descried
> Hangs in the clouds, by equinoctial winds
> Close sailing from Bengala, or the isles
> Of Ternate or Tidore, whence merchants bring
> Their spicy drugs.   (II. 634–40)

There is nothing that quite matches the imaginative perfection of the word 'hangs' (recalling Virgil's use of *pendere*) in the flight of Uriel or Raphael.

The problem (if such it is) is not easily resolved, but two points may be made. First, there is one obvious sense in which Milton and the reader must be of the devil's party. For both are fallen, and, before Book IX, we are inevitably more directly reflected in Satan than in any other character. It is theologically and psychologically right that he should be our way into the poem and that it is first with his vision that we see the Earthly Paradise. The psychological meanderings of his great soliloquy (IV. 32ff) are all too close to home; the reader recognises the workings of his own mind, for in all his doubts about God Satan has preceded him. As soon as we have a fallen Adam and Eve to empathise with, there is no more need for a psychologically plausible and delicately human Satan, and he can be bundled unceremoniously out of the poem. Secondly we must resist a presumption, which our ancestors seem not to have shared, that beauty is truth. In the words of J.R.R. Tolkien: 'We find it difficult to conceive of evil and beauty together. The fear of the beautiful fay that ran through the elder ages almost eludes our grasp.'[50] (Tolkien apparently connects this shift in response with the sheer increase in the physical ugliness of the environment which accompanied industrialisation.) An instructive parallel from painting suggests that we are dealing not with individual idiosyncrasy only but with the sensibility of an age. Among the paintings by Tintoretto (1518–94) in the Scuola di San Rocco in Venice is a fine Temptation of Christ.[51] The Saviour, clothed, sits with his face sideways, partly in shadow, bearded and expressionless. Satan by contrast is shown as a beautiful youth with large roseate wings, wearing skin-tight and transparent armour that reveals his naked body beneath; the figure shows a pagan delight in youthful male beauty. Satan reaches out towards Christ in a gesture of yearning, holding the stones to be made bread; the expression on his face, which is of some loveliness, seems tinged with a noble melancholy, an indefinable sadness. Although Satan is positioned at the lower left side of the painting, the composition makes him the inevitable focus of the viewer's attention. Here, then, is a remarkable visual analogue for the exquisite verses that accompany the prince of darkness in *Paradise Lost*. Yet no one has ever suggested, so far as I am aware, that the pious Tintoretto was secretly of the devil's party.

Finally, while the paganism of the classical world and the literary forms in which it had found expression were not simply rejected by Milton, they were clearly to him provisional and inadequate. The opening two books of *Paradise Lost* employ a predominantly heroic mode closely reminiscent of Homer and Virgil, a mode in which Satan can appear at his most impressive. But these epic tones increasingly give place to other notes, at once more Biblical and more inward, and these necessarily widen the perspective from which Satan must be seen and judged. This is not to say that the portrayal of Satan, any more than the poem as a whole, can be reduced to perfect orderliness. Doubtless Milton's was a divided sensibility, torn between a sense of the beauty of pagan literature and of its inadequacy, and doubtless these divisions played their part in making Satan so spell-binding a figure. But there is also conscious design as Milton pours new wine into old bottles, wrenching pagan epic to new Biblical purposes and forcing on recalcitrant material a new meaning and a new inwardness. Inevitably, strains result; to quote Fisch again, *Paradise Lost* is 'one of the least harmonious poems in the English language', one that is 'full of profound unrest, of unresolved intentions, of contradictory emphases'.[52] But that is not to criticise the poem, but rather to point to the very centre of its power.

## Milton the Metaphrast

*Paradise Lost* is not a poem for scholars only, but it was written by a scholar. This shows itself not so much in the allusions and references, since these are characteristic of the bulk of Renaissance poetry, as in certain curious qualities of the language. Johnson claimed that Milton 'formed his style by a perverse and pedantic principle', the desire 'to use English words with a foreign idiom'; thus 'of him, at last, may be said what Jonson says of Spenser, that "he wrote no language", but has formed what Butler calls "a Babylonish dialect", in itself harsh and barbarous, but made, by exalted genius and extensive learning, the vehicle of so much instruction and so much pleasure that, like other lovers, we find grace in its deformity'.[53] Addison, though much less critically, had also stressed the importance of this element in the style of *Paradise Lost*:

Another way of raising the language and giving it a poetical turn is to make use of the idioms of other tongues . . . Milton, in conformity with the practice of the ancient poets and with Aristotle's rule, has infused a great many Latinisms as well as Grecisms and sometimes Hebraisms into the language of his poem . . .[54]

Addison thought that Milton aimed in this way 'to give his verse the greater sound and throw it out of prose', providing 'pomp of sound and energy of expression' to compensate for the lack of rhyme. Certainly the use of foreign idioms is a determining factor for the

41

overall timbre of the verse, as Milton uses departures from normal English syntax and word order to give that calculated roughness, that *asprezza*, which Tasso had recommended as a way of achieving the requisite heroic magnificence.[55] The modification of English syntax is used as an expressive device in particular contexts, as Ricks has shown in detail, and also in general to energise the verse, to maintain its powerful flow. The result is not in any sense a pastiche of Latin — or Greek or Hebrew — but a completely fresh creation in which, in Coleridge's words, 'the connection of the sentences and the position of the words are exquisitely artificial, but the position is rather according to the logic of passion or universal logic than to the logic of grammar'.[56] The creation of this style required a poet's imagination, but also perhaps a scholar's nicety in regard to the particularities of languages other than his own. Perhaps the closest parallel is the verse of another poet-scholar, Hopkins, who likewise strained the expressive resources of English, although largely lacking Milton's exact ear for verbal music. The consequence, as Eliot observed, is that Milton's style 'is not a *classic* style, in that it is not the elevation of a *common* style, by the final touch of genius, to greatness. It is, from the foundation, and in every particular, a personal style.'[57] The paradox is that Milton, by sheer force of his genius and subsequent prestige, was able to make this idiosyncratic creation into one of the norms of English verse.

Milton's fascination with the alien properties of other languages is shown in his translation of Horace's Pyrrha Ode (I. 5), in which Horace observes with amusement the flirtatious antics of a former mistress. In the *Preface to Ovid's Epistles* of 1680 Dryden uses the word 'metaphrase' to describe the kind of translation where word-for-word equivalence is sought, in contrast to 'paraphrase', a freer translation, where 'the author is kept in view by the translator so as never to be lost but his words are not so strictly followed as his sense'.[58] Dryden, like many since, thought that metaphrase was pedantic and servile, whereas in paraphrase the spirit of the original could be captured. There is, however, a sense in which only in metaphrase can a detailed encounter with the original work take place, since only the metaphrast respects its alien and (in the case of the classics) its ancient character, and tries to reproduce its linguistic texture exactly and in detail. Thereby he may also extend the capacities of his native language (as happens with the Hebraisms and Grecisms of the Authorised Version of the Bible) and with it the sensibilities of the reader. It is significant that this was the path that

Milton chose to tread in his version of the Pyrrha Ode, which may usefully be compared with another translation from the period which Dryden would presumably have categorised as a paraphrase:

Quis multa gracilis te puer in rosa
perfusus liquidis urget odoribus
    grato, Pyrrha, sub antro?
      cui flavam religas comam,
simplex munditiis? Heu quotiens fidem
mutatosque deos flebit et aspera
    nigris aequora ventis
      emirabitur insolens
qui nunc te fruitur credulus aurea,
qui semper vacuam, semper amabilem
    sperat, nescius aurae
      fallacis. miseris, quibus
intemptata nites; me tabula sacer
votiva paries indicat uvida
    suspendisse potenti
      vestimenta maris deo.


What stripling now thee discomposes,
In woodbine rooms, on beds of roses,
    For whom thy auburn hair,
    Is spread, unpainted fair?
How will he one day curse thy oaths
And heaven that witnessed your betroaths!
    How will the poor cuckold,
    That deems thee perfect gold,
Bearing no stamp but his, be mazed
To see a sudden tempest raised!
    He dreams not of the winds,
    And thinks all gold that shines.
For me my votive table shows
That I have hung up my wet clothes
    Upon the temple wall
    Of sea's great admiral.

                            (Fanshawe)

What slender youth bedewed with liquid odours
Courts thee on roses in some pleasant cave,
   Pyrrha, for whom bindest thou
   In wreaths thy golden hair,
Plain in thy neatness? O how oft shall he
On faith and changed gods complain, and seas
   Rough with black winds and storms
   Unwonted shall admire,
Who now enjoys thee credulous, all gold,
Who always vacant, always amiable
   Hopes thee, of flattering gales
   Unmindful! Hapless they
To whom thou untried seem'st fair. Me in my vowed
Picture the sacred wall declares to have hung
   My dark and dropping weeds
   To the stern god of sea.

('Rendered almost word for word without rhyme according to the Latin measure, as near as the language will permit')

In the version by Sir Richard Fanshawe (1608–66) the whole approach seems one of unsatisfactory compromise. On the one hand there is a lack of really striking phrase making, on the other much that is in Horace's poem has simply disappeared: in the first stanza, for example, specific mention of the grotto, and the perfume that drenches the young man. The dominant sea image is weakened, and on one occasion diluted by imagery not in the original ('bearing no stamp but his'). On the credit side Fanshawe has tried to provide an appropriate stanza form, in fact the same stanza form that Marvell also used with far greater skill, presumably to represent Horatian Alcaics, in his famous 'Horatian Ode' for Cromwell. Unfortunately in Fanshawe the couplets assert themselves to the cost of the stanza, and the original's complex unity is thereby dissipated; the tensions in the verse are held and released within the couplet, and thus it is difficult for Fanshawe to obtain the rhythmic momentum that characterises Horace's poem. Fanshawe was praised by a contemporary for preserving the flame in his translations,[59] but actually the tone of Horace's poem eludes him, above all the avuncular and amiable malice; the phrase 'poor cuckold' is a disaster from which the poem could never have quite recovered. In sum Fanshawe's paraphrase tells us too little about the original, while at the same time not floating free of it to become as it were a fresh creation (which is what happens with many of the great translations, including some of Dryden's own).

By contrast I find it difficult to be altogether temperate in my admiration for Milton's metaphrase. It is not known when Milton wrote it, the suggestions ranging from 1626, a couple of years before the 'Nativity Ode', to 1655, by which time the poet had almost certainly begun work on *Paradise Lost*. This uncertainty is interesting in view of the radical changes in Milton's style over these years. The explanation is, I think, that the style of his Pyrrha is dictated by the original rather than imposed upon it; hence the difficulty of dating the piece on purely stylistic grounds (external evidence is lacking). It might be tempting to urge the translation's 'modernity' — certainly it is astonishingly innovatory both linguistically and rhythmically in terms of normal seventeenth-century practice — but I would prefer to see a sort of timelessness. We hear so much about Milton's personal arrogance that it is worth stressing the strange humility of his procedure here. A poet, whose sensitivity and originality in the use of the English language is comparable only with Shakespeare's, 'empties himself', if such theological language may be excused, before the genius of another.

Like Fanshawe, Milton employs an appropriate stanza form, one in fact a little closer to Horace's in terms of relative line lengths (two iambic pentameters followed by two iambic trimeters), but unlike Fanshawe he makes no use of rhyme. More importantly he reproduces the way that Horace's complex sentences cut across stanza divisions, thus helping to cement the poem into a single unified structure. For example the climactic effect of holding back the phrase 'simplex munditiis' to the beginning of the second stanza, thereby creating a considerable release of verbal energy at this point by the run-on effect, is precisely caught. Milton too seeks to reproduce as much as possible of the word order and syntactic movement of the original. There are obvious limits to what is possible as a result of the differences between Latin and English syntax, and the fact that Latin, unlike English, is a fully inflected language, thereby facilitating a much greater freedom in word order. One could not translate the first line of the Pyrrha Ode as 'What many slender you boy among a rose', since clearly the syntactic relationship between the words, indicated in Horace's densely clotted textures by the case endings, would be wholly obscure. In fact Horace's word order here is mimetic: the 'gracilis

45

puer' surrounds the girl ('te'), and the roses ('multa in rosa') in turn surround the lovers.[60] Milton does not imitate this effect, which perhaps is not really imitable. The sudden and unexpected revelation that Horace has been one of Pyrrha's lovers requires the shock effect of beginning the final sentence with 'me', and both Fanshawe and Milton reproduce this abrupt transition, Milton much more boldly. Milton also tries to avoid, as far as is possible, the use of the definite and indefinite article (four examples in Fanshawe, two in Milton), which helps to make English a less monumental and compressed language than Latin, which has no such articles; hence 'the stern god of sea'. Other English poets have tried to drive out that irritating mass of small words, including Hopkins, who, for example, in 'Heaven-Haven' writes 'I have desired to go / Where springs not fail' or, in the sonnet, 'Thou art indeed just, Lord', 'birds build but not I build'. In line 9 Milton retains the striking juxtaposition of adjectives 'credulus aurea', even at the risk of initial unintelligibility. It may take the Latinless reader a moment or two to work out that the boy is 'credulous', the girl 'all gold' (although the difficulty is often exaggerated), but the inversions of the next two lines, though convoluted, pose no such problems. Horace's lyric poetry is anyway difficult, and some effort in unravelling it is usually required. Milton's version is really no more complicated than the original, where too the word order in no way corresponds to normal Latin usage.

Milton's version is not perfect. 'Plain in thy neatness' seems too puritanical for 'simplex munditiis', but if Milton fails here, he fails with the nation, since I know no satisfactory rendering of this phrase; Ronald Storrs, in the introduction to his collection of translations of this poem, cites what must be two of the very worst: 'Bright charmer, nicely clean though plain' and Christopher Smart's 'so seeming in your cleanly vest, / Whose plainness is the pink of taste'.[61] Milton does not imitate the word play 'aurea: aurae'. 'Golden' hair is a mistake for 'flavam', since it detracts from the effect of 'aurea' later in the poem; 'yellow' would be preferable. More significantly Milton does not capture the elegance that rather unexpectedly goes with the dense and difficult textures of the original (though Nisbet and Hubbard are right to observe that Horace's poem is not 'particularly pretty')[62] nor the brio and bounce of the final stanza. But it remains true that Milton's is the only version that I know that even begins to tell us what is happening in detail in the Ode and to capture its linguistic tension, above all by reproducing its splendid periods. It also shows Milton's sense of the radical differences between Latin and English verse — comparable with his sense of the difference between a pagan and a Christian culture — and of the value of not seeking to accommodate them in bland synthesis.[63]

The sensibility and habits of mind that produced the Pyrrha translation are everywhere evident in *Paradise Lost* and indeed in Milton's works as a whole. Furthermore much of Milton's poetic career could be seen as a series of acts of metaphrase, by which aspects of Milton's beloved ancient literature, both classical and Hebrew, could be brought, with as little damage as possible, into his native tongue. Despite the Biblicising that I have described, *Paradise Lost* is still more radically like a classical epic than anything else in English or indeed in any other modern language. By contrast Spenser's 'epic' the *Faerie Queene* would hardly have been recognised by Virgil as belonging to the same genre as the *Aeneid*. *Samson Agonistes* is almost unique in giving some idea of the alien qualities of Greek drama, while 'Lycidas' is another piece of poetic archaeology — a revival of the pastoral elegy — a point that becomes clear if we compare it with the more fashionable tributes to Edward King that originally appeared alongside it. When it was published after the Restoration *Paradise Lost* must have appeared like an impressive but weird anachronism, something written out of its time or rather oddly timeless. One might compare the late works of J.S. Bach, in one sense old-fashioned in their indifference to contemporary interests, in another so advanced that it was many years before they could receive their proper due. Bach too took a defunct form — in his case the fugue — and brought it to unimagined heights of complexity and richness. I end this section on Milton the metaphrast with the pleasant allegory of A.D. Nuttall:

One might compare the translator with a man who is asked to carry a large awkwardly-shaped burden through a narrow gate into his native city. The modern man, Procrustes-like, lops off the corners and passes easily through the gate. Milton, on the contrary, carries his burden as though it were sacred, and after great strain and some damage to the gate-posts gets it within his city walls.[64]

# Introduction

## Notes

1. See Addison, 'Notes upon the Twelve Books of Paradise Lost', (*The Spectator*, 1712): in John T. Shawcross (ed.), *Milton: The Critical Heritage* (Routledge & Kegan Paul, London, 1970), p. 168, and Donald F. Bond (ed.), *The Spectator* (5 vols, Clarendon Press, Oxford, 1965), vol. 3, p. 62.
2. Bond (ed.), *Spectator*, vol. 1, p. 297.
3. See Douglas Bush, 'Ironic and Ambiguous Allusion in *Paradise Lost*', *Journal of English and Germanic Philology*, vol. 60 (1961), pp. 631–40. Bush also instances Adam's words to Eve (IV. 481–2) which may recall, with deliberate inappropriateness, Apollo's pursuit of Daphne in *Met.* I, especially 504, 514 (p. 638).
4. See G.S. Kirk, *Homer and the Oral Tradition* (Cambridge University Press, 1976) p. 89.
5. Francis C. Blessington, *Paradise Lost and the Classical Epic* (Routledge & Kegan Paul, Boston and London, 1979) pp. 1ff.
6. Ibid., pp. 7–8. For the sources see James A. Freeman, 'The Roof Was Fretted Gold', *Comparative Literature*, vol. 27 (1975), pp. 254–66; Claes Schaar, *The Full Voic'd Quire Below: Vertical Context Systems in Paradise Lost*, Lund Studies in English 60 (Gleerup, Lund, 1982), pp. 288–305.
7. There is a parallel in an ode of Bacchylides (5. 65–7) not discovered until 1896; see C.M. Bowra, *From Virgil to Milton* (Macmillan and St. Martin's Press, London and New York, 1945), pp. 240–1. For the sources see James P. Holoka, ' "Thick as Autumnal Leaves": The Structure and Generic Potentials of an Epic Simile', *Milton Quarterly*, vol. 10 (1976), pp. 78–83; Schaar, *Full Voic'd Quire*, pp. 52–8.
8. See e.g. (for Helen and Nausicaa) William B. Hunter Jr (ed.), *A Milton Encyclopedia*, (8 vols, Bucknell University Press and Associated University Presses, Lewisburg and London, 1978–80), vol. 4, pp. 22–3.
9. This and other citations from the translations of Richmond Lattimore are from *The Odyssey of Homer* (Harper & Row, New York, 1967) and *The Iliad of Homer* (University of Chicago Press, 1951).
10. Christopher Ricks, *Milton's Grand Style* (Oxford University Press, London, Oxford, New York, 1963), pp. 97–9.
11. For instances of this *topos* see John S. Coolidge, 'Great Things and Small: The Virgilian Progression', *Comparative Literature*, vol. 17 (1965) pp. 1–16, p. 2 note 3, and for Milton's use of it, pp. 18–19.
12. See J.C. Bramble, *Persius and the Programmatic Satire: A Study in Form and Imagery* (Cambridge University Press, 1974) pp. 156–73.
13. Addison, 'Notes': in Shawcross (ed.), *Milton*, p. 166, and Bond (ed.), *Spectator*, vol. 3, p. 60.
14. 'The Life of Milton' in Samuel Johnson, *Lives of the English Poets*, ed. G.B. Hill (3 vols, Clarendon Press, Oxford, 1905), vol. 1, p. 187.
15. Addison, 'Notes': in Shawcross (ed.), *Milton*, p. 181, and Bond (ed.), *Spectator*, vol. 3, pp. 145–6.
16. George Wither, *A Preparation to the Psalter* (London, 1619), p. 77.
17. Cf. also, for example, Statius, *Thebaid* VII. 706–8; Valerius Flaccus, IV. 398; and see Schaar, *Full Voic'd Quire*, pp. 191–4.
18. Blessington, *Paradise Lost and the Classical Epic*, p. 3.
19. 'Hebraic Style and Motifs in *Paradise Lost*' in R.D. Emma and J.T. Shawcross (eds), *Language and Style in Milton: A Symposium in Honor of the Tercentenary of Paradise Lost* (Frederick Ungar Publishing Co., New York, 1967), p. 40. I am also indebted to a lecture that Professor Fisch gave at the University of Sussex.
20. For Jonson's theory and practice of imitation see Richard S. Peterson, *Imitation and Praise in the Poems of Ben Jonson* (Yale University Press, New Haven and London, 1981), especially ch. 1. For a discussion of some of the theoretical

problems involved see the introduction to Schaar, *Full Voic'd Quire*, pp. 11–33; however, Schaar's attempt to collapse the distinction between an allusion to a particular passage and the use of traditional material and motifs is misguided.

21. See Frank Kermode's Arden edition of *The Tempest* (Methuen, London, 1954), appendix D, pp. 147–50.

22. For some representative Renaissance texts see Joanna Martindale (ed.), *English Humanism: Wyatt to Cowley* (Croom Helm, Beckenham, 1985), pp. 98–156.

23. Some examples are given in D.A. Russell and M. Winterbottom (eds), *Ancient Literary Criticism: The Principal Texts in New Translations* (Clarendon Press, Oxford, 1972), pp. 548–51; and D.A. Russell, *Criticism in Antiquity* (Duckworth, London, 1981) pp. 193–7. For some more sophisticated comparisons see Longinus, *On the Sublime*, 10. 4–6; 15. 6; 16. 2–3.

24. Roger Ascham, *The Schoolmaster* (1570), ed. J.E.B. Mayer (London, 1863; reprinted AMS Press, New York, 1967), p. 141.

25. D.A. Russell, 'De Imitatione' in David West and Tony Woodman (eds), *Creative Imitation and Latin Literature* (Cambridge University Press, 1979) pp. 1–16 (p. 9).

26. See *The Works of John Milton*, ed. F.A. Patterson *et al.* (18 vols and 2 vols index, Columbia University Press, New York, 1931–40), vol. 18, pp. 128ff. (Hereafter *Columbia Milton*.)

27. D.T.Starnes and E.W.Talbert, *Classical Myth and Legend in Renaissance Dictionaries: A Study of Renaissance Dictionaries in their Relation to the Classical Learning of Contemporary English Writers* (University of North Carolina Press, Chapel Hill, 1955), pp. 243–4. This study has too narrow a focus to be entirely convincing (e.g. in the present instance the authors ignore the fact that Sandys also has the form Hermione).

28. Joseph A. Wittreich Jr (ed.), *The Romantics on Milton: Formal Essays and Critical Asides* (Case Western Reserve University Press, Cleveland and London, 1970), p. 157; S.T. Coleridge, *Collected Letters*, ed. E.L. Griggs (Oxford University Press, 1956), vol. 1, p. 164.

29. John Carey, *Milton*, Literature in Perspective Series (Evans Brothers, London, 1969), p. 76.

30. *Columbia Milton*, vol. 3, p. 238.

31. John Donne, *Sermons*, ed. G.R. Potter and E.M. Simpson (10 vols, University of California Press, Berkeley and Los Angeles, 1959), vol. 4, p. 167.

32. See C.G.Osgood, *The Classical Mythology of Milton's English Poems*, Yale Studies in English 8 (Henry Holt, New York, 1900), Introduction, pp. xlv-li; Douglas Bush, *Mythology and the Renaissance Tradition in English Poetry* (University of Minnesota Press and Oxford University Press, Minneapolis and London, 1932), pp. 267–70; D.P. Harding 'Milton and the Renaissance Ovid', *Illinois Studies in Language and Literature*, vol. 30 (1946), pp. 93–5.

33. In *De Doctrina Christiana* I. 12 Milton makes the same point, rather more positively (*Columbia Milton*, vol. 15, p. 209).

34. *The Rambler* 140 (20 July 1751) in W.J. Bate and A.B. Strauss (eds), *The Yale Edition of Samuel Johnson* (Yale University Press, New Haven and London, 1969), vol. 4, p. 378.

35. See E.A.J. Honigmann (ed.), *Milton's Sonnets* (Macmillan, London and New York, 1966), pp. 177–81.

36. J.B. Broadbent, *Some Graver Subject: An Essay on Paradise Lost* (Chatto & Windus, London, 1960), p. 7.

37. A.D.Nuttall, Introduction to *John Milton: The Minor Poems in English*, with notes by Douglas Bush (Macmillan, London, 1972), pp. 46–53.

38. E.R.Curtius, *European Literature and the Latin Middle Ages*, trs. Willard R. Trask (Routledge & Kegan Paul, London and Henley, 1953; paperback 1979), p. 462. For Tasso's approach to these problems see Judith A. Kates, 'The Revaluation

# Introduction

of the Classical Heroic in Tasso and Milton', *Comparative Literature*, vol. 26 (1974), pp. 299–317. She argues that both poets had 'a complex sense of the conflicting allegiances involved in that enterprise', i.e. Christian epic (p. 300). I have not seen her book *Tasso and Milton: The Problem of Christian Epic* (Bucknell University Press, Lewisburg, 1984).

39. The account is by Paolo Tartessio; see Maria A. Di Cesare, *Vida's Christiad and Vergilian Epic* (Columbia University Press, New York and London, 1964), p. 25.

40. See my introduction to *Virgil and his Influence: Bimillennial Studies* (Bristol Classical Press, 1984), pp. 4–5.

41. 'The Life of Cowley' in Johnson, *Lives of the English Poets*, ed. Hill, vol. 1, p. 53.

42. Addison, 'Notes': in Shawcross (ed.), *Milton*, p. 207, and Bond (ed.), *Spectator*, vol. 3, pp. 330–1.

43. 'Hebraic Style' in Emma and Shawcross, *Language and Style in Milton*, p. 56; cf. Thomas Greene, *The Descent from Heaven: A Study in Epic Continuity* (Yale University Press, New Haven and London, 1963), pp. 380ff.

44. Blessington, *Paradise Lost and the Classical Epic*, p. 76.

45. 'The Life of Waller' in Johnson, *Lives of the English Poets*, ed. Hill, vol. 1, pp. 292–3.

46. C.S. Lewis, *A Preface to Paradise Lost* (Oxford University Press, London, Oxford, New York, 1942) p. 132.

47. For hell as both place and condition see C.A. Patrides, *Premises and Motifs in Renaissance Thought and Literature* (Princeton University Press, 1982), ch. 11, pp. 182–99.

48. Wittreich, *Romantics on Milton*, p. 35.

49. See Stella Purce Revard, *The War in Heaven: Paradise Lost and the Tradition of Satan's Rebellion* (Cornell University Press, Ithaca and London, 1980), ch. 6.

50. J.R.R.Tolkien, 'On Fairy-Stories' in *J.R.R. Tolkien: The Monsters and the Critics and Other Essays*, ed. Christopher Tolkien (Allen & Unwin, London, 1983), p. 151.

51. Reproduced in R.M. Frye, *Milton's Imagery and the Visual Arts: Iconographic Tradition in the Epic Poems* (Princeton University Press, 1978), plate 251, or in colour in Carlo Bernari and Pierluigi de Vecchi, *L'Opera Completa del Tintoretto* (Rizzoli Editore, Milan, 1970), plate 34.

52. Emma and Shawcross, *Language and Style in Milton*, p. 58. Those who like T.J.B. Spenser hold that *Paradise Lost* is a species of anti-epic ('*Paradise Lost*: The Anti-Epic' in C.A. Patrides (ed.), *Approaches to Paradise Lost*, The York Tercentenary Lectures (Edward Arnold, London, 1968), pp. 81–98) are thus as guilty of oversimplification as those who treat it as continuously and epically sublime.

53. 'The Life of Milton' in Johnson, *Lives of the Poets*, ed. Hill, vol. 1, pp. 190–1.

54. Addison, 'Notes': in Shawcross (ed.), *Milton*, pp. 160–1, and Bond (ed.), *Spectator*, vol. 3, pp. 12–14.

55. See F.T. Prince, *The Italian Element in Milton's Verse* (Clarendon Press, Oxford, 1954).

56. Wittreich, *Romantics on Milton*, p. 244.

57. T.S.Eliot, 'Milton II', in Frank Kermode (ed.), *Selected Prose of T.S.Eliot* (Faber & Faber, London, 1975), pp. 267–8.

58. John Dryden, *Of Dramatic Poesy and Other Critical Essays*, ed. George Watson (2 vols, Dent, London and New York, 1962), vol. 1, p. 268.

59. John Denham, cited by Dryden; see note 58.

60. See Gilbert Highet, *Poets in a Landscape* (Penguin Books, Harmondsworth, 1959), p. 128.

61. *Ad Pyrrham: A Polyglot Collection of Translations of Horace's Ode to Pyrrha (Book I, Ode 5)*, assembled with an introduction by Ronald Storrs (Oxford University Press, London, New York and Toronto, 1959), pp. 22–3.

50

62. R.G.M. Nisbet and Margaret Hubbard (eds), *A Commentary on Horace: Odes Book I* (Clarendon Press, Oxford, 1973), p. 73.

63. For an excellent discussion see D.P. Harding, *The Club of Hercules: Studies in the Classical Background of Paradise Lost* (University of Illinois Press, Urbana, 1962), pp. 128ff.

64. *John Milton: The Minor Poems*, p. 43.

# 2
# HOMER

## Renaissance Homer

Homer seems to have been Milton's favourite classical poet. It is recorded that Homer was the author that he most liked having read to him in his old age: 'The books in which his daughter . . . represented him as most delighting, after Homer, which he could almost repeat, were Ovid's *Metamorphoses* and Euripides.'[1] According to his admirers the Richardsons, who published an important commentary on *Paradise Lost* in 1734, Milton regretted that he had never visited Greece and Athens, since 'he was more a Greek than a Roman'.[2] Addison comments that 'no poet seems ever to have studied Homer more, or to have more resembled him in the greatness of genius, than Milton'.[3] It is true that in an early Latin poem (*Elegia Prima*, 23–4) Milton grants Virgil the first glory (*laus prima*), but this seems a conventional placement rather than a considered personal judgement. Many Renaissance critics, in particular the Italians (moved perhaps by patriotic zeal) preferred Virgil to Homer on the grounds of the superior artistry and moral usefulness of the *Aeneid*.[4] In particular Julius Caesar Scaliger (1484–1558) included in his influential *Poetices libri septem* (published 1561) an extended comparison of the two poets, in Virgil's favour, and often scornful of Homer. Many of these criticisms were revived and extended in France in the seventeenth and eighteenth centuries. England, however, has usually managed to avoid the worst excesses of Neoclassicism, and Chapman (the translator of Homer), Dryden and Pope all, perhaps surprisingly, agreed that Homer was the greater poet because of his greater originality and fire; for Pope Homer is the poet of 'invention', Virgil of 'judgement', a characteristically neat if misleading Augustan antithesis.[5] Chapman is indignant at the 'impalsied diminution' of Homer by 'Ajantical' critics (that is critics like Homer's lumbering Ajax), chief among them 'soul-blind' Scaliger: 'The majesty he [Homer] enthrones and the spirit he infuseth into the scope of his work so far outshining Virgil that his skirmishes are but mere scramblings of boys to Homer's, the silken body of Virgil's muse curiously drest in gilt and embroidered silver, but Homer's in plain, massy and unvalued [invaluable] gold.'[6]

Homer's Renaissance admirers, who included Erasmus, greatest of the humanists, did not take the view of him that has been widespread over the last two centuries. Since the publication, in 1795, of F.A. Wolf's epoch-making *Prolegomena ad Homerum*, which gave scholarly justification for views more casually advanced earlier in the century by Robert Wood, Thomas Blackwell and others, the *Iliad* and *Odyssey* have often been seen as primitive poems, if indeed really poems at all and not collections of lays stitched together by more or less incompetent editors.[7] (Scholars who think thus are called analysts, in contrast to unitarians who, in Johann Heinrich Voss's words, 'believe in *one* Homer! *One* Iliad! *One* Odyssey!') The analyst case has been weakened by Milman Parry's demonstration that the technique of the Homeric poems is oral (which accounts for many of the features previously put down to multiple authorship); while some recent studies are again presenting the *Iliad* and *Odyssey* as works cunningly put together and embodying a profound vision of life. Certainly many humanists were convinced that the poems were masterly exemplary compositions that offered models of good and bad conduct. Thus Thomas Elyot, who moved in humanist circles and shared much of the vision of Erasmus, recommended them in *The Book Named The Governor* (1531) thus:

> For in his books be contained and most perfectly expressed, not only the documents martial and discipline of arms, but also incomparable wisdoms and instructions for politic governance of people, with the worthy commendation and laud of noble princes; wherewith the readers shall be so all inflamed that they most fervently shall desire and covet, by the imitation of their virtues, to acquire semblable glory. For the which occasion Aristotle, most sharpest witted and excellent learned philosopher, as soon as he had received Alexander from King Philip his father, he before any other thing taught him the most noble works of Homer; wherein Alexander found such sweetness and fruit that ever after he had Homer not only with him in all his journeys but also laid him under his pillow when he went to rest . . . Therefore I now conclude that there is no lesson for a young

gentleman to be compared with Homer, if he be plainly and substantially expounded and declared by the master.[8]

We should not suppose that in stressing the moral value of poetry humanists were not alive to its more direct pleasures. In *De Copia* Erasmus praises Homer for his skill in characterisation — for example the speeches at the opening of *Iliad* XXII reveal 'a wonderful mastery of what is appropriate to each character' — and for his graphic descriptions: 'Is there anything he does not display vividly before our eyes by putting in the appropriate circumstantial detail?' Erasmus also shows a lively appreciation of Homer's quiet narrative skills in a detailed discussion of the famous meeting of Hector and Andromache in *Iliad* VI, concluding 'No one has ever had enough of Homer but is led on by continual delights as he reads'.[9] Erasmus accepts the traditional, and as such things go plausible, allegorisations of Odysseus' wanderings, but avoids the more bizarre allegorical flights favoured by some other Renaissance interpreters.

Milton used the massive Byzantine commentary on Homer of Eustathius,[10] the twelfth-century archbishop, which contains much allegorical exegesis (the Greekless reader can most easily make Eustathius's acquaintance in the notes to Pope's Homer), together, in all likelihood, with the important Renaissance edition by Spondanus (Jean de Sponde), a characteristic humanist production first published in Basle in 1583. This contains a Greek text with facing Latin translation and a reasonably compact commentary marked by considerable good sense. In the preface, dedicated to Henry IV of France, Spondanus advances characteristic humanist perceptions: the *Iliad* is a mirror of courage ('fortitudinis speculum') exemplified in Achilles and the other heroes. (In *Epistles* I. 2 Horace had rather presented the *Iliad* as a negative exemplum: the people pay the price of their leaders' folly and lack of self-control.) In the *Prolegomena*, which includes a defence of poetry, Spondanus displays a theoretical openness to allegorical as well as exemplary understandings.[11] Christian truths are veiled in pagan myths; for example Minerva could be taken as a pagan perversion of *Sapientia*, Wisdom, the second person of the Trinity. Even in the Bible truth is often revealed enigmatically; the obscurities of Scripture ensure that only those understand on whom God has bestowed the ability to penetrate the mysteries. Similarly pagan poetry has hidden beneath the poison of fables much honeyed doctrine which it has revealed only to the worthy. A Christian spirit breathes widely in ancient literature, although mixed with much dross. However in the commentary Spondanus has less use for allegory. In *Iliad* VIII. 17ff Zeus challenges Hera to a contest. If all the other gods fastened a golden chain from heaven and tried to draw him down to earth, they would fail in their attempt; but he could draw them up, together with earth and sea, and suspend them in space from the peaks of Olympus. The golden chain was understood allegorically in antiquity and thereafter, but to Spondanus the episode is merely a demonstration of Zeus' pre-eminence. Spondanus recognises, without fuss, that Homer's theology is far removed from Christianity. For example, of Achilles' pessimistic attitude to death in *Odyssey* XI. 488ff he comments, 'Obviously Homer did not understand about the eternal bliss of souls', while on the lines about the nature of the gods that follow the wounding of Aphrodite in *Iliad* V. 339ff he remarks, 'Our blind Homer is still blind in his understanding of God' ('caecus noster Melesigenes adhuc in Dei cognitione caecutit'). But Zeus' chain is to Spondanus an instance where the gap closes: 'this is one of those places in which Homer thinks well of God, when he asserts that he is omnipotent', whereas elsewhere impiously he makes him subject to Fate. In a longish note on *Odyssey* XIII. 96ff Spondanus expounds an allegorical reading of the poem which he rejects, but adds, 'if anyone is delighted by it, he can use it as far as I am concerned'. Likewise he refers readers to the Neoplatonist Porphyry's famous allegorisation of the Cave of the Nymphs, but makes it clear that in his view it contributes nothing to the understanding of Homer.

Moralistic interpretations are much more to Spondanus's taste. He is particularly eloquent in his praise of the description of the shield of Achilles in *Iliad* XVIII, recommending the interpretation of the scholar J. Goropius, according to which, whereas the device on a shield normally indicates nobility of birth, Homer shows by the scenes on this shield what most ennobles a man. Hephaestus depicts there all the variety of the heavens which lead our minds to the contemplation of the Creator and then 'all the arts and duties of peace and war'. Homer 'does not praise a leisured and idle philosophy, but one which he has brought down from the ordered movements of the stars to the governing of the state'. Chapman follows Spondanus in enthusing about the shield which he regards as figuring 'the universal world',[12] and it may be partly this conception that led Milton to include reminiscences of passages from the shield for the vision of the life of fallen man in *Paradise Lost* XI. 638–711. Curiously such moralising interpretations are again in fashion, if under a different disguise. For example Oliver Taplin has recently argued that the shield provides an implicit criticism of the martial world of the *Iliad*. Homer is thus accommodated to the anti-war ethos of twentieth-century liberalism, and thereby made available to a new generation of readers.[13]

Chapman's great translations, which famously provided for Keats the key to a new golden world, were almost certainly known to Milton, possibly influencing the occasional turn of phrase in *Paradise Lost*.[14] Chapman made extensive use of Spondanus' Latin translation and notes, but he was rather more receptive than Spondanus to allegory. The *Iliad* shows 'the body's fervour and fashion of outward fortitude to all possible height of heroical action', while the theme of the *Odyssey* is the 'fashion of an absolute man, and necessary or fatal passage through many afflictions . . . to his natural haven and country', a pilgrim's progress. Odysseus is an exemplary hero, representing 'the mind's inward, constant and unconquered empire, unbroken, unaltered with any most insolent and tyrannous infliction'. 'Flowers of precept' are strewn everywhere, for example in the depiction of the 'shamefastness' (modesty) of Nausicaa. The more extreme fictions in the poems are to be understood allegorically: 'if the body, being the letter or history, seems fictive and beyond possibility to bring into act, the sense then and allegory, which is the soul, is to be sought.' For example the obstacles to Odysseus' return are the things that hinder us from arriving at the 'only true natural country of every worthy man, whose haven is heaven and the next life, to which this life is but a sea in continual aesture [surging] and vexation'. Chapman felt free to expand and alter the original extensively so as to bring out the full force of what he believed to be Homer's true moral meaning.

How is Milton likely to have read Homer? There is no reason to suppose that he would have been any less delighted than Erasmus by the vividness and narrative skills of the *Iliad* and *Odyssey*. Likewise he read closely and as a scholar, as we know from his brief but learned annotations to Euripides and other ancient writers. The great Columbia edition prints as Milton's some more extensive marginal notes on Pindar taken from a copy of a text of Pindar's Odes believed to have been in the possession of Milton and now at Harvard. However for a number of reasons, including the fact that Milton's normal Greek script is subtly different, it seems probable that these marginalia are in another hand,[15] but even so they are not without interest because they show how a scholarly reader of the period approached an ancient text and the kind of details he was trained to notice. In a note on Pindar's 5th *Olympian* the writer cites no less than 21 parallels for a particular kind of poetic locution commonly found in grander types of poetry whereby, for example, 'the strength of Telemachus' is put for 'the strong Telemachus'; of these 13 come from Homer.[16] A similar scrupulous attention to the diction of ancient poetry left its mark when Milton came to compose his own epic. If we take the figure under discussion, in *Paradise Lost* VI. 355 we find 'where the might of Gabriel fought' for 'the mighty Gabriel'. One could compare too V. 371, 'the angelic virtue answered mild', where 'the angelic virtue' means primarily 'the virtuous angel', although there may also be a kind of pun, since 'virtues' constituted one of the angelic orders.

Milton, who shared the characteristic Renaissance view that poetry in a delightful fashion presents, in his words, 'the whole book of sanctity and virtue through all the instances of example',[17] evidently regarded Homer as one of those ancients by whom 'moral virtue is expressed / By light of nature not in all quite lost' (*PR* IV. 351–2), and thus as a source of pagan wisdom (this contrasts with the common medieval stress on Homer's mendacity). In the *First Defence* Homer is cited as an authority alongside Solomon.[18] In *The Reason of Church Government* an episode from the *Iliad* is used to illustrate a general moral proposition:

> It was thought of old in philosophy that shame, or to call it better the reverence of our elders, our brethren and friends, was the greatest incitement to virtuous deeds and the greatest dissuasion from unworthy attempts that might be. Hence we may read in the *Iliad* where Hector being wished to retire from the battle, many of his forces being routed, makes answer that he durst not for shame, lest the Trojan knights and dames should think he did ignobly.[19]

In *De Doctrina Christiana* Milton quotes with approval the passage in *Odyssey* I (32ff) in which Zeus denies that the gods are to blame for the sufferings of men.[20]

There is a small but instructive instance of Milton's use of Homer in the invocation to *Paradise Lost* VII, where Bellerophon's attempt to ride to heaven exemplifies sinful aspiration. This was the

usual Renaissance interpretation. Alexander Ross, the author of
*Mystagogus Poeticus or the Muses' Interpreter*, a mythological
handbook in regular school use until late in the seventeenth
century, writes: 'By the example of Bellerophon beware of pride,
which will spoil all good actions in us and at last will give us a fall.'[21]
Milton articulates the moral by means of a pun. Bellerophon falls on
the Aleian plain, 'Erroneous there to wander and forlorn'.
'Erroneous' bears both its etymological non-moral and its
developed moral meaning, that is both 'wandering' and 'in error'.
Two passages of classical poetry contributed. In *Odes* IV. 11. 26–9,
in advising a girl not to aim too high in love matters, Horace uses the
story of Bellerophon as a (humorous) example, and points the
moral by a pun, though a different one from Milton's: 'Pegasus who
refused the *weight* of his earthly rider Bellerophon affords a *weighty*
example that you should always follow things worthy of you'
('exemplum *grave* praebet ales / Pegasus terrenum equitem *gravatus*
/ Bellerophontem / semper ut te digna sequare'). Of greater
importance is Glaucus' account of Bellerophon's eventual fate in
*Iliad* VI. When Bellerophon came to be hated of the gods, 'he
wandered (alāto) alone over the Aleian plain' (201). The apparent
word play led commentators, including Eustathius and Spondanus,
to take the Aleian plain to mean the plain of wandering, and this
interpretation obviously gives extra point to Milton's lines.

Again, like Erasmus, Milton was open to some of the traditional
allegorisations of Homer. In *Prolusions* 2 Milton accepts, where, as
we have seen, Spondanus had not, an allegorical sense for Zeus'
golden chain: 'this complete concord and lovely agreement of the
universe, which Pythagoras covertly introduced in poetic fashion,
by means of the word Harmony, Homer too strikingly and
appropriately shadowed forth by means of that golden chain of
Jupiter suspended from heaven.'[22] Certainly in *Paradise Lost* II.
1051 this image comes bearing its traditional freight of post-
Homeric interpretation. Similarly in *Comus* Milton builds on the
time-hallowed allegorisations of the Circe episode in the *Odyssey*.
But there is no evidence that he would have had much sympathy for
more recherché allegorisations, particularly if they lacked ancient
authority.

This point may have some bearing on whether Milton's own
strategies in *Paradise Lost* can reasonably be viewed as allegorical.
Literary historians customarily distinguish between 'primary epic',
poems like the *Iliad* orally composed or at any rate orally delivered

that are part of a living tradition of heroic song, and 'secondary epic', the artificial and self-conscious recreation of such heroic poetry, in far more sophisticated environments, by fully literate poets. Alastair Fowler proposes a third category, 'tertiary epic', the allegorical development of literary epic, and raises the question of 'the extent to which *Paradise Lost* allegorizes the inherited epic images, in the Neoplatonic manner of a Landino or a Spenser — that is, the extent to which the poem is tertiary rather than secondary epic'.[23] Fowler's own notes, including those on the similes, suggest that in his view Milton indeed allegorises to a quite considerable degree (elsewhere I shall be querying some of these interpretations). In one sense only does *Paradise Lost* seem evidently tertiary, and that is in the degree and the self-consciousness with which Milton gathers together the grand spectrum of previous heroic literature: classical epic, Italian romantic epic and the Arthurian romances (e.g. I. 576ff). Particularly striking is the way that he comments *directly* on the heroic tradition in the prologue to Book IX. (*Thebaid* XII. 816–17, where Statius mentions by name the *Aeneid* he so revered, provides only the tiniest and most half-hearted of classical precedents.) But this does not make Milton an allegorist. It is likely that Milton thought that the allegorical manner of a Spenser, however appropriate in the *Faerie Queene* with its romance elements, was foreign to the central classical epic tradition within which he had chosen to locate *Paradise Lost*.

The only undoubtedly allegorical scenes in the poem are the two involving Sin and Death. There was a precedent in *Aeneid* VI. 273ff for the presence at the gate of Hell of certain ghostly personifications. Other personifications in classical epic include Fama (Renown) who spreads the report of the affair between Dido and Aeneas in *Aeneid* IV. 173ff, Somnus (Sleep) who pushes Palinurus overboard in *Aeneid* V. 838ff, and Sleep and Death who bury Sarpedon in *Iliad* XVI (453ff; 671ff). However, by developing such figures into significant and startlingly concrete characters in II. 648ff Milton goes beyond the ancients in a way that aroused a predictably hostile response from Johnson. Yet even here the result is quite unSpenserian, because Milton heavily underlines the resulting incongruities. The episode employs a sort of 'Gothic' manner, at times genuinely mysterious — leading Coleridge to praise the writing for creating 'a sublime feeling of the unimaginable' by 'hovering between images' and thereby 'keeping the mind in a state of activity':[24] 'The other shape, / If shape it might be called that shape had none / . . . Or substance might be called that shadow seemed' (666–9); 'what seemed his head / The likeness of a kingly crown had on' (672–3). In the main, however, the writing is deliberately ponderous, grotesque, blackly humorous, even parodic (Satan, Sin and Death constitute an infernal parody of the Trinity). We are curiously close at one moment to space fiction, with its extraterrestrial monsters, at another to strip cartoon, particularly at the moment when Satan changes from disgust at the ugliness of Sin and Death to unctuous flattery, when he learns their identity (815ff), a transition of remarkable and clearly deliberate crudity far removed from the subtler analysis of Satan's psychological make-up elsewhere. A similar semi-humorous, ponderous style characterises the bridge-building activities of Sin and Death in X. 229ff. The treatment of Sin and Death is something of a *tour de force*, but it is not characteristic of *Paradise Lost* as a whole and it does not suggest a poet who is working relaxedly within an allegorical medium.

Milton's handling of the epic journey may serve as an example to suggest that *Paradise Lost* is to be aligned with 'secondary' rather than with 'tertiary' epic. The account of Odysseus' wanderings, a series of adventures that tests to the full the hero's mental and physical prowess, is one of the unchallenged triumphs of Homeric narrative. Virgil realised that such direct excitements would not suit the different temper and style of the *Aeneid*.[25] It would not be decorous to present the founder of the Roman race twirling a red-hot stake in a giant's eye or escaping from his cave under a ram. The obstacles that Aeneas must overcome in his voyage from Troy in *Aeneid* III are essentially psychological: he must learn to re-orientate himself from a Trojan past to a Roman future, as divine hints and warnings prod him on his way. In the long central episode at Buthrotum (293ff) Aeneas is in no physical danger at all, but the miniature Troy which Andromache and Helenus have constructed for themselves arouses his longing for a peace based solely on the past, and thus constitutes a kind of temptation. The problem is that Virgil also wants to align Aeneas' journey closely with Odysseus'; accordingly the Homeric ingredients — Scylla and Charybdis and the Cyclops — are there, but to no very clear purpose. Virgil, it may be felt, has difficulty in devising a compelling *narrative* that meets his quite different conception of the journey and its significance. There seem to be metaphorical reverberations to some episodes; in

particular when the Harpies snatch away the Trojans' food (210ff),
we discern the glimmerings of a story pattern suggestive of greed
and lack of self-control, but such resonances hang uncertainly in the
air, and are never resolved into specific meanings. Spenser in *Faerie
Queene* II. 12 straightforwardly allegorises the journey; Guyon's
voyage to the Bower of Bliss is an allegory of the tribulations and
trials that beset the true, wayfaring Christian on his path through
life. The results are bland and lack narrative tension.

Milton's solution to the problem is characteristically audacious.
He devises a literal but novel journey which is perfectly adapted to
the new subject of the epic as a whole, and which without strain can
bear the necessary moral and theological implications — unlike
Virgil Milton is not tied to Homer's apron-strings. The literary
ancestry of Satan's voyage through the abyss is carefully signalled to
the reader lest he miss the point (II. 1017–20):

> more endangered than when Argo passed
> Through Bosporus betwixt the jostling rocks,
> Or when Ulysses on the larboard shunned
> Charybdis, and by the other whirlpool steered.

This brilliant piece of early science-fiction allows Milton to write
some of his most dazzling 'scientific' poetry. We are taken into a
world of whirling atoms which derives ultimately from the
Epicurean Lucretius' great philosophical poem *De Rerum Natura*,
in which the universe is explained in terms of the atomic theory of
Democritus. For the description of chaos Milton employs military
imagery suggested by his sources (e.g. Lucretius I. 606; II. 118–19,
573–4; Ovid *Met.* I. 19) to describe the clashing of the atoms
(898–903):

> For hot, cold, moist and dry, four champions fierce,
> Strive here for mastery, and to battle bring
> Their embryon atoms; they around the flag
> Of each his faction, in their several clans,
> Light-armed or heavy, sharp, smooth, swift or slow,
> Swarm populous . . .

The sensuous concreteness of Milton's imaginings throughout the
episode leads him to much striking if unepic writing (947–50):

> so eagerly the fiend
> O'er bog or steep, through straight, rough, dense or rare,

With head, hands, wings or feet pursues his way,
And swims or sinks or wades or creeps or flies . . .

It took Pope only minor stylistic adjustments to adapt line 950 to the bizarre, chaotic, teeming satiric world of the *Dunciad* (II. 63–5):

As when a dabchick waddles through the copse,
On feet and wings, and flies and wades and hops;
So labouring on, with shoulders, hands and head . . .

Milton has returned us to Homeric immediacy, if by the most unexpected of paths.

That Milton did not dislike allegory as such is suggested by his great and enduring love of the *Faerie Queene*. Nevertheless the nature of the Homeric epic tradition combined with a number of other factors to encourage literalism. In all his late works Milton chose Biblical subjects to whose literal truthfulness he was committed. Moreover the bent of his imagination, as well as of his intellect, was always towards concreteness. When Adam and Eve eat we can almost hear the champing of their jaws (IV. 335–6):

The savoury pulp they chew, and in the rind
Still as they thirsted scoop the brimming stream.

The lines have an almost Keatsian character, possibly embarrassing to some, but characteristic of much that is best in Milton. It is true that many would argue that large parts of *Paradise Lost* must be regarded as symbolic, accommodated narrative, in which the descriptions of the spiritual realities with which the poem deals are adapted to our limited perceptions (this, the 'theory of accommodation', helped commentators to deal with some of the cruder anthropomorphisms of Scripture). Certainly passages suggestive of 'accommodation' can be cited in support (V. 570ff; VI. 297ff; VII. 176ff; XII. 386ff), but in the first and most important of these formulations Raphael lurches oddly from a symbolic back to a more literalist position, which seems closer to Milton's own belief:

Yet for thy good
This is dispensed, and what surmounts the reach
Of human sense, I shall delineate so,
By likening spiritual to corporeal forms,
As may express them best; though what if earth
Be but the shadow of heaven, and things therein

Each to other like, more than on earth is thought?

In *De Doctrina Christiana* Milton argues, with inexorable logic, that if God does accommodate himself to us, we cannot expect to go behind the accommodated picture:

> Our safest way is to form in our minds such a conception of God, as shall correspond with his own delineation and representation of himself in the sacred writings. For granting that both in the literal and figurative descriptions of God, he is exhibited not as he really is, but in such a manner as may be within the scope of our comprehensions, yet we ought to entertain such a conception of him, as he, in condescending to accommodate himself to our capacities, has shown that he desires we should conceive.[26]

This argument, which perhaps helps to explain the concreteness of *Paradise Lost*, is extremely telling. If we call God 'father' then much of the normal force of the word must be retained for it to be worth using at all. Excessive insistence on the metaphorical quality of religious language looks suspiciously like evasion, a desire to have things both ways; the cry of some of Milton's critics that he should have more often resorted to vagueness can be seen as an invitation to intellectual dishonesty. In conclusion both epic decorum and the bent of Milton's mind and imagination would suggest that *Paradise Lost* is not, in any interesting sense, 'tertiary epic'.

### The Blind Bard

It is reasonable to speculate that Milton's blindness may have brought him closer to Homer. Amid the mass of material, all of it of legendary not historical character, about Homer's life nothing seemed more firmly established than his blindness.[27] According to one etymology his very name meant 'the one who does not see' ('ho mē horōn'). Pope argues, common-sensically, that Homer could hardly have been born blind, since it would then be difficult to account for the extraordinary visual clarity of his descriptive writing: 'He must certainly have beheld the creation, considered it with a long attention, and enriched his fancy by the most sensible knowledge of those ideas which he makes the reader see while he but describes them.'[28] Accordingly Pope argues that Homer became blind only in his old age, conceivably as a result of his exertions in composing the *Iliad* (was he thinking of Milton?). But any prosaic objections to the traditional picture paled before the potent image of the sightless singer. Moreover Demodocus, the blind poet at the Phaeacian court in the *Odyssey*, was often taken, despite objections by scholars such as Spondanus, to be Homer's self-portrait. C.S. Lewis argues that the passages about the poet's blindness in *Paradise Lost* are not to be regarded as primarily autobiographical:

> Even the poet, when he appears in the first person within his own poem, is not to be taken as the private individual John Milton. If he were that, he would be an irrelevance. He also becomes an image — the image of the Blind Bard — and we are told about him nothing that does not help that archetypal pattern. It is his office, not his person, that is sung. It would be a gross error to regard the opening of *Samson* and the opening of Book III as giving us respectively what Milton really felt, and what he would be thought to feel, about his blindness. The real man, of course, being a man, felt many more things, and less interesting things, about it than are expressed in either.[29]

One move in the argument is curiously feeble from so skilfully combative a critic. That Milton will have felt much about his blindness that does not find expression in *Paradise Lost* is obvious, but has no logical bearing on whether those feelings that do find expression are personal or not. Otherwise Lewis gives a clear statement of a widely held view which, however attractive, is vulnerable on several counts. There is about the whole paragraph a strong whiff of the New Criticism, of the doctrine that the critic should be concerned only with the words on the page and not with the writer's times and life. A *tour de force* of this method is Leo Spitzer's analysis of Milton's sonnet on his dead wife ('Methought I saw my late espoused saint'), an analysis which tries altogether to ignore the fact that Milton, outside the poem, was blind, to concentrate on theme and convention:[30] 'When faced with the sonnet . . . the "poor-blind-twice-widowed-Milton-wrote-this-poem-in-a-dreary-apartment-alone-with-his-small-children" school of thought . . . must definitely yield to that of the less sentimental and more factual literary historians concerned with the *dolce stil nuovo* of Dante and Petrarch' (the rhetorical bludgeoning and misrepresentation of his opponents' position is very evident here). According to Spitzer the poem does not really deal with

Milton's blindness and his wife's death, but with the more 'generally human problem of the Ideal in our world', of which Milton's blindness is only 'a metaphor'. (With such bland and abstract generalities do literary critics seek to insulate poems and their readers from the specific pains of a real existence.) We are not to be allowed to entertain any thoughts of ordinary human sympathy: 'in view of this grandiose picture of man between two separated worlds how irrelevant would be the personal detail that Milton was blind at the time of his second marriage and hence had never seen his wife!' The poem could, as it were, have been written by a sighted poet, or at any rate would be intelligible even if we did not know that Milton was blind. The common reader will probably think that it takes a literary critic to believe such sophistries, and that Milton wrote obsessively about blindness because he was himself blind. Obviously the sonnet would not be worth reading if it were not a carefully wrought literary artifact, and it is the poem and not biographical details external to it that must be the focus of our attention, but that does not mean that it must be impersonal or supra-personal, or cannot reflect a precise human situation. If it could be proved that Milton was not blind, the sonnet and the invocation to *Paradise Lost* III would lose much of their power to move. Most readers automatically relate what they read to their own and the writer's world and experience, and it can be argued that any theory of reading ought to take into account the practice of readers.[31]

It is true that the first person in the invocation to Book I can be taken simply as the impersonal epic voice, the office not the individual. But the invocation to Book III goes beyond any impersonal thematic concerns, in particular beyond the contrast, important as it is, between external blindness and inner sight. Lines 25–6 giving the cause of blindness, with its reference to *gutta serena*, refer specifically to Milton's own case, and not to that of any blind poet, while in general to call this passage an invocation is to make it seem more epical, and more epically conventional, than in fact it is. What we have is more a prayer than an invocation, a prayer by the blind poet John Milton to the God who had let him go blind. There is a marvellous conflation between God as light and the physical light that beats uselessly on Milton's eyes, and there is a strong sense of the eyeball as a frail physical object which reflects the experience of a blind man, who, as the blind regularly report, has his other senses strengthened in intensity ('feel', 'roll', 'thick' and 'quenched' are all key words):

> thee I revisit safe,
> And feel thy sovereign vital lamp; but thou
> Revisitest not these eyes that roll in vain
> To find thy piercing ray, and find no dawn;
> So thick a drop serene hath quenched their orbs
> Or dim suffusion veiled.     (21–6)

Similarly in *Samson* Milton writes 'why was the sight / To such a tender ball as the eye confined? / So obvious and so easy to be quenched . . .' (93–5). Significantly the only comparably powerful passage on the eyeball in English poetry descends directly from Milton: 'like this sleek and seeing ball / But a prick will make no eye at all' (Hopkins, 'Binsey Poplars', 15–16).

Such a personal passage invariably brings a change of stylistic register. The syntax and especially the diction are simplified, epic pomp and circumstance laid aside, and the poet writes with a directness and simplicity that few seventeenth-century poets can match. The effect would be almost prosaic, were it not for Milton's mastery of rhythm and sheer auditory imagination. Even the repetition 'thus return . . . not to me returns' seems less a rhetorical device than a touching stumbling, almost a clumsiness, that gives an appropriately halting, uncertain rhythm to the line:

> Thus with the year
> Seasons return, but not to me returns
> Day, or the sweet approach of even or morn,
> Or sight of vernal bloom, or summer's rose,
> Or flocks, or herds, or human face divine;
> But cloud instead and ever-during dark
> Surrounds me, from the cheerful ways of men
> Cut off, and for the book of knowledge fair
> Presented with a universal blank . . .     (40–8)

There is, as in this passage, a modulation in the first invocation from epic grandeur to prayerful simplicity, a movement which mirrors the wider movement of the poem as a whole from the glamour of the Earthly Paradise to the chastened glory of the paradise within —

> what in me is dark
> Illumine, what is low raise and support.     (22–3)

Nor can we doubt that what is dark includes the ever-during darkness of Milton's eyes.

In general C.S. Lewis seems to mistake the kind of poet that Milton is, one that is at the opposite extreme from the 'negative capability', in Keats's phrase, and from the openness to others, that is the mark of Shakespeare. Milton is an example, the supreme in English letters, of the 'personal' poet, the poet who stamps his personality, indelibly and for some excessively, on whatever he writes. We can never be sure that we have found the real Shakespeare, for, most godlike of makers, he hides himself most completely in his creation. Milton by contrast is easy to find, despite a preference for formally impersonal genres, pastoral, epic or tragedy. He thus foreshadows the Romantic movement in general, and particularly the sublime egotism of Wordsworth, for whom the only proper subject for heroic song is the story of his own life. Milton's defects, as well as his strengths, reside in this, for example his comparative weakness in characterisation. It is commonplace to say that there is much of Milton in Satan; but the truth is that there is much of Milton in most of his characters, even or perhaps especially in his God, who shares with his creator a fondness for heavy sarcasm at the expense of his opponents. Dante, who could certainly match the personal arrogance of Milton, was able to create in the *Divine Comedy* a galaxy of contrasted personalities, to bring to life, often with a few bold strokes, characters wholly different from himself. Milton prudently chose another path; Eliot was right to say that in his choice of subject Milton displayed 'his inerrancy, conscious or unconscious, in writing so as to make the best display of his talents, and the best concealment of his weaknesses'.[32]

Anyone who goes blind is likely to reflect on the reasons for it. But Milton, with his extraordinary sense of poetic vocation and manifest personal destiny, must have done so with especial intensity. Already, in his early twenties, he was meditating in a sonnet ('How soon hath time the subtle thief of youth') on his slow start, and the requirements of his 'great task-master'. The death of his friend Edward King raised the spectre of a more momentous loss, and Milton exorcised his fears in 'Lycidas'. The upward progression through the genres on the model of Virgil as recorded in his epitaph ('Cecini pascua, rura, duces'; I sang of pastures, the countryside, chiefs — i.e. pastoral, georgic, epic) was under way. But with the loss of his sight the blind Fury must have seemed to strike a terrible blow to his career. In one of the two sonnets which he wrote about his blindness ('To Mr Cyriack Skinner upon his Blindness') he sees it as a sacrifice made 'In liberty's defence, my noble task' (in *Defensio Secunda* he compares himself with Achilles who was given the famous choice between long life and glory). In the other ('When I consider how my light is spent'), a more ambitious attempt to justify God's ways to Milton, he comforts himself with the thought that God does not need anything we can do for him (even poems like *Paradise Lost*), and that 'They also serve who only stand and wait.' In *Samson* — blindness surely determined the choice of subject here — he presents us with a blinded hero who is still able to perform one mighty work for God, and there is no doubt that among Greek plays Milton particularly studied Sophocles' *Oedipus at Colonus* in which the old sightless king receives a final mysterious call from heaven.

Blindness could be understood in various ways. It could, for example, be regarded as a punishment. In *Paradise Lost* III. 35 Milton mentions not only Homer but, more ominously, Thamyris. In *Iliad* II. 594–600 Homer tells how the bard Thamyris offended the Muses by challenging them to a contest, and was punished by them; in later accounts the punishment was blindness. Milton's enemies could claim that his blindness was God's vengeance on his wickedness. Milton responded with an indignation that might suggest unease. In *Defensio Secunda*, after rebutting a charge of ugliness, he ruminates eloquently on his blindness, giving an extraordinarily extensive list of all the worthy blind, and insisting that he is not conscious of any offence, 'though often and as much as I could I have carefully examined myself on this point'.[33] As we have seen, in *Paradise Lost* VII. 15ff he prays that he may avoid the fate of Bellerophon, whose attempt to scale heaven was punished with a heavy fall. Milton does not mention, but doubtless was aware (the detail is in Spondanus and in Natale Conti's *Mythologiae*, one of the standard reference books for mythology in the Renaissance), that the gods also blinded Bellerophon.

There were, however, more hopeful possibilities, and in particular the notion of compensatory blindness. Poets and prophets, at the price of their sight, were granted special insight. Homer in one account had been blinded by a radiant vision of Achilles. St. Paul's enlightenment on the Damascus road temporarily cost him his eyes. One of the most familiar treatments of the paradoxes of blindness and sight is in Sophocles' Oedipus plays. In a tremendous scene in *Oedipus the King* the blind Teiresias hurls the truth at the sighted, confident, uncomprehending king; 'you are blind in ears and in wits and in eyes' had been Oedipus' angry taunt (371). When Oedipus learns the truth he blinds himself, only now knowing who he is. In *Oedipus at Colonus* the tables are turned. Oedipus enters blind and helpless, dependent on stick and guide, but at the end, at the summons of the gods, he leads the way out, the blind guiding the sighted. He is given strange new powers to help and harm, and can foresee the fate of his sons. One might compare this exchange between an old man and Gloucester in *King Lear* (IV. i. 17–19):

— You cannot see your way.
— I have no way, and therefore want no eyes;
I stumbled when I saw.

The idea finds one of its most moving expressions in the figure of Homer's Demodocus, 'whom the Muse loved beyond others, and gave both good and evil — she deprived him of his eyes, but she gave him sweet song' (*Od.* VIII. 63–4). Similarly Teiresias is blinded by an angry Juno but given the gift of prophecy in compensation (Ovid *Met.* III. 334ff). Edgar Wind, in a discussion of the figure of the blind Cupid, quotes the Neoplatonist Pico della Mirandola (1463–94): 'Many who were rapt to the vision of spiritual beauty were by the same cause blinded in their corporal eyes.'[34] Reflecting on ideas such as these may have enabled Milton to make sense of God's apparent rebuff, to see his blindness as part of the ordered pattern of his experience; in *Defensio Secunda* he speaks of 'an inner and far superior light'. God had truly made him the English Homer to tell of things invisible to mortal sight; though he was outwardly blind, the Holy Spirit shone inward.

One obvious result of Milton's blindness was that he composed in his head and not on paper. This constitutes a further link with the oral poetry of Homer. Apparently Milton normally composed at night or early in the morning, and complained if his amanuensis was late, saying 'he wanted to be milked'.[35] It is reasonable to suppose that he meant seriously his claim that his 'celestial patroness' (IX. 21) dictated to him nightly, that is that he composed spontaneously under divine inspiration (III. 32; VII. 28–9). His patroness is the Heavenly Muse, Urania (*ouranios* is Greek for heavenly, and Urania had previously been the muse of astronomy), the Christian muse introduced by the French Huguenot poet Guillaume de Salluste du Bartas (1544–90) in *La Muse Chrétienne* (1574).[36] In

1605 a translation of 'L'Uranie', which together with an epic about Judith made up this volume, was included by Joshua Sylvester in his version of du Bartas's poem on the Creation and sacred history of the world, translated as *Du Bartas his Divine Weeks and Works*, which had a great influence on Milton. In the last resort Milton's heavenly muse is probably to be taken as an aspect of the Holy Spirit. In *The Reason of Church Government* Milton describes how he had schooled himself to produce literary work

> not to be raised from the heat of youth or the vapours of wine . . . nor to be obtained by the invocation of Dame Memory and her Siren daughters [i.e. the muses], but by devout prayer to that eternal Spirit who can enrich with all utterance and knowledge, and sends out his seraphim with the hallowed fire of his altar to touch and purify the lips of whom he pleases.[37]

In the invocation to Book I Milton addresses first the Muse and then the Spirit, in a way that might suggest that the two are not identical, and this had led some to identify the Muse with the second person of the Trinity, the Logos. But Urania was often conflated with the Holy Spirit, and Milton is following a common pattern in ancient prayers in which the deity is addressed under a variety of names significant in cult. Milton is also gradually moving from the classical grandeur of the opening to the simple Biblical prayer, and as the style modulates, so the object of the invocation changes, from the Muse — still partly a pagan concept, however much Christianised — to the purely Biblical, now specifically the Holy Spirit 'that dost prefer / Before all temples the upright heart and pure' (17–18).

This exordium is a conflation of the openings of the *Iliad, Odyssey* and *Aeneid* (though with many Biblical elements injected);[38] but Milton keeps closer to the Homeric than to the Virgilian format. Virgil first announces the theme of the *Aeneid* as his own ('arms and the man I sing'), and only later calls on the Muse to aid him. This separation by Virgil of *propositio* (statement of theme) and *invocatio* (address to muse) which are fused in Homer was noticed by ancient and Renaissance commentators; La Cerda mentions a debate about which of these two models should be followed, and the Virgilian pattern was deliberately adopted by Cowley in the *Davideis* as superior. Milton, however, follows Homer in immediately calling on the muse; without such inspiration from outside, without such inbreathing of the divine, the poet cannot even begin to sing. It is thus significant that both Homer and Milton are more bardic than Virgil. In one sense their styles might seem at opposite extremes, Milton's orotund tones so different from the relaxed and leisurely Homeric manner. Yet there is an obvious oral character to *Paradise Lost* which the *Aeneid* lacks. Anyone who has read *Paradise Lost* aloud will know how difficult it is to stop, once one has started reading; the verse has a seemingly endless momentum which carries one relentlessly onwards, the ebb and flow of tensions maintained through the long, syntactically loose sentences. In the bardic quality of his verse Milton is Homer's truest son.

### Mulciber's Fall

Milton might have made more obvious use of Homer but for his awareness that Greek was to a degree a minority language.[39] However, in a prominent position towards the end of *Paradise Lost* I Milton risks publicly paying Homer a unique if double-edged tribute. It is comparatively rare for Milton to translate freely his predecessors' work in the common Renaissance way — Johnson is right to stress that 'of all the borrowers from Homer [i.e. epic poets] Milton is perhaps the least indebted' being 'naturally a thinker for himself, confident of his own abilities and distainful of help or hindrance'[40] — but in this famous passage he does so with something of a flourish (738–51):

> Nor was his name unheard or unadored
> In ancient Greece, and in Ausonian land
> 740 Men called him Mulciber, and how he fell
> From heaven, they fabled, thrown by angry Jove
> Sheer o'er the crystal battlements; from morn
> To noon he fell, from noon to dewy eve,
> A summer's day, and with the setting sun
> 745 Dropped from the zenith like a falling star,
> On Lemnos, the Aegean isle; thus they relate,
> Erring — for he with this rebellious rout
> Fell long before, nor aught availed him now
> To have built in heaven high towers, nor did he scape
> By all his engines, but was headlong sent
> With his industrious crew to build in hell.

Lines 740–6 are a close imitation of *Iliad* I. 589–94. In an episode rich in comedy Hephaestus (Latin form ; Vulcan or Mulciber) intervenes in a quarrel between Zeus and Hera, and persuades his mother to yield to her husband's greater power:

> For hard is the Olympian to oppose.
> For already me also on another occasion eager to rescue (you)
> 591 Hurled he catching me by the foot from the divine threshold;
>     All day I was borne down, and together with the setting sun
> Fell in Lemnos, and little life was still in me.
> There me the Sintian men immediately cared for when I fell.

Milton ignores the context, and was evidently attracted primarily by the cosmic grandeur of the idea of a divine being thrown out of heaven (he had already used this myth, if in a rather routine way, in an early Latin poem *Naturam non pati senium*, 23–4 and also in *Elegy* 7. 81–2). Among the chief glories of *Paradise Lost* are the various descriptions of angels flying through space. The Mulciber passage looks back to the famous lines on the fall of Satan himself: 'Him the almighty power / Hurled headlong flaming from the ethereal sky . . .' (I. 44ff). Indeed it is part of Milton's point that the pagan poets distorted the truth about the fall of the angels. Milton's imitation is more self-consciously poetic than the original. Of all great poets Homer seems to achieve his effects with the least effort and fuss, something that probably reflects in part the easy rapport between the oral poet and his audience and the fact that he inherits from his predecessors a rich and flexible traditional language. Yet there can be no doubt about the poet's art, revealed for example in the emphatic positioning of the two key verbs 'hurled' and 'fell' at the beginning of lines 591 and 593 (which I have reproduced in my literal version), and by the lovely assonance of 594 ('entha me Sinties andres aphar komisanto pesonta'), where the sound suits the touch of human sympathy so simply and quietly conveyed. The natural, unforced quality of such poetry might make us exclaim with Verlaine 'Et tout le reste est littérature'.[41]

By contrast Milton aims to dazzle. Again the verse movement enacts the fall of Hephaestus, as Milton engages in emulous rivalry with Homer, particularly in the superb placement, mimetically, of the verb 'dropped'. Milton removes the warmly human touch with which Homer ends, but enlarges the sense of cosmic drama. He also introduces a linguistic opulence and wistful romantic lyricism not in Homer — 'crystal battlements', 'noon to dewy eve, / A summer's day'. This glittering Homeric recreation is then placed by its context. Having imitated so lovingly, Milton now dismisses the story as pagan falsity: 'erring' in its emphatic position comes as a hammer blow to shatter the mood of frail beauty and there is then a marked change of tone for the contemptuous dismissal. The effect, though disliked by some readers including Walter Savage Landor ('My good Milton! Why in a passion?'),[42] has a colossal power. Neither mood destroys the other but they rather exist in a tense and urgent conjunction.

Some scholars think that a passage from Lucretius lies behind this rhetorical movement (I. 391–3):[43]

quod si forte aliquis, cum corpora dissiluere,
tum putat id fieri quia se condenseat aer,
errat.

(But if by chance anyone supposes that when bodies have leapt apart, this is because the air condenses, he errs.)

There may be a ghost of an echo here ('erring' and 'errat'), but the effect in this passage of Lucretius is different, since there is no juxtaposition of styles. Nevertheless, a Lucretian influence is likely; there are indeed wide analogies between the two poets. Like Milton, though for different reasons, the materialist Lucretius was, intellectually at least, hostile to mythology, in general treating myths with scorn (for example the stories about the underworld, III. 978ff) or at best as unsatisfactory allegory (for example the myth of Cybele, II. 600ff). Nevertheless there are times when he uses mythological material for richly poetic effect without apology, as in the famous opening invocation to Venus or the description of spring in V. 737ff which lies behind Horace's Sestius Ode (I. 4) and Botticelli's *Primavera*. Such passages suggest to some that, emotionally, there is an anti-Lucretius devoted to the old stories inside the austere rationalist. Perhaps the closest analogy, rhetorically, to the Mulciber passage occurs in V. 392ff. Lucretius speaks of the 'war' between heat and moisture, and then observes that there were two occasions on which, as the story goes ('ut fama est') one or other gained the upper hand. He then summarises, with considerable power and heightened epic diction, the story of Phaethon who set the world on fire. So far only the phrase 'ut fama est' has given any hint that the myth is to be rejected, but, the story told, Lucretius concludes that it cannot be true:

scilicet ut veteres Graium cecinere poetae
quod procul a vera nimis est ratione repulsum.

(So indeed sang the old poets of Greece, but it is very far from truth and reason.)

After stating the rational objections to the myth Lucretius next refers to the story of the flood, with a second and now clearly ironical 'ut fama est'. Similarly in IV. 570ff, during the course of a discussion of echoes, Lucretius magically evokes a picture of satyrs and nymphs and Pan playing his pipes in lonely places by night, only to reject it with contempt: the local inhabitants invent the stories 'as all mankind is too greedy to get attention' ('ut omne / humanum genus est avidum nimis auricularum' — the scornful diminutive 'little ears' is particularly effective). In both these passages the best poetry is given by Lucretius to the stories that are being dismissed.

Milton thus could well have learned the technique from Lucretius, but it is to Homer not to Lucretius that he directs the reader's attention in lines 747ff. Milton's rebuttal of Homer is itself conducted in Homeric terms, since he apparently has in mind two common Homeric formulae. The first is a motif used, to create an effect of irony and sometimes pathos, about the minor victims of war who are said not to be saved by their possessions, endowments or achievements:

Atreus' son Menelaus slew with his sharp spear Scamandrius, son of Strophius, skilful in the chase, a good hunter; for Artemis herself taught him to shoot all wild things which the mountain woods nurture — but archer Artemis did not avail him then, nor his archery in which before he excelled, but Atreus' son spear-famed Menelaus hit him in the back as he fled before him . . .

(*Iliad* V. 49ff and cf. Virgil's imitation in *Aen.* XI. 843–4
'nec . . . profuit', 'nor aught availed him')

The second is a corrective formula which Homer uses when a character is acting in ignorance of the reality of the situation, and which is always introduced by the word 'nēpios' ('fool') emphatically at the beginning of the line like Milton's 'erring' (e.g. *Iliad* XX. 463–9). The two motifs are combined in *Iliad* II. 872–5: 'who [Nastes] came to the war dressed in gold like a girl, / fool, but in no way did this avail to keep dreadful destruction from him, / but he was conquered beneath the hands of the swift-footed son of Aeacus [Achilles] / in the river, and wise-hearted Achilles carried off the gold'. The effect of using Homeric rhetoric against Homer himself is unnerving; Milton's relationship with his classical models is complex and devious.

It has been maintained that Milton is criticising only the Homeric chronology, and nothing else,[44] but this is surely to trivialise the whole passage and to ignore the marked change of style between the lines in imitation of the passage from the *Iliad* and the abrasive rebuttal. Likewise it is inadequate to argue that Milton's procedure is merely the standard one of at once illustrating the benighted errors of paganism and showing how they pre-echo the Christian truth. This would be to ignore the curious edginess of Milton's relationship with the ancients, the evident sense of tension and strain. In fact the Mulciber passage provides much of the initial charge for a rhetorical strategy that is sustained, however, much it may clash with other elements in the poem, until the prologue to Book IX where the poet comes (rhetorically) clean, denouncing the values both moral and aesthetic of previous epics. The Fall, it is now asserted, is a theme more heroic than those of the *Iliad, Odyssey* or *Aeneid* (13ff). Milton scorns even the romantic epics of Spenser and the Italians, since he is (27–37)

> Not sedulous by nature to indite
> Wars, hitherto the only argument
> Heroic deemed, chief mastery to dissect
> With long and tedious havoc fabled knights
> In battles feigned — the better fortitude
> Of patience and heroic martyrdom
> Unsung — or to describe races and games,
> Or tilting furniture, emblazoned shields,
> Impreses quaint, caparisons and steeds,
> Bases and tinsel trappings, gorgeous knights
> At joust and tournament . . .

Milton's belief that Spenser was a better teacher than Scotus or Aquinas suggests that these lines should be taken not literally, but as the rhetorical climax of an attempt to cut the ground from under the poet's and the reader's feet. There is nothing standard about such a strategy.

The ideas of the prologue to Book IX are in themselves conventional enough in the Biblical poetry of the period. For example Sylvester writes in *Job Triumphant in his Trial*:

'Twere labour lost to fable (Homer-like)
The strange long voyage of a wily Greek,
The pains, the perils and extreme disease
That he endured both by land and seas,
Sith sacred truth's heaven-prompted books present
In constant Job a worthier argument.[45]

So expressed such sentiments seem merely bland, even banal, partly because of the flaccid quality of the writing, but more because the lines convey no sense that paganism is a real threat. Milton had to bring life to the dry bones of classical story before he could inject power into their abandonment or overtopping. It is just because Milton adopts the manner and matter of classical epic with an almost pedantic thoroughness that the denunciations of Book IX are so devastatingly effective and disconcerting.

There are parallels to such creative tensions in other Protestant poems, for example Herbert's 'Jordan I' which leaves little room for art at all:

Who says that fictions only and false hair
Become a verse? Is there in truth no beauty?
Is all good structure in a winding stair?
May no lines pass except they do their duty
    Not to a true but painted chair?

Is it no verse except enchanted groves
And sudden arbours shadow coarse-spun lines?
Must purling streams refresh a lover's loves?
Must all be veiled, while he that reads divines,
    Catching the sense at two removes?

Shepherds are honest people — let them sing;
Riddle who list for me and pull for prime;
I envy no man's nightingale or spring;
Nor let them punish me with loss of rhyme
    Who plainly say, 'My God, my King'.

This is indeed a more bizarre and extreme example of the phenomenon than anything in Milton. The Christian poet's job, if we are to believe Herbert, is to say plainly and unadornedly 'My God, my King'. But, as A.D. Nuttall has observed, this is not to make a poem at all, and 'Jordan' thus *necessarily* devotes all its imaginative energies to what is rejected.[46] The poem's potent images and the gyrating complexities of the argument are a denial of what is being argued; the poem is inevitably trapped in its own inconsistencies. In comparison Milton's approach seems almost a moderate one, since he is free and able to bring Biblical and Christian material into imaginative life. I do not imply that Milton reduces the tension to something orderly and contained — *Paradise Lost* would be a less exciting poem if that were so — but he is not carried, like Herbert, completely out of control.

'How he fell / from heaven, they fabled': from this moment the words 'feign' and 'fable' take on an insistent suggestion of falsity.[47] Sometimes there is little more than a distant drum beat, the most lightly insinuated dubiety, a hint of unease; for example, in 'herself more lovely fair / Than wood-nymph or the fairest goddess feigned' (V. 380–1). Elsewhere there is a tauter knottiness (IV. 705–8):

In shady bower
More sacred and sequestered, though but feigned,
Pan or Silvanus never slept, nor nymph
Nor Faunus haunted.

Here the negatives are oddly contorted; on the surface the lines mean that no pagan deity ever inhabited a more sacred bower, but, since Milton starts by telling us that the bowers of paganism were feigned, the alternative meaning seems to suggest itself that Pan and Silvanus never slept, that nymph and Faunus never haunted, because they never existed. The logic of the comparison requires a definite though inferior beauty from which to measure. Instead we have a comparison that does not compare, or compares something with nothing.

## Some Homeric Echoes

Recognising the passing Homeric echoes — for those who do — is hardly among the more intense pleasures of reading *Paradise Lost*.[48] Such echoes are in fact comparatively infrequent. Book II. 868, 'the gods who live at ease' translates one Homeric formula ('theoi rheia zōontes', *Il.* VI. 138, etc.), VI. 236 'the ridges of grim war' apparently another ('polemoio gephurai', *Il.* IV. 371, etc., the dykes of war, a curious phrase apparently referring to open spaces on the battlefield). These are little more than grace notes to a melody, perhaps giving the learned reader an innocently pleasant shock of recognition, a slight incantation of the epic. The voice of the wise counsellor Nestor is sweeter than honey (*Il.* I. 249); Milton produces an ingenious, faintly parodic variant for Belial: 'his tongue / Dropped manna' (II. 112–13). Adam has 'hyacinthine locks' (IV. 301), which recall the curly hair of Odysseus 'like a hyacinth flower' (*Od.* VI. 231). After the creation of vegetation 'earth now / Seemed like to heaven, a seat where gods might dwell, / Or wander with delight and love to haunt / Her sacred shades' (VII. 328–31). The phrasing recalls some lines from the great primary source for the *locus amoenus* (the description of a spot of idyllic beauty) in *Odyssey* V, the description of Calypso's island, at whose soft meadows blooming with flowers 'even an immortal if he came would wonder as he looked and be delighted in his heart' (73–4). The similarity of context and of content makes the allusion a graceful one. In none of these instances does it greatly matter if the reader misses the echo.

On occasion a more substantial resonance may be added. In IX. 892 Adam drops the garland he has woven for his now sinful wife. This recalls, harrowingly, the gestures of Andromache in dropping the shuttle and then casting off her headdress in grief at Hector's death at a similarly climactic moment in the *Iliad* (XXII. 447ff). The invocation to *Paradise Lost* I contains a sustained play on the opening word of the *Odyssey*, 'andra', 'the man' ('Sing, Muse, of the man of many ways'). The *Aeneid's* famous opening phrase, 'Arms and the man I sing', contains an implicit claim that the epic is to be both *Iliad* and *Odyssey*, while what follows shows that Virgil has a greater theme, not merely a man, Aeneas, but the founding of a mighty empire made possible by his efforts. Milton overgoes both his predecessors. His subject concerns not a man but all men —

'man's first disobedience' — and that disobedience will be made good not by a hero like Odysseus or Aeneas, but by 'one greater man', the Son of God himself.

Elsewhere it is less a question of echoing than of employing a Homeric motif. For example gods in Homer are regularly surrounded by mist or cloud. Milton uses the motif for Satan in Book IX to suggest his delusive, slippery nature — in line 75 he is 'involved in rising mist', in 180 he is 'like a black mist low creeping', while in a magical simile he is compared to *ignis fatuus* (633–42):

joy
Brightens his crest, as when a wandering fire,
Compact of unctuous vapour, which the night
Condenses and the cold environs round,
Kindled through agitation to a flame,
Which oft, they say, some evil spirit attends
Hovering and blazing with delusive light,
Misleads the amazed night-wanderer from his way
To bogs and mires and oft through pond or pool,
There swallowed up and lost, from succour far.

Obviously central to the simile's meaning is the traditional moral interpretation of *ignis fatuus* — a sinister delusive light which leads travellers astray, associated, though Milton distances himself from this, with evil spirits. The mood shifts interestingly: we begin with the scientific technicalities, and then Milton's imagination kindles to the mysterious, magical close reminiscent of *The Tempest*. The simile gives a sinister backdrop to the seemingly cheerful daytime scene in the foregound, as Eve follows Satan happily to her doom in the sunlight. When Adam has been alienated from God and driven from Paradise, the good angels assume an equivalent elusiveness: 'as evening mist / Risen from a river o'er the marish glides' (XII. 629–30). Certain quasi-formulaic narrative devices also have a Homeric origin. For example 'and now all heaven / Had gone to wrack . . . / Had not the almightly Father . . .' (VI. 669ff) derives from such transitional formulae as *Iliad* VIII. 130ff: 'Then had there been ruin and deeds irremediable . . . had not the father of gods and men been quick to notice . . .' The Homeric poems provided authoritative models of how to articulate epic structure, though, as we shall see, Milton does not use them mechanically.

Homer may also take the credit, or the blame, for the few

humorous moments in *Paradise Lost*. Addison, while noting the presence of burlesque elements in Homer, rather ponderously avers that 'Sentiments which raise laughter can very seldom be admitted with any decency into an heroic poem, whose business is to excite passions of a much nobler nature'.[49] He is severe on the punning exchange between Satan and Belial in VI. 609ff. Humour on the battlefield is apt to be rather heavy-handed, but in general we may agree that Homer has a defter touch when it comes to such pleasantries. Examples include Hephaestus arousing the unquenchable laughter of the gods in *Iliad* I. 595ff, or the wrestling match between Odysseus and the beggar Irus in *Odyssey* XVIII. lff.

In general Milton treats Homer, like his other sources, with considerable freedom, as in the shimmering description of Satan's shield and spear, Homeric in origin (I. 284–95):

> his ponderous shield
> Ethereal temper, massy, large and round,
> Behind him cast; the broad circumference
> Hung on his shoulders like the moon, whose orb
> Through optic glass the Tuscan artist views
> At evening from the top of Fesole
> Or in Valdarno, to descry new lands,
> Rivers or mountains in her spotty globe.
> His spear, to equal which the tallest pine
> Hewn on Norwegian hills to be the mast
> Of some great admiral were but a wand,
> He walked with . . .

Achilles' shield gleams like the moon in *Iliad* XIX. 374, while the club of the Cyclops is compared to the mast of a merchant-ship of twenty oars in *Odyssey* IX. 321ff. From these straightforward similes Milton weaves a mannered web of complexities. Stanley Fish, in a now famous analysis, draws our attention to the oddly confusing quality of such comparisons, which conceal as much as reveal.[50] If the shield is as large as the moon, then we may ask how large that is. The moon after all, when seen from earth, does not appear of great size. Clearly it depends on who is looking and from where; size in *Paradise Lost* is always relative. Throughout this first book Milton plays baffling tricks with perspective, as the devils at one moment seem to loom incalculably large, only to appear at another as small as bees or elves (Voltaire thought the effect mock-heroic). Similarly, if more straightforwardly, Satan's spear is not the size of a tall pine tree but, rather, the pine tree would be but a wand in comparison with the spear. Homeric precision and concreteness is seemingly evoked but actually denied.

In the first simile we find ourselves looking dizzyingly through a telescope at previously unknown sights, the undiscovered landscapes on the spotty globe of the moon. The moon's orb shrinks and grows, as we move from the moon as a planet to the astronomer in his specific earthly setting looking up at the heavens from a distance, back to the moon as it grows in telescopic sight and thus is enlarged again. It is not even clear whether the point of comparison is size or rather roundness and even mysteriousness. The verse quickens into a peculiar vividness as happens elsewhere when Milton is recalling his Italian visit or thinking about the excitements of contemporary astronomical or territorial discovery, apprehended as much in sensual as in intellectual terms, not least in the marvellous 'spotty' (Donne's much-bruited interest in the new science is almost one-dimensional in comparison). The simile combines the scientific with the romance of Italy — an evening in Fiesole. The figure of Galileo, 'the Tuscan artist', echoes through the poem, a symbol at once of man's intellectual mastery as artist and explorer, and of the ominousness of aspiring knowledge. In V. 261ff the glass of Galileo is 'less assured' than the unclouded vision of Raphael. In III. 588ff Satan is like a sunspot seen through a telescope. Again the syntax is oddly involuted — 'a spot like which perhaps / Astronomer . . . yet never saw' — so that, beyond the surface meaning (no astronomer has yet seen a sunspot like this), the lines seem weirdly to flicker and hesitate ('perhaps', 'never saw'). However exciting, scientific knowledge is uncertain and possibly insignificant.

Curiously (in view of the allusion to the Cyclops) the wavering about the size of Satan's weapons reflects a comparable complexity in *Odyssey* IX as a whole in the presentation of Polyphemus, his stature and nature. At some points his monstrous size is emphasised; he is like 'a wooded peak of lofty mountains' (191–2), and he can lift a rock that 22 waggons could not shift (240ff). But at others it is underplayed; there is no clear hint that his sheep or the milk-pails and other accoutrements of his cave are in any way abnormal in size, and Odysseus has no difficulty in conversing with him. The fact that Cyclops has only one eye, his most remarkable feature, is never directly mentioned and only emerges obliquely when the plan to blind him is mooted. This doubleness about the

Cyclops' size reflects a wider doubleness. The Cyclopes are lawless monsters who flout Zeus and all his works (including the laws of hospitality), but they also lead a pastoral and idyllic life-style, in which, without effort on their part, the land produces all their needs (105–15). Cyclops is a grisly monster who enjoys eating the human flesh of Odysseus' crewmen, but he normally lives a well-ordered shepherd's life and could be seen almost as a noble savage. Though in one sense 'lawless' he organises his life in a manner which is meticulously ordered. When he speaks in accents of tenderness to his favourite ram, under which ironically Odysseus is making his escape, Odysseus' attitude to him seems momentarily coarse (447ff). In short he is a kind of Caliban — it is significant that both Cyclops and Caliban are corrupted by drink brought by the newcomers to their islands. One would like to think that Milton noticed some of this, and used it in his own fashion when initiating us into analogous confusions about Satan.

## The Garden and the Bower

Critics are increasingly aware of the extent to which Milton breaks generic barriers in *Paradise Lost*. Such 'mixing of the genres', to use W. Kroll's designation of it, had been a regular feature of ancient and, in a more relaxed way, of Renaissance poetry. But Milton's feeling for generic distinction was strong, and in his case the generic mixing is unusually self-conscious. An obvious instance of the phenomenon is the strong pastoral colouring given to the description of Eden in Books IV and V. There was ancient precedent in the quasi-pastoral elements in the *Odyssey*. These are in fact of two distinct kinds. First, there is the essentially naturalistic presentation of the life of the farmer, particularly in the loving description of Eumaeus, Odysseus' loyal pigman, and his steading (the opening of Book XIV is particularly masterly). Closer in some respects to Renaissance pastoral, because less homely and more idealised, is the demi-paradise of Phaeacia. Phaeacia provides the perfect way for Homer to modulate from the fairy-tale world of the Great Wanderings to the realism of his Ithacan scenes. Phaeacia is a human community, without witches or ogres, but one freed from most of the cares and constraints that beset other men. The Phaeacians spend their time feasting, dancing, playing games and listening to poetry, and there are touches of magic like the

self-steering ships and the famous never-failing gardens of their king
Alcinous (VII. 112ff, Chapman):

> Without the hall and close upon the gate
> A goodly orchard-ground was situate,
> Of near ten acres, about which was led
> A lofty quickset. In it flourished
> High and broad fruit trees that pomegranates bore,
> Sweet figs, pears, olives, and a number more
> Most useful plants did there produce their store,
> Whose fruits the hardest winter could not kill,
> Nor hottest summer wither. There was still
> Fruit in his proper season all the year.
> Sweet Zephyr breathed upon them blasts that were
> Of varied tempers: these he made to bear
> Ripe fruits, these blossoms; pear grew after pear,
> Apple succeeded apple, grape the grape,
> Fig after fig came; time made never rape
> Of any dainty there. A spritely vine
> Spread here his root, whose fruit a hot sunshine
> Made ripe betimes; here grew another green.
> Here some were gathering, here some pressing, seen.
> A large-allotted several each fruit had;
> And all the adorned grounds their appearance made
> In flower and fruit, at which the king did aim
> To the precisest order he could claim.

There is a sense too of pastoral, frozen time, or rather timelessness,
in the episode, in contrast to Ithaca where we find an ordinary world
of time and change. The two modes of existence excitingly interlock
when Demodocus sings episodes from the tale of Troy, for the
Phaeacians merely a thread in the tapestry of their entertainment,
but for Odysseus part of his experience and of history (VIII. 71ff,
499ff). The gardens of Alcinous are certainly present in the
background to Milton's Eden, and receive direct mention on two
occasions. The fruits which Eve offers Raphael are like those 'In
Pontus or the Punic coast, or where / Alcinous reigned' (V. 340–1),
while in IX. 439–41 Satan approaches Eve in 'Spot more delicious
than those gardens feigned / Or of revived Adonis, or renowned /
Alcinous'.
    There is an oddly disturbing conclusion to Homer's story of

Phaeacia (XIII. 125ff). When the Phaeacians return Odysseus to Ithaca, they are heeding the laws of hospitality upheld by Zeus. On the other hand the ease with which they can accomplish such tasks in their half-magical ships is an interference in the natural order. Poseidon, god of the sea, angry for the safe conduct given to Odysseus and others, asks Zeus' permission to turn the ship to stone on its return and to throw a mountain about the city (the text leaves it uncertain whether or not he carries out this second action). The Phaeacians in alarm at the ship's metamorphosis resolve to cease giving passage to strangers. Thus if Phaeacia is a kind of Homeric earthly paradise, it becomes, as regards the rest of mortals, a paradise lost.[51] We may recall the moving lines in which Milton describes the fate of the physical Eden lost forever to mankind (XI. 829–35):

> then shall this mount
> Of Paradise by might of waves be moved
> Out of his place, pushed by the horned flood,
> With all his verdure spoiled and trees adrift
> Down the great river to the opening gulf,
> And there take root an island salt and bare,
> The haunt of seals and orcs and sea-mews' clang.

Line 833 seems to recall, in rhythm and movement, a line from the Orpheus passage in 'Lycidas' (63): 'Down the swift Hebrus to the Lesbian shore'. This presumably accidental self-echo could have resulted from an unconscious association of the Orpheus myth with loss, here with the loss of Paradise. Part of the pastoral quality of Milton's Eden lies in its precariousness, and the consequent mingling of joy and sorrow, of longing and exile, in our sense of it.

Virgil too has a quasi-pastoral episode, in *Aeneid* VIII, Aeneas' visit to Evander and his Arcadians (resonant name) at Pallanteum, site of future Rome. Again there is an exciting clash between the epic world of city and history and the rural scene; the primitive settlement embodies the values of simplicity and virtuous poverty. Cattle low in what will be the Roman forum, and the Capitol is still a wooded spot, unimproved or unspoiled — the ambiguity is Virgil's — by the grandiose monuments of Rome: 'golden now, once bristling with woody thickets' (348). Evander receives Aeneas in a narrow home, and gives him a seat of leaves and bear-skin, telling him to dare to embrace poverty (362ff). Virgil recalls, with a heavier moralising hand, the reception of Odysseus by the good Eumaeus with seat of brushwood and goat-skin (XIV. 48ff). Milton's Paradise in a sense combines the two sorts of Homeric pastoral, the glamorous, essentially amoral life of pleasure of the Phaeacians and the virtuous rural existence of Eumaeus.[52] Eden is a place of plenty and simplicity, of frugal delight. Following a hint in Genesis (man was put in Eden 'to dress it and to keep it', 2: 15), Milton makes Adam and Eve active gardeners in God's garden, so that the golden times are seen not as mere idleness but as the full realisation of a happiness that is truly moral.

One might have expected Milton, with his taste for romance and faerie, as witnessed by his special affection for *A Midsummer Night's Dream*, to have preferred the *Odyssey* to the martial *Iliad*. Certainly, before *Paradise Lost*, it is the *Odyssey* to which he turned for inspiration, particularly in *Comus* where he uses the story of Circe. For example the herb haemony, which the Attendant Spirit gives the brothers, is a version of the plant moly that Hermes brings Odysseus as a protection against Circe's spells (X. 302ff), often interpreted as a symbol of temperance. But, where Homer is comparatively down-to-earth, Milton weaves a passage of rich suggestiveness, stylistically closer to Virgil's description of the plant amellus (*Georgics* IV. 271ff):

> The leaf was darkish, and had prickles on it,
> But in another country, as he said,
> Bore a bright golden flower, but not in this soil,
> Unknown and like esteemed, and the dull swain
> Treads on it daily with his clouted shoon,
> And yet more medicinal is it than that moly
> That Hermes once to wise Ulysses gave.   (630–6)

'In another country' could mean merely 'in a country other than Britain', the Mediterranean as it might be, often seen in the Renaissance as a more natural soil, because of the climate, for beauty and culture (cf *PL* IX. 44–5), but the wistfulness and the sense of waste in what follows hints at another meaning — 'in heaven'. Milton gives a pastoral melancholy, with Christian overtones, to the Homeric motif. The romantic quality of his response to the *Odyssey* is shown even more clearly in some haunting lines from the early 'At a Vacation Exercise' (47–52):

And last of kings and queens and heroes old,
Such as the wise Demodocus once told
In solemn songs at king Alcinous' feast,
While sad Ulysses' soul and all the rest
Are held with his melodious harmony
In willing chains and sweet captivity.

This passage bears something of the relationship to the *Odyssey* that the *Idylls of the King* bears to Malory and the medieval Arthurian stories; both the undertow of bitter-sweet melancholy and the artful oxymorons of the final line take us far from 'the strong vertical light' of the Homeric style.[53]

One scene from the *Iliad* which caught Milton's imagination has something of an Odyssean flavour, namely the deception of Zeus by Hera (XIV. 153ff). What is particularly Odyssean about this episode is not so much its witty handling of the gods — divine comedy is the norm·in Homer — as a certain artfulness, even a hint of parody, in the narrative style. The *Odyssey* contains a number of incidents which have what might be termed a sub-heroic character. For example in Book VI Odysseus, shipwrecked on Phaeacia, wakes to the sound of girlish laughter. He emerges from the bush where he had been sleeping, naked and holding a branch to conceal his genitals, to address an adroitly diplomatic speech to princess Nausicaa (VI. 130–6, Chapman):

> Look how from his den
> A mountain lion looks that, all embrued
> With drops of trees and weather-beaten-hued,
> Bold of his strength, goes on, and in his eye
> A burning furnace glows, all bent to prey
> On sheep or oxen or the upland hart,
> His belly charging him, and he must part
> Stakes with the herdsman in the beasts' attempt,
> Even where from rape their strengths are most exempt;
> So wet, so weather-beat, so stung with need
> Even to the home-fields of the country's breed
> Ulysses was to force forth his access,
> Though merely naked . . .

Warriors in the *Iliad* are frequently compared to wild animals, but the application of such a simile in the quite different context of

*Odyssey* VI is playful and irreverent. Similar sophistications, which would be at odds with the serious human story of the *Iliad*, mark the scene in Book XIV. Hera, to distract Zeus' attention from the battle, decides to seduce him. She goes to her boudoir to adorn herself, and under a false pretext borrows from Aphrodite the famous girdle or cestus which arouses desire. Having bribed Sleep to aid her, she goes to Ida and pretends to Zeus that she is leaving on a visit. He is aroused, and the pair sleep together under a cloud, while the earth burgeons beneath them. The shift from near-farcical humour to sublimity is a characteristic one in scenes involving the gods. So in *Iliad* I when Thetis appeals to Zeus he is first the henpecked husband but then, when he nods assent to her request, he is the great cloud-gatherer, the sky-god whose manifestations are as awful as those of Jahweh on Mount Sinai: 'The son of Cronus spoke and nodded his dark brows in assent, and the ambrosial hair waved from the king's immortal head and he made great Olympus shake' (528–30).

Similarly the lovemaking of Zeus and Hera has suggested to many the pattern of a sacred marriage (*hieros gamos*) between sky and earth, and so it was interpreted by Virgil in *Georgics* II. 325–7:

tum pater omnipotens fecundis imbribus Aether
coniugis in gremium laetae descendit et omnes
magnus alit magno commixtus corpore fetus.

(Then the almightly father Aether with fruitful showers descends on the lap of his joyful wife and in his might mixed with her mighty body nourishes all the produce.)

Virgil also recalls an earlier, less thoroughly anthropomorphised and mythologised treatment by Lucretius, with similar sexual undertones (I. 250–1):

postremo pereunt imbres, ubi eos pater Aether
in gremium matris Terrai praecipitavit.

(Finally the rains end, when father Aether has thrown them headlong on the lap of mother earth.)

All these passages fused in Milton's imagination when in IV. 497–501 he gives us an idea of the fulfilled sexual love of Adam and Eve:

he in delight
Both of her beauty and submissive charms
Smiled with superior love, as Jupiter
On Juno smiles, when he impregns the clouds
That shed May flowers . . .

The lovemaking of the gods is depicted in terms of the operations of natural forces, in this case probably the marriage of Aether and Air. There is a considerable erotic charge: 'smiles' is powerful in its suggestive reticence, 'superior' hints at physical position as well as moral and intellectual elevation, while 'impregns' is even more specific than anything in the classical exemplars. As often in Milton's more lyrical writing there is a curious surrealism when the literal force of the words shines through, in the phrase 'clouds that shed May flowers' (one might compare the 'quaint enamelled eyes' that 'suck the honied showers' in 'Lycidas' 139–40). The passage momentarily gives an elemental quality to the relationship between Adam and Eve, elsewhere presented in personal terms, and suggests too their grandeur and importance as lords of creation.

The episode of Zeus' deception frequently roused the moral hackles of commentators. Plato had condemned it for showing Zeus so overcome by passion that he indulged it lying on the ground (*Republic* III. 390 B-C). To Spondanus it was particularly offensive that Zeus should boast about his extra-marital successes, while other commentators resorted to allegory as an interpretative escape route. Pope bows gravely to the objections — 'I don't know a bolder fiction in all antiquity . . . or that has a greater air of impiety and absurdity', and 'upon the whole' he is forced to give up the morality.[54] However the episode clearly delighted him as 'one of the most beautiful pieces that ever was produced by poetry', and in his extensive annotations he is at his most arch and feline, indulging in constant banter at the expense of the 'fair sex'. For example when Zeus tells Hera that he desires her more than all his conquests, whom he then lists — 'Ma in Ispagna son già mille e tre' — Pope offers these sage comments:

This courtship of Jupiter to Juno may possibly be thought pretty singular . . . A great many people will look upon this as no very likely method to recommend himself to Juno's favour. Yet, after all, something may be said in defence of Jupiter's way of thinking with respect to the ladies. Perhaps a man's love to the sex in general may be no ill recommendation of him to a particular. And to be known, or thought, to have been successful with a good many is what some moderns have found no unfortunate qualification in gaining a lady, even a most virtuous one like Juno, especially one who, like her, has had the experience of a married state.[55]

Throughout these notes we find ourselves in the world of *The Rape of the Lock*, and never more so than when Hera performs her toilette (169ff). This sequence relates to, and perhaps parodies, a common type-sequence, of which there are a number of examples in the *Iliad*, the arming of a hero for battle, a point noted by Spondanus as well as more recent commentators. As Pope says Hera 'comes from her apartment against her spouse in complete armour':[56]

Thus while she breathed of heaven, with decent pride
Her artful hands the radiant tresses tied;
Part on her head in shining ringlets rolled,
Part o'er her shoulders waved like melted gold.
Around her next a heavenly mantle flowed,
That rich with Pallas' laboured colours glowed;
Large clasps of gold the foldings gathered round,
A golden zone her swelling bosom bound.
Far-beaming pendants tremble in her ear,
Each gem illumined with a triple star.
Then o'er her head she casts a veil more white
Than new fallen snow and dazzling as the light.
Last her fair feet celestial sandals grace.
Thus issuing radiant, with majestic pace,
Forth from the dome the imperial goddess moves . . .

It is not so large a step to the boudoir of a more recent belle. Belinda is of course not literally a goddess like Homer's queen of heaven, but the ancestry is clear and the atmosphere of the two scenes is similar. In each case there is both an authentic glamour and a deft touch of parody that never threatens to spill over into burlesque. Homer was regarded by the ancients as the father of all the genres; in *Iliad* XIV he fathers the mock-heroic.

Part of Milton must have shared the Renaissance doubts about the Deception of Zeus; in *An Apology for Smectymnuus* he mentions the fault attributed to Homer 'to have written undecent things of the gods'.[57] However he was at least as susceptible as Pope to the pleasing sorcery of poetry, while the Deception also provided a rare model for the treatment of sexual coition in epic. (The scene in the cave where Dido and Aeneas make love in *Aeneid* IV. 165ff is too oblique for his uses.) In carefully balanced scenes in *Paradise Lost*, before and after the Fall, Milton describes the lovemaking of Adam and Eve, and in both cases Homer is in the background. In IV. 690ff the lovers enter the bower:

> it was a place
> Chosen by the sovereign planter, when he framed
> All things to man's delightful use; the roof
> Of thickest covert was inwoven shade
> Laurel and myrtle, and what higher grew
> Of firm and fragrant leaf; on either side
> Acanthus and each odorous bushy shrub
> Fenced up the verdant wall; each bounteous flower,
> Iris all hues, roses and jessamine
> Reared high their flourished heads between and wrought
> Mosaic; underfoot the violet,
> Crocus and hyacinth with rich inlay
> Broidered the ground, more coloured than with stone
> Of costliest emblem . . .

The bower combines natural growth with the adornments deliberately placed there by Eve (708–10), but even nature is described in terms of culture and artistry, since it is the work of the 'sovereign planter'. The bower's natural features recall the later artifacts of civilised man: 'roof', 'inwoven shade', 'verdant wall', 'mosaic', 'rich inlay', 'broidered'. Such exotic paradoxes point back beyond the fissipations introduced by the Fall to a time when nature and culture were one. The flower catalogue clearly recalls that in *Iliad* XIV. 346–9 which includes crocus and hyacinth — as Pope says 'the very turn of Homer's verses is observed and the cadence' — so that Zeus and Hera are also suggested, if only at this stage obliquely. In Book IX the flowers feature again (1039–41), while Adam's lustful proposal to Eve clearly echoes the words of Zeus to Hera (which in turn recall Paris' words to Helen in *Iliad* III. 441ff):

> For never did thy beauty since the day
> I saw thee first and wedded thee, adorned
> With all perfections, so inflame my sense
> With ardour to enjoy thee. (*PL* IX. 1029–32)

For never yet has desire so for goddess or woman
overcome the heart in my breast    (*Iliad* XIV. 315–16)

In Pope's words Milton makes Homer's 'impious fiction' into 'a
moral lesson'.[58]

Some modern critics think that neither scene in Milton is
successful. For example C.S. Lewis argues that Milton should have
treated prelapsarian sex in much more vague and mysterious terms,
and that the two scenes of lovemaking are too similar: 'he has made
the unfallen already so voluptuous and kept the fallen still so
poetical that the contrast is not so sharp as it ought to have been.'[59]
Further he regards the lovely Homeric flower catalogue in the
postlapsarian scene as not to the purpose. We may grant that in one
obvious sense Milton must fail: any depiction of unfallen man (as of
God) must be inadequate. Nevertheless these particular objections
are bad literary criticism and, more particularly, bad theology. A
retreat into vagueness would not have served for the description of
prelapsarian sex. Adam and Eve perform the same physical act as
their descendants, and that act is more not less sensuous and joyful
because free from guilt and exploitation. Likewise it is sound of
Milton to keep a certain similarity between the two scenes, since
nothing has changed except the frame of mind in which Adam and
Eve approach their lovemaking. Moreover that change, though
crucial, is in another sense slight. Although fallen the couple are still
far from the hideous depravities of our world (there is no question
yet of the bought smile of harlots) — they are still young in deed.
Yet 'the gallantries of Paradise', in Addison's fine phrase,[60] have
degenerated into the innuendos and puns of Adam's proposal to
'play' (1027; how coarse this word seems in comparison with Book
IV):

> Eve, now I see thou art exact of taste,
> And elegant, of sapience no small part,
> Since to each meaning savour we apply
> And palate call judicious . . .    (1017–20)

Adam still loves Eve — 'How can I live without thee, how forgo /
Thy sweet converse and love so dearly joined' (908–9) — but that
love is now partly selfish, partly a fear of loneliness (910), while love
and sex have begun, as in the world we know, to shed their
prelapsarian harmony.

The double reference to Homer is also presumably a kind of foreshadowing. Milton alludes to the passage in *Iliad* XIV before it becomes fully relevant, so that there is momentarily a prolepsis, a hint of danger to come amid the delights of Paradise. Moreover, when Adam and Eve enter their blissful bower, readers of Spenser may well think of the Bower of Bliss, a haven of corrupt and artificial pleasures (*FQ* II. 12), only to realise how incongruous, how Satanic is that thought. Milton in other words invites us to strive to see beyond our fallen perceptions and fallen language to the possibility of bliss. Ricks has well observed that a phrase like IV. 239 'with mazy error' (of the streams of Paradise) 'takes us back to a time when there were no infected words because there were no infected actions'.[61] We toy with the modern fallen meaning of 'error' only to reject it as irrelevant and grasp again the purer prelapsarian sense of 'wandering'. Similarly Eve's 'wanton ringlets' (IV. 306) are luxuriant and not immodest. It is vital to Milton's strategy that we first see Paradise through Satan's eyes, for our eyes too are fallen. Any sophisticated embarrassment that we may feel at Adam and Eve in Book IV is hence an index of how far we are from beatitude. Similarly in the *Divine Comedy* we must journey through Hell and Purgatory before we can savour the riches of Paradise; sin must be acknowledged and confronted before it can be transcended. We learn that the dark wood of *Inferno* I is only a perverse reflection of the benign wood of the Earthly Paradise; before the beatific vision the crooked must be made straight, and we must return to the childhood of our race when all woods gave delight. In both poems the reader must be re-educated for felicity.

## Homeric Warfare

In treating of war[62] Milton turned inevitably to the *Iliad*. It is today sometimes suggested that Milton should be regarded as an anti-war poet.[63] This is certainly misleading if by 'anti-war' is meant an unconditional opposition to the use of force in the conduct of human affairs. Milton believed that war, as one of the evil consequences of the Fall, was of Satanic origin, and Satan in *Paradise Lost* is specifically associated with gunpowder and its invention, first in an anticipatory simile in IV. 814ff and then in a striking episode in the War in Heaven. But Milton accepted that in a fallen world warfare in a righteous cause was justified. For example in the sonnet for

Cromwell, when he praises 'our chief of men' for his military
victories, the language is surprisingly brutal — 'God's trophies'
include 'Darwin's stream with blood of Scots imbrued'. The
younger Milton had liked to wear a sword, and had a considerable
interest in the technicalities of duelling which served him well when
writing the Harapha scene in *Samson*. In *Paradise Lost* Milton
makes extensive use of a language of Christian warfare and
heroism, partly of Biblical origin, which it is difficult to regard as
wholly metaphorical (e.g. VI. 63–8). Abdiel, who as Addison
observed is 'a pattern to those who live among mankind in their
present state of degeneracy and corruption',[64] shows his heroism by
defying Satan and confronting him in battle. The Son's victory
involves the use of God's ultimate weapon 'the chariot of paternal
deity' (VI. 750) and he returns to heaven like a triumphant general.
Milton, moreover, responded imaginatively to the more chivalric
trappings of warfare. An example is the romantic description of the
unfurling of Satan's banner (I. 531ff). The comparison with a comet
is sinister in an unfocused way, but the overall effect is authentically
glamorous, stately and ceremonial:

> Then straight commands that at the warlike sound
> Of trumpets loud and clarions be upreared
> His mightly standard; that proud honour claimed
> Azazel as his right, a cherub tall,
> Who forthwith from the glittering staff unfurled
> The imperial ensign, which full high advanced
> Shone like a meteor streaming to the wind,
> With gems and golden lustre rich imblazed,
> Seraphic arms and trophies.

Milton's practice is at once to give considerable attention to celestial
warfare, and at the same time to launch periodic attacks on war and
eventually, in the prologue to Book IX, to repudiate its suitability as
a subject for heroic song. The first direct criticism of war occurs in
II. 496ff at the council of the devils, when Milton contrasts the
concord reached in Hell with the warlike divisions among men. The
most extended and important passage is XI. 638ff, and has,
significantly, a Homeric basis, the description of scenes of war on
the shield of Achilles. Adam sees visions of horrid violence and
Michael denounces the heroic ethos that lies behind them (689–97):

For in those days might only shall be admired,
And valour and heroic virtue called;
To overcome in battle and subdue
Nations and bring home spoils with infinite
Manslaughter shall be held the highest pitch
Of human glory, and for glory done
Of triumph, to be styled great conquerors,
Patrons of mankind, gods and sons of gods,
Destroyers rightlier called and plagues of men.

The drabness of the language in this section means that heroic warfare is now wholly stripped of the excitements accorded to it in the earlier books. War is seen as sordid, its heroic possibilities are no longer present and what we might call the 'epic angle' has simply been suppressed. Similarly the Christian language of warfare now takes on a more purely metaphorical quality; in XII. 490ff Christian armour is unambiguously spiritual, as in the famous passage in Paul's Epistle to the Ephesians (6: 11–17). Unfortunately Milton fails to energise the purely Christian passages in these final books; contemplation of 'the better fortitude of patience and heroic martyrdom' does not in general draw great poetry from him. Thus it is unclear whether we are dealing with a deliberate attempt to undermine the allure of pagan heroism or simply declining poetic powers.

Milton certainly implies in the early books that even the finest martial values are in themselves worthless unless exercised for a good purpose. In *The Faerie Queene* II. 9. 12ff the assailants of the castle of Alma are an ill-organised and ill-equipped rabble (reminiscent, perhaps, of the hated Irish rebels), and this is in general how the forces of evil are presented in the literature of the period. (The disciplined fascist parade is for us so familiar and potent an image that we do not always realise how apt our ancestors were to associate military *disorder* with evil.) At the opening of *Iliad* III Homer contrasts the quiet disciplined advance of the Greeks with the birdlike babble of voices coming from the Trojans; this is one of the few places where Homer seems to display a pro-Greek bias. The passage lies behind the balanced descriptions in *Paradise Lost* of the marching order of the devils and of the good angels:

thus they
Breathing united force with fixed thought

95

Moved on in silence to soft pipes . . .   (I. 559–61)

> the powers militant,
> That stood for heaven, in mighty quadrate joined
> Of union irresistible, moved on
> In silence their bright legions, to the sound
> Of instrumental harmony . . .   (VI. 61–5)

We might have expected Milton to make his devils behave like the Trojans and his angels like Greeks, but in fact both sides of the celestial divide march quietly and in good order. Satan commands a superb military organisation; goodness and good soldiery are thus seen to be quite distinct.

For the War in Heaven Milton gives us, fought between angels, a fully-fledged Homeric battle, complete with taunts, counter-taunts and single combats. There are numerous echoes both of Iliadic phrasing and of the typical routines of Homeric warfare. For example Satan's taunting of the angels knocked over by cannon-balls, 'As they would dance, yet for a dance they seemed / Somewhat extravagant and wild, perhaps / For joy of offered peace' (VI. 615–17), recalls Patroclus' mockery when he strikes Cebriones, one of Priam's sons, and fells him from his chariot (*Iliad* XVI. 745ff, Chapman):

> O heavens! For truth this Trojan was a passing active man!
> With what exceeding ease he dives, as if at work he were
> Within the fishy seas! This man alone would furnish cheer
> For twenty men, though 'twere a storm, to leap out of a sail
> And gather oysters for them all, he does it here as well.

Similarly the angel Zophiel employs a characteristically grim heroic humour: 'this day will pour down, / If I conjecture ought, no drizzling shower, / But rattling storm of arrows barbed with fire' (VI. 544–6). The results are, however, unlike a typical Iliadic battle, partly because the style is quite un-Homeric, owing more to the baroque manner of post-Augustan Latin poetry (a matter I shall pursue in the chapter on Lucan) but also because the combatants are not men but angels. The effect is not widely popular. Carey's comments are typical: 'The slapstick war in Heaven can be debited to the classical tradition: epics were meant to have battles.'[65]

It would be tempting to regard the episode merely as a parody of an epic battle, but the episode is structurally too important to be a kind of farce, though some have taken it as such.[66] R.M. Frye has reminded us that physical battles between anthropoid angels in armour are a commonplace of the visual arts, both of Milton's day and of previous centuries.[67] Seen in its full European context Milton's work can often seem less eccentric than when viewed against an exclusively English literary background. Nevertheless I cannot accept Frye's view that, seen in its context, there is nothing peculiar or incongruous about the war (after all, the Father in Raphael's narrative talks about 'wild work in heaven' and 'perverse commotion' (VI. 698 and 706)). Rather, once again Milton is putting the epic form and the epic style under deliberate pressure. The charge of absurdity is an old one. Johnson's often quoted criticism that 'the confusion of spirit and matter which pervades the whole narration of the War in Heaven fills it with incongruity'[68] is in fact very much to the point, so long as 'confusion' is not taken to imply that the poet himself was confused. The episode is a *tour de force* in which Milton pushes the basic idea of spiritual beings fighting a very physical battle to its extreme, deliberately skirting absurdity.

Milton's approach is not a wholly novel one, for Homer himself had already pointed the way with his *theomachia* (battle of the gods) in *Iliad* XXI. 388ff. Here too gods fight like men. Thus Ares insults Athena and hurls a spear at her; she then fells him with a stone and vaunts over him. Apollo and Poseidon exchange pleasantries and agree not to fight, as in Book VI Glaucus and Diomedes have done. The final sequence is close to burlesque; Artemis is beaten about the ears by Hera, and runs to Olympus to sit weeping on Zeus' knees. A fight beween beings who are immortal and cannot be killed necessarily lacks elements of seriousness, and the whole episode has a humorous flavour with more than a hint of parody. We should not draw the wrong conclusions. Homer's gods may amuse us in their dealings with each other, but when Apollo comes down in anger to inflict plague on the Greeks 'and his coming was like the night' (I. 47), or when Poseidon rides out in his chariot and the sea-beasts gambol about him (XIII. 18ff), no one is laughing. At all events Milton evidently took Homer's *theomachia* as his model, even if he toned down its more farcical elements.

The *theomachia* shares certain features with the fight between Diomedes and the gods, from which Milton took one curious detail. When Aphrodite is pierced in the hand by Diomedes' spear, ichor,

the divine equivalent of blood, flows from the wound (*Iliad* V.
339–40). Aphrodite returns to Olympus, where she is healed by
Dione and comforted, rather patronisingly, by Zeus. The episode
lies behind the wounding of Satan (VI. 328–34):

> So sore
> The griding sword with discontinuous wound
> Passed through him, but the ethereal substance closed
> Not long divisible, and from the gash
> A stream of nectarous humour issuing flowed
> Sanguine, such as celestial spirits may bleed,
> And all his armour stained erewhile so bright.

There is a hint of absurdity about both episodes, as Pope must have
seen when he scaled down the motif to make a perfect mock-heroic
moment in *The Rape of the Lock*. The sylph Ariel is cut through by a
pair of scissors, 'But airy substance soon unites again' (III. 152).
Miltonic levity is, as always, somewhat more elephantine.

The War in Heaven contains some impressive bravura writing,
but it is not, perhaps, the part of *Paradise Lost* to which the lover of
Milton finds himself most often returning. A more fully achieved
martial sequence of broadly Homeric character occurs at the end of
Book IV (776ff). An angelic squadron patrolling Eden apprehends
Satan and brings him to Gabriel. There follows a notable and
extended Homeric flyting in which the figures of the two adversaries
loom ever larger as they insult each other. The unexpected
conclusion of the episode is amongst the beauties of the poem
(977ff):

> While thus he spake, the angelic squadron bright
> Turned fiery red, sharpening in mooned horns
> Their phalanx, and began to hem him round
> With ported spears, as thick as when a field
> Of Ceres ripe for harvest waving bends
> Her bearded grove of ears, which way the wind
> Sways them; the careful ploughman doubting stands
> Lest on the threshing floor his hopeful sheaves
> Prove chaff. On the other side Satan alarmed
> Collecting all his might dilated stood,
> Like Teneriff or Atlas unremoved;
> His stature reached the sky, and on his crest

Sat horror plumed; nor wanted in his grasp
What seemed both spear and shield — now dreadful deeds
Might have ensued, nor only Paradise
In this commotion, but the starry cope
Of heaven perhaps, or all the elements
At least had gone to wrack, disturbed and torn
With violence of this conflict, had not soon
The eternal, to prevent such horrid fray,
Hung forth in heaven his golden scales, yet seen
Betwixt Astraea and the Scorpion sign,
Wherein all things created first he weighed,
The pendulous round earth with balanced air
In counterpoise, now ponders all events,
Battles and realms; in these he put two weights,
The sequel each of parting and of fight.
The latter quick up flew and kicked the beam,
Which Gabriel spying, thus bespake the fiend:
Satan, I know thy strength and thou know'st mine,
Neither our own but given; what folly then
To boast what arms can do, since thine no more
Than heaven permits, nor mine, though doubled now
To trample thee as mire; for proof look up,
And read thy lot in yon celestial sign
Where thou art weighed and shown how light, how weak,
If thou resist. The fiend looked up and knew
His mounted scale aloft, nor more, but fled
Murmuring, and with him fled the shades of night.

Johnson objected to 'the conduct of the narrative' in this episode:
'Satan is with great expectation brought before Gabriel in Paradise,
and is suffered to go away unmolested.'[69] The observation is
characteristically just, but the objection misses the mark. The
pattern of thwarted combat, of expectations aroused and then
disappointed, recurs, puncturing the heroic pretensions of Satan.
The same Homeric formula (discussed above, p. 80) is employ-
ed three times for the same reason. There has already been the
interrupted duel between Satan and Death, where again there is
a flyting but no action: 'and now great deeds / Had been achieved,
whereof all hell had rung, / Had not . . .' (II. 722ff). Later, in Book
VI, the contest in angelic mountain-throwing will likewise be
broken off: 'and now all heaven / Had gone to wrack, with ruin

overspread, / Had not the almighty Father . . .' (669ff). On that occasion, however, there will be a firm closure, with the decisive intervention of the Son. In all three cases epic expectations are undermined, but only in the third are the tensions fully resolved, as heroic warfare gives place to Biblical triumph. In Book IV, as elsewhere, the size of Satan is underlined with epical vulgarity. Heroes in Homer are bigger and stronger than ordinary men. 'Ingens' (huge) is one of Virgil's favourite adjectives, as the Victorian commentator James Henry pointed out with characteristic panache in a famous seven-page note, of which here is a sample: 'Ingens is our author's maid of all work — cook, slut, and butler at once . . . Seville's famous barber was never busier: it is Ingens here, Ingens there, everywhere Ingens . . . Serpents hiss Ingens . . . Swine grunt Ingens . . . Bulls bellow Ingens . . . None but a heart of adamant had worked any unfortunate biped in such a manner. Many a time I have pitied her, but small good to her a pity of which she knew nothing.'[70] Milton can easily overtop his predecessors; the conventional epic comprison of hero and mountain (*Iliad* XIII. 754; *Aeneid* XII. 701–3) may in his case be taken literally. There is a graphic science-fiction touch in the picture of Satan, surrounded by the red cherubim, growing in size; 'dilated' is physical as well as psychological, though the physicality is questioned by the hint that Satan's spear and shield are not real. But when the balance is hung out, the perspective suddenly and radically shifts, and Satan is completely diminished.

The whole passage is of considerable complexity, and has become something of a critical battleground. The simile especially has seen some notable skirmishing, but often the right questions are not raised. Thus it is not necessary to identify the ploughman with one of the characters in the narrative in order to save the simile's appropriateness to its context.[71] The ploughman is not God (Empson delightedly argued that, if so, God's powerlessness was exposed). The simile is one that most closely resembles its analogues in classical epic. Stylistically it is nearest to Virgil, in particular in the linguistic piquancy that results from the partial personifying of corn as the goddess Ceres ('her bearded grove of ears'). But in structure and content it is Homeric (its most immediate source is *Iliad* II. 147–50). In a number of similes Homer introduces a human observer to focus the response to a natural phenomenon. So too Milton's ploughman suggests a mood of anxiety over the possible destruction of the fruits of careful labour.

Milton excitingly confuses the reader by arousing in him a double response, on the one hand fear that a combat between Satan and Gabriel might shatter the universe, on the other an underlying sense, sustained throughout the poem, of Satan's essential weakness. The simile supports the former response, since it suggests a lack of order and control; the 'doubting' ploughman might thus be said to stand for the reader, if he must stand for anyone. The initial point of comparison concerns the shape and thickness of the angelic phalanx, although there is also a suggestion of serried ranks of corn. If the implication of the crescent shape continues, we may imagine a crescent-shaped swathe of corn blown by the wind. However the simile quickly moves away from the initial comparison, replacing an impression of orderly preparation for battle with a picture of a field disordered by storm. If a memory of the crescent shape lingers, there might be a hint of a farmer's sickle and thus an image of judgement. Certainly the language of the second part of the simile ('threshing floor', 'sheaves', 'chaff') has such Biblical undertones hinting at judgement, but it would be wrong to try to fix them too tightly in terms of strict narrative logic. Thus our emotions are manipulated in complex ways, so that it is misleading of Ricks to complain about the lack of exact fit between this simile and the narrative.

The apparent solidity of the whole description is undermined by the fact that Milton does not allow us to hold on to a single picture. After the statement about how shattering the conflict could have been, the perspective changes, comparatively quietly and delicately, as God's presence is made manifest in the balance. The hitherto restricted location opens out, while long vistas of time present themselves, as we are referred in turn to the continual presence of the constellation, to the Creation, and to the present fallen world. The scales have a double ancestry. In the *Iliad* Zeus, unknown to the human actors, twice weighs the outcome of fighting, first between the Greeks and Trojans, and then between Hector and Achilles in their climactic duel (VIII. 69–77; XXII. 208–13). The motif is imitated, rather mechanically perhaps, by Virgil for the structurally equivalent single-combat between Aeneas and Turnus (XII. 725–7). In each case it is the scale of the loser that drops. This motif is corrected by Milton in accordance with the authority of Scripture; in line 1012 Gabriel echoes the famous writing on the wall at Belshazzar's Feast (Daniel 5: 27), 'Thou art weighed in the balances, and art found wanting' when he tells Satan to read his lot in the sign, 'Where thou art weighed and shown how light, how weak'. Accordingly Satan's side of the scales leaps up rather than sinks. However, the full significance of the scales is not fully determined by its complex origins. Gabriel in his speech, while he points out the powerlessness of himself and Satan, retains his former stance of heroic vaunting, and both he and Satan seem to see the sign as an indication about their own strength and the outcome of the fight. But Fowler is surely right to suggest that God's message in the sign is not limited to either Gabriel's or Satan's interpretation of it. God is rather making manifest his will that Satan may go unmolested and thus be able to tempt man. He thereby establishes the choice for free-will, and this is what makes the moment so overwhelmingly important. The worry about the safety of the universe is ultimately beside the point (God could doubtless have ensured this anyway). The last three lines are exquisitely compressed and understated. It is striking that the verbose Satan should be so utterly silenced ('murmuring' is most eloquent); he seems to melt away.

## Notes

1. 'The Life of Milton' in Samuel Johnson, *Lives of the English Poets*, ed. G.B. Hill (3 vols, Clarendon Press, Oxford, 1905), vol. 1, p. 154.

2. *Explanatory Notes and Remarks on Milton's Paradise Lost* (London, 1734; repr. Garland, New York, 1970), preface, pp xx-xxi.

3. Addison, 'Notes upon the Twelve Books of Paradise Lost' (*The Spectator*, 1712): in John T. Shawcross (ed.), *Milton: The Critical Heritage* (Routledge & Kegan Paul, London, 1970), p. 206, and Donald F. Bond (ed.), *The Spectator* (5 vols, Clarendon Press, Oxford, 1965), vol. 3, p. 312.

4. See Howard Clarke, *Homer's Readers: A Historical Introduction to the Iliad and the Odyssey* (Associated University Presses, London and Toronto, 1981), ch. 3 ('Homer Criticized').

5. *The Iliad of Homer*, ed. Maynard Mack, vols 7 and 8 in *The Twickenham Edition of the Poems of Alexander Pope*, general editor John Butt (11 vols, Methuen and Yale University Press, London and New Haven, 1967), vol. 7, preface p. 12.

6. *Chapman's Homer*, ed. Allardyce Nicoll (2 vols, Routledge & Kegan Paul, London, 1957), vol. 1, pp. 544-5 and 346.

7. See Clarke, *Homer's Readers*, ch. 4 ('Homer Analyzed'); p. 159 for Voss.

8. Thomas Elyot, *The Book named the Governor* (London, 1531), ed. S.E. Lehmberg (Dent, London, 1962), p. 30.

9. Vol. 24 of *Collected Works of Erasmus*, ed. Craig R. Thompson (University of Toronto Press, 1978), pp. 649, 580, 655, 612 (translations by Betty I. Knott).

10. See *The Works of John Milton*, ed. F.A.Patterson *et al.* (18 vols and 2 vols index, Columbia University Press, New York, 1931-40), vol. 18, p. 305. (Hereafter *Columbia Milton*.) No conclusive evidence that Milton used Spondanus has been adduced (the only references to him are in the annotations to the Harvard Pindar, now assigned to another hand).

11. For the allegorisations see Clarke, *Homer's Readers*, ch. 2 ('Homer Allegorized'): the chain, pp. 78–9, the cave of the nymphs, pp. 96–7, the deception of Zeus, pp. 79–80.

12. *Chapman's Homer*, ed. Nicoll, vol. 1, p. 543. For Homer's shield as an allegory of creation see George Kurman, 'Ecphrasis in Epic Poetry', *Comparative Literature*, vol. 26 (1974), pp. 1–13.

13. 'The Shield of Achilles Within the Iliad', *Greece and Rome*, vol. 27 (1980), pp. 1–21.

14. See George G. Loane, 'Milton and Chapman', *Notes and Queries*, vol. 175 (1938), pp. 456–7. Chapman's translation, together with Eustasthius, is recommended for school use by Charles Hoole, *A New Discovery of the Old Art of Teaching School* (1660, repr. Scolar Press, Menston, 1969), p. 196. A readable study of Chapman's *Odyssey* is George deF. Lord, *Homeric Renaissance: The Odyssey of George Chapman* (Chatto & Windus, London 1956), but Lord's view that Chapman's reading of the *Odyssey* as a dynamic allegory is essentially correct is mistaken; for example Odysseus' speech to Amphinomus (XVIII. 198–211) is clearly an *ad hoc* invention, not an admission of error (p. 68). See also Phyllis Bartlett, 'Chapman's Revisions in his *Iliads*', *ELH*, vol. 2 (1935), pp. 92–119; Donald Smalley, 'The Ethical Bias of Chapman's *Homer*', *Studies in Philology*, vol. 36 (1939), pp. 169–91. The quotations from Chapman are from vol. 2, pp. 4, 11, 107, 5, 14.

15. Milton's authorship is questioned by Maurice Kelley and Samuel D. Atkins, 'Milton and the Harvard Pindar', *Studies in Bibliography*, vol. 17 (1964), pp. 77–82. This removes the evidence for Milton's use of Spondanus (cf. Harris Fletcher, 'Milton's Homer', *Journal of English and Germanic Philology*, vol. 38 (1939), pp. 229–32). For the Euripides notes, see Kelley and Atkins, 'Milton's Annotations of Euripides', *JEGP*, vol. 60 (1961), pp. 680–7.

16. *Columbia Milton*, vol. 18, pp. 283–5.

17. *Reason of Church Government*, *Columbia Milton*, vol. 3, p. 239.

18. *Columbia Milton*, vol. 7, p. 111.

19. Ibid., vol. 3, p. 259.

20. Ibid., vol. 14, p. 175.

21. Alexander Ross, *Mystagogus Poeticus or the Muses' Interpreter: Explaining the Historical Mysteries, and Mystical Histories of the Ancient Greek and Latin Poets* (enlarged edn, London, 1675), p. 46.

22. *Columbia Milton*, vol. 12, p. 150.

23. *The Poems of John Milton*, ed. John Carey and Alastair Fowler (Longman, London, 1968), p. 429. See further Michael Murrin, *The Allegorical Epic: Essays in its Rise and Decline* (University of Chicago Press, 1980), pp. 153–71. There is the odd allegorical detail in *Paradise Lost* like the stairs 'mysteriously [i.e. symbolically] meant' in III. 516, but these are not developed in the manner of a Dante or a Spenser.

24. Joseph A. Wittreich, Jr (ed.), *The Romantics on Milton: Formal Essays and Critical Asides* (Case Western Reserve University Press, Cleveland and London, 1970), pp. 200–1.

25. For my reading of this book I am indebted to Steele Commager (ed.), *Virgil: A Collection of Critical Essays*, Twentieth Century Views Series, (Prentice-Hall, Englewood Cliffs, N.J., 1966), pp. 6–7; Kenneth Quinn, *Virgil's Aeneid: A Critical Description* (Routledge & Kegan Paul, London, 1968), pp. 121ff; Brooks Otis, *Virgil: A Study in Civilized Poetry* (Clarendon Press, Oxford, 1964), ch. 6; and the introduction to R.D.Williams's edition of *The Aeneid Book III* (Clarendon Press, Oxford, 1962).

26. *Columbia Milton*, vol. 14, pp. 31–3 (translation by Charles R. Sumner); see also A.D. Nuttall, *Overheard by God: Fiction and Prayer in Herbert, Milton, Dante and St John* (Methuen, London, 1980), pp. 98–100.

27. For a number of points in this section I am indebted to Penelope Murray,

'Homer and the Bard' in Tom Winnifrith, P. Murray and K.W.Gransden (eds), *Aspects of the Epic* (Macmillan, London and Basingstoke, 1983), pp. 1–15. See also Mary R. Lefkowitz, *The Lives of the Greek Poets* (Duckworth, London, 1981), ch. 2 and appendix 1.

28. Alexander Pope, 'An Essay on Homer' in *The Twickenham Edition of the Poems of Alexander Pope,* vol. 7, p. 46; cf. pp. 31 and 49.

29. C.S.Lewis, *A Preface to Paradise Lost* (Oxford University Press, London, Oxford, New York, 1942), p. 59.

30. 'Understanding Milton' in Anna Hatcher (ed.), *Essays on English and American Literature by Leo Spitzer* (Princeton University Press, 1962), pp. 116–31 (the quotations are from pp. 127–8 and 126).

31. For a sophisticated defence of the position adumbrated here see A.D. Nuttall, *A New Mimesis: Shakespeare and the Representation of Reality* (Methuen, London and New York, 1983).

32. T.S.Eliot, 'Milton II' in Frank Kermode (ed.), *Selected Prose of T.S.Eliot* (Faber & Faber, London, 1975), p. 269.

33. *Columbia Milton,* vol. 8, pp. 63ff.

34. Edgar Wind, *Pagan Mysteries in the Renaissance* (new edn, Faber & Faber, London, 1968), p. 58.

35. See Helen Darbishire (ed.), *The Early Lives of Milton* (Constable, London, 1932), p. 33.

36. See Lily B. Campbell, 'The Christian Muse', *Huntingdon Library Bulletin,* vol. 8 (1935), pp. 29–70.

37. *Columbia Milton,* vol. 3, p. 241.

38. See R.W. Condee, 'The Formalized Openings of Milton's Epic Poems', *Journal of English and Germanic Philology,* vol. 50 (1951), pp. 502–8.

39. See Davis P. Harding, *The Club of Hercules: Studies in the Classical Background of Paradise Lost* (University of Illinois Press, Urbana, 1962), p. 3.

40. 'The Life of Milton' in Johnson, *Lives of the English Poets,* ed. Hill, vol. 1, p. 194.

41. So C.M. Bowra, *From Virgil to Milton* (Macmillan and St Martin's Press, London and New York, 1945), p. 1.

42. Wittreich, *Romantics on Milton,* p. 313.

43. See, for example, Richard Jenkyns, *Three Classical Poets: Sappho, Catullus and Juvenal* (Duckworth, London, 1982), pp. 129–30.

44. See J.H. Collett, 'Milton's Use of Classical Mythology in *Paradise Lost*', *PMLA,* vol. 85 (1970), p. 92.

45. Quoted by Burton O. Kurth, *Milton and Christian Heroism: Biblical Epic Themes and Forms in Seventeenth-Century England* (Archon Books, Hamden, Conn., 1966), p. 69.

46. Nuttall, *Overheard by God,* pp. 14ff. See too H.R. Swardson, *Poetry and the Fountain of Light: Observations on the Conflict between Christian and Classical Traditions in Seventeenth-Century Poetry* (Allen & Unwin, London, 1962), ch. 3 (Swardson argues that the tensions are resolved in 'The Flower').

47. Collett's attempt to distinguish sharply between 'fable' and 'feign' would seem to founder on *PL* IX. 30–1 'fabled knights / In battles feigned'.

48. For a list of echoes, some certain, some probable or possible, see *Columbia Milton* index under 'Homer'. Two articles that stress and, in my view, exaggerate, the structural similarities between *PL* and the Homeric epics are Manoocher Aryanpur, '*Paradise Lost* and the *Odyssey*', *Texas Studies in Literature and Language,* vol. 9 (1967), pp. 151–66; and Martin Mueller, '*Paradise Lost* and the *Iliad*', *Comparative Literature Studies,* vol. 6 (1969), pp. 292–316. For Milton's use of 'amerce' in its Greek/Homeric sense in I. 609, see Carter and Stella Revard, 'Milton's Amerc't: The Lost Greek Connection', *Milton Quarterly,* vol. 12 (1978), pp. 105–6.

49. Addison, 'Notes': in Shawcross (ed.), *Milton*, p. 157, and Bond (ed.), *Spectator*, vol. 2, p. 589.

50. Stanley Eugene Fish, *Surprised by Sin: the Reader in Paradise Lost* (MacMillan, London and New York, 1967), pp. 22ff.

51. There is an analogous episode in *Iliad* VII. 443ff when Zeus agrees that Poseidon may eventually destroy the Greek wall, since this brings too much fame to men and thus constitutes a threat to the divine prerogative.

52. For the complexities and ambiguities of the material utilised by Milton see Frank Kermode, *Shakespeare, Spenser, Donne: Renaissance Essays* (Routledge & Kegan Paul, London, 1971), pp. 286–7 (with further references). For the tensions between two aesthetics (picturesque baroque landscape versus formal *hortus conclusus*) see G.Stanley Koehler, 'Milton and the Art of Landscape', *Milton Studies*, vol. 8 (1975), pp. 3–40.

53. The phrase is Alexander Kinglake's in *Eothen* (repr. Oxford University Press, Oxford and New York, 1982), p. 44.

54. *Homer's Iliad*, in *The Twickenham Edition of the Poems of Alexander Pope*, vol. 8, pp. 165ff.

55. Ibid., p. 180.

56. Ibid., p. 170.

57. *Columbia Milton*, vol. 3, p. 304.

58. *Homer's Iliad*, in *The Twickenham Edition of the Poems of Alexander Pope*, vol. 8, p. 182.

59. C.S.Lewis, *A Preface to Paradise Lost* (Oxford University Press, London, Oxford, New York, 1942), p. 70; cf. pp. 122–4 and 128.

60. Addison, 'Notes': in Shawcross (ed.), *Milton*, p. 186, and Bond (ed.), *Spectator*, vol. 3, p. 175.

61. Christopher Ricks, *Milton's Grand Style* (Oxford University Press, London, Oxford, New York, 1963), p. 110.

62. Two good modern treatments of the subject, though without much reference to Homer, are Stella Purce Revard, *The War in Heaven: Paradise Lost and the Tradition of Satan's Rebellion* (Cornell University Press, Ithaca and London, 1980) and James A. Freeman, *Milton and the Martial Muse: Paradise Lost and European Traditions of War* (Princeton University Press, 1980).

63. So, for example, Freeman, *Milton and the Martial Muse*, introduction and ch. 1. Contrast John E. Seaman, 'The Chivalric Cast of Milton's Epic Hero', *English Studies*, vol. 49 (1968), pp. 97–107, who points out that the heroic presentation of Christ in *PL* illustrates 'martial prowess . . . in a good cause' (p. 104), though obviously much depends on how literally one takes Christ's victory over the devils in Book VI. See too Alan Sinfield, *Literature in Protestant England 1560–1660* (Croom Helm, Beckenham, 1983), pp. 39–44.

64. Addison, 'Notes': in Shawcross (ed.), *Milton*, p. 191, and Bond (ed.), *Spectator*, vol. 3, p. 204.

65. John Carey, *Milton*, Literature in Perspective Series (Evans Brothers, London, 1969), p. 120.

66. So Arnold Stein, *Answerable Style: Essays on Paradise Lost* (University of Minnesota Press, Minneapolis, 1953), p. 22.

67. Roland Mushat Frye, *Milton's Imagery and the Visual Arts: Iconographic Tradition in the Epic Poems* (Princeton University Press, 1980), pp. 43ff.

68. 'The Life of Milton' in Johnson, *Lives of the English Poets*, ed. Hill, vol. 1, p. 185.

69. Ibid., p. 186.

70. James Henry, *Aeneidea or Critical, Exegetical, and Aesthetical Remarks on the Aeneis*, vol. 3 (Dublin, 1889), note on V. 118, pp. 39ff. For the mountain simile see Claes Schaar, *The Full Voic'd Quire Below: Vertical Context Systems in Paradise Lost*, Lund Studies in English 60 (Gleerup, Lund, 1982), pp. 205–8.

71. See Fowler's notes in Carey and Fowler (eds), *The Poems of John Milton*; Ricks, *Milton's Grand Style*, pp. 129–30; Schaar, *The Full Voic'd Quire*, pp. 83–8.

# 3
# VIRGIL

## Style

The purpose of this chapter is, in part, a negative one, to argue that, whereas the presence of Homer in *Paradise Lost* has not always been given its full recognition, the influence of Virgil is often exaggerated, or at any rate not described with sufficient precision. In particular certain features of the style of *Paradise Lost* — for example the frequent occurrence of enjambement and the partly Latinate syntax — are not due to Virgil alone. Some of the trouble lies in the customary modern division of epics into 'primary' and 'secondary', or 'primitive' and 'literary', with Homer in the first category and Virgil in the second, and thus in the fracturing of the tradition that leads directly from Homer to Milton.[1] For in terms of that tradition Homer belongs with Virgil and Milton, and not with the *Song of Roland* or the *Nibelungenlied*. The *Iliad* and *Odyssey* may not have been conceived as Epics as later generations came to understand the term — just as stories about the famous deeds of men — but they became such as a result of their later reception, a process facilitated by their profundity of vision and poetic quality and by Virgil's great indebtedness to them.

There is no reason to doubt Milton's admiration for Virgil. While there is no extended celebration of Virgil in Milton's works[2] and the *Aeneid* is not mentioned in the treatise *Of Education* (only the *Georgics*), nevertheless Virgil is frequently cited in the prose works, and on one occasion described as 'summus artifex decori', the great master of what is appropriate, a quality which Milton rated highly.[3] It might be suspected that Milton's republicanism would have led him to have reservations about a poet who had put his pen at the service of Augustus, the man who had replaced the Republic with a thinly concealed monarchy. However, the republican Gibbon did not regard Virgil as an upholder of monarchy, and both Gibbon and Milton cite with approval the episode from *Aeneid* VIII (489ff) about the expulsion of the tyrant Mezentius.[4] Moreover, like Spenser before him, Milton shaped his poetic career, with characteristic self-consciousness, on Virgil's example, preparing himself for his great epic by cutting his poetic teeth on lesser genres. To the men of the Renaissance Virgil's career had a quality of inevitability about it, and the apparently relentless upward march through the genres seemed to have been planned from the first. In fact Virgil had started by declaring an allegiance to what is often known as the Neoteric movement which had rejected epic for slighter but more highly polished forms (of particular importance is the opening of *Eclogue* VI which was modelled on the prologue to Callimachus' *Aetia*, the foundation text of the new poetics). His eventual decision to embark on a 'big book', something for which Callimachus had explicitly expressed dislike, may well have surprised and even disconcerted many of his contemporaries. But in hindsight the neat shape of his poetic career provided a uniquely authoritative model for an aspiring young poet.[5]

We cannot know for certain how Milton read Virgil, but it is likely that he did so as a scholar, a humanist and a poet concerned with the mechanics of his craft and of imitation as a creative process. It has been argued that Milton may have been influenced by the allegorical commentaries of the grammarian Fulgentius (5th–6th century) and the Renaissance Neoplatonist Cristoforo Landino (1424–92).[6] However no clear connection has been established, and we are offered merely vague analogies that prove nothing. As I have suggested Milton could have consulted, among other editions, the standard Renaissance commentary of the Spanish Jesuit J.L. de La Cerda first published in Madrid in 1608–17. This was in regular school use, and is recommended by Charles Hoole in *A New Discovery of the Old Art of Teaching School* (1660), along with the famous commentary of Servius (4th–5th century) and Thomas Farnaby's *Notes on Vergil*.[7] In a letter to Milton, Carlo Dati, one of Milton's learned Italian friends, mentions La Cerda and he was consulted by the author of the annotations of the Harvard Pindar, whether Milton or not.[8]

La Cerda's edition differs little from a modern one. The full notes offer glosses, explanations and numerous parallels from both Latin and Greek writings. La Cerda includes the Greek parallels to show Virgil as the perfect imitator of Greek poetry: 'he adds what is lacking in the Greek authors, takes away what is redundant, renders what is imperfect and lacking in dignity more perfect and polished by his careful efforts' ('ut quae in Graecis desunt, addat, quae in illis redundant, adimat, quae in illis sunt imperfecta et parum alta, perfectiora et nitidiora labore suo et industria reddat'. 'Ad Lectorem'). For example, following J.C. Scaliger, La Cerda prefers the simile in *Aeneid* II. 304ff, because the details are in his opinion more relevant and judiciously chosen, to its Homeric source (the two similes are discussed below, pp. 123–5) and in general shares Scaliger's view of Virgil's superiority to Homer. Thus by observing Virgil's adaptation of Greek material and the qualities so revealed — judgement, propriety, sublimity, vividness and so forth — one can learn the art of imitation. The introduction is rather more alien in character than the notes; Virgil is here presented not only as the greatest poet of antiquity but as a universal genius skilled in such matters as philosophy, astrology, medicine and mathematics (La Cerda rejects the common medieval view of Virgil as a magician) and a man of supreme virtue, as shown for example by the fine moral qualities exhibited throughout his works. The *Aeneid* sets forth the power of wisdom and goodness, and contains examples of all the virtues. Milton agreed with La Cerda that a good poet needed to be a good man,[9] a view that, however unconvincing, is at least preferable to a prevalent modern belief that poets are not bound by ordinary morality.

The style of *Paradise Lost* is often regarded as Virgilian.[10] However, as Mario Di Cesare has rightly observed, 'every great poem creates its own language',[11] and the language of *Paradise Lost* is of course not Virgilian but Miltonic. Certainly many influences went into its making, including Virgil. Milton also inevitably owed much to earlier English poetry, especially to his three favourites, Spenser, Shakespeare (who sometimes writes in a way that is more like the later Milton than is generally recognised, for example in some parts of *Troilus and Cressida*) and Cowley. Milton also studied those Italian poets, in particular Tasso, who had struggled to create a vernacular equivalent of a Latin style, above all by studied manipulation of syntax. Milton's diction — as opposed to his syntax — is not, even in *Paradise Lost*, as Latinate as has sometimes been thought. However, attempts to reduce the number of Latinisms to a minimum (for example Fowler's apparent assumption that a word in *Paradise Lost* cannot be a Latinism if it is used in the same sense by any other seventeenth-century writer) probably spring from a desire to rescue the poem from the charge of the anti-Miltonists that Milton's writing is un-English. A better answer to Leavis would be that all English Renaissance poets use Latinisms, and that the use of foreign idioms can be an enrichment rather than an impoverishment of our language. Milton likes to exploit, like many other English poets before and since, striking juxtapositions of words that grandly proclaim their Latin origin with simpler, more basic vocabulary that belongs to a different linguistic stratum (though in some cases also deriving from Latin). There is a classic instance in *Macbeth* II. ii. 61–2, 'the multitudinous seas incarnadine, / Making the green one red'. Two such phrases from *Paradise Lost* are 'aggregrated soil' and 'mace petrific' (X. 293–4).[12]

Certain features of the style of *Paradise Lost* are positively un-Virgilian. The neoclassical writers may have failed to notice what we would call the romantic aspect of Virgil's sensibility but they were surely right to stress the element of control, of careful art, in Virgil's writing. In *The Temple of Fame*, after lines on Homer, Pope characterises Virgil in this way (196–201):

A golden column next in rank appeared,
On which a shrine of purest gold was reared,
Finished the whole and laboured every part,
With patient touches of unwearied art;
The Mantuan there in sober triumph sate,
Composed his posture and his look sedate.

Similarly in *The Battle of the Books*, Swift gives his sense of Virgil's sobriety thus: 'He was mounted on a dapple-grey steed, the slowness of whose pace was an effect of the highest mettle and vigour.'[13] Control, sobriety, sedateness, a temperately contained potential power and energy — this may not be the whole truth about Virgil, but it is an important part of the truth. No one would, I think, characterise Milton in quite this way. The style of *Paradise Lost* is not patient or sedate; rather it has a baroque quality of deliberate and heady excess, and it is marked by articulate energy rather than by stasis. Milton has a fondness for long, sinewy, sometimes trailing sentences. The famous first sentence of *Paradise Lost* is 16 lines in length, more than twice as long as the grand opening sentences of the *Iliad* and *Aeneid*, and the verb 'sing' is almost unbearably held back until line six. The energy thus built up is relesased in the remainder of the sentence in a manner that resembles the arching and breaking of a wave.

One element in Milton's verse which is often regarded as Virgilian is the extensive employment of enjambement (the carrying of sentences across line divisions without a pause). Milton

regarded this as a matter of considerable importance, and draws our
attention to it in a note on the verse:

> The measure [i.e. metre] is English heroic verse without rhyme,
> as that of Homer in Greek and of Virgil in Latin, rhyme being no
> necessary adjunct or true ornament of poem or good verse, in
> longer works especially, but the invention of a barbarous age to
> set off wretched matter and lame metre . . . Not without cause
> therefore some both Italian and Spanish poets of prime note have
> rejected rhyme both in longer and shorter works, as have also
> long since our best English tragedies, as a thing of itself, to all
> judicious ears, trivial and of no true musical delight, which
> consists only in apt numbers, fit quantity of syllables and *the sense
> variously drawn out from one verse into another* [my italics], not
> in the jingling sound of like endings, a fault avoided by the
> learned ancients both in poetry and all good oratory. This neglect
> then of rhyme so little is to be taken for a defect, though it may
> seem so perhaps to vulgar readers, that it rather is to be esteemed
> an example set, the first in English, of ancient liberty recovered
> to heroic poem from the troublesome and modern bondage of
> rhyming.

A comparison of two passages from sixteenth-century poetry
both deriving from Virgil should help to make clear the reasons for
Milton's insistence:

> Aeneas, I'll repair thy Trojan ships,
> Conditionally that thou wilt stay with me,
> And let Achates sail to Italy.
> I'll give thee tackling made of rivelled gold,
> Wound on the barks of odoriferous trees;
> Oars of massy ivory, full of holes,
> Through which the water shall delight to play;
> Thy anchors shall be hewed from crystal rocks,
> Which if thou loose shall shine above the waves;
> Thy masts whereon thy swelling sails shall hang,
> Hollow pyramides of silver plate;
> The sails of folded lawn, where shall be wrought
> The wars of Troy, but not Troy's overthrow;
> For ballast empty Dido's treasury,
> Take what ye will, but leave Aeneas here.    (III. i. 112–26)

1030 'What helps to yield unto such furious rage,
Sweet spouse?' quoth she. 'Without will of the gods
This chanced not; nor leful [lawful] was for thee
To lead away Creusa hence with thee —
The king of the high heaven suffreth it not.
A long exile thou art assigned to bear,
Long to furrow large space of stormy seas;
So shalt thou reach at last Hesperian land,
Where Lydian Tiber with his gentle stream
Mildly doth flow along the fruitful fields.
1040 There mirthful wealth, there kingdom is for thee,
There a king's child prepared to be thy make [mate].
For thy beloved Creusa stint they tears.
For now shall I not see the proud abodes
Of Myrmidons nor yet of Dolopes;
Ne I, a Trojan lady and the wife
Unto the son of Venus the goddess,
Shall go a slave to serve the Greekish dames.
Me here the gods' great mother holds.
And now farewell, and keep in father's breast
1050 The tender love of thy young son and mine.'
        This having said, she left me all in tears
And minding much to speak; but she was gone
And subtly fled into the weightless air.
Thrice wrought I with mine arms to accoll [embrace] her
    neck,
Thrice did my hands' vain hold the image escape,
Like nimble winds and like the fleeing dream.
So night spent out, return I to my feres [companions].
And there wandering I find together swarmed
A new number of mates, mothers and men,
1060 A rout exiled, a wretched multitude,
From each where flocked together, prest (ready) to pass,
With heart and goods, to whatsoever land
By sliding seas me listed [pleased] them to lead.
And now rose Lucifer above the ridge
Of lusty Ide, and brought the dawning light.
The Greeks held the entries of the gates beset;
Of help there was no hope. Then gave I place,
Took up my sire and hasted to the hill.

## Virgil

The first passage is one of the best speeches from Marlowe's *Dido Queen of Carthage*, published in 1594, which turns material from *Aeneid* Books I, II and IV into a play; the second is from the Earl of Surrey's translation, published in 1557, of *Aeneid* II. At a first glance one might be tempted to prefer the Marlowe because of its more gorgeous language and the evident zest of the mighty line. Further acquaintance, however, may well revise one's estimate. Marlowe offers a rather unfocused lyric glamour and the relentless end-stopping (pauses at the end of each line) contributes to the overall rhythmic monotony of what is only an assemblage of individual fine lines. By contrast Surrey, though sober at times to the point of drabness, thinks in longer units, in paragraphs rather than in single lines, and in imitating Virgil's enjambed style, if without Virgil's finesse, sustains a measure of neoclassic poise, rhythmic variety and epic movement.[14] For example line 1034 gains in weight and impressiveness because it contrasts with the more fluid movement of the preceding lines. The final paragraph is particularly impressive; as in Virgil, a quickening of the pulse of the verse creates a mood of hope as Aeneas and the Trojan remnant set out for exile, an effect of the metre and rhythmic subtlety as much as of anything that Aeneas is saying (one could compare the closing lines of 'Lycidas'). In comparison with Milton, or Shakespeare, another supreme master of enjambement, Surrey is a tiro, but his somewhat fumbling efforts point the way to later achievements.

The kind of enjambement where the sense is carried across the line division without any pause at all and where the first line makes no sense on its own is somewhat commoner in Virgil than in Homer, but Homer too is a master of it. Geoffrey Kirk has devoted a useful essay to Homer's use of enjambement which he divides into two basic types; 'progressive', where the first line could constitute a complete sense unit on its own, and 'necessary', where it could not. He further subdivides the second category into 'periodic' where the first line is a subordinate clause (e.g. *Iliad* XVI. 36–7), 'integral' where a clause is carried across a line division (e.g. ibid. 81–2), and 'violent' where this happens in a particularly extreme way (e.g. ibid. 396–7, where a preposition is divided from the nouns it governs).[15] Kirk observes that enjambement is used sometimes for a particular expressive purpose, and sometimes simply to secure a variety of rhythmic movement. Homer makes particular use of progressive enjambement, and on occasion uses it to powerful effect. For example the *Iliad*'s first line seems complete in itself, 'Sing, goddess, the wrath of Peleus' son Achilles', but is then dramatically modified by the enjambed adjective 'accursed' ('oulomenēn'), thereby given unusual force (Milton's 'thus they relate / Erring' is similar). Elsewhere progressive enjambement is used for the leisurely accumulation of detail, and thus seems connected with the oral nature of the poetry. Addison thought that Milton's use of enjambement was essentially Homeric: 'Milton has copied after Homer rather than Virgil in the length of his periods, the copiousness of his phrases, and the running of his verses into one another.'[16] Kirk shares this view, and cites II. 557–61 as an example of Milton's composing 'in a ruminative oral way':[17]

> Others apart sat on a hill retired,
> In thoughts more elevate, and reasoned high
> Of providence, foreknowledge, will and fate,
> Fixed fate, free will, foreknowledge absolute,
> And found no end, in wandering mazes lost.

However, the mannered repetitions that seem to weave a net in which the fallen angels are trapped is unlike the less self-conscious art of Homer. A more convincing instance of such Homeric cumulative writing occurs in III. 440ff, where three times the sentence seems to come to rest only to be injected with a fresh input of energy:

> So on this windy sea of land the fiend
> Walked up and down alone bent on his prey,
> Alone, for other creature in this place
> Living or lifeless to be found was none,
> None yet, but store hereafter from the earth
> Up hither like aerial vapours flew
> Of all things transitory and vain, when sin
> With vanity had filled the works of men,
> Both all things vain, and all who in vain things
> Built their fond hopes of glory or lasting fame . . .

In general, in Kirk's words, it is 'Milton's capacity for varying the tone and feeling of his poetry that makes him resemble Homer rather than the consistently intense and artifice-dominated Virgil'.[18] At all events Milton's use of enjambement should be seen as an epic rather than specifically a Virgilian feature.

Similarly the Latinate syntax of *Paradise Lost* is not due to Virgil alone. In his masterly study F.T. Prince has shown the extent of Milton's debt to Italian poets, especially Tasso (1544–95) and Giovanni Della Casa (1503–56). In the sonnets, where to a degree the style of *Paradise Lost* was forged, Milton was composing with one eye on Della Casa and the other on Horace. The combination of an unusually spare vocabulary with departures from normal syntax creates a ruggedness, that 'asprezza' that Tasso had sought but hardly fully attained, that is in its ultimate effect not especially Virgilian. An extreme example is the sonnet 'On the Late Massacre in Piedmont':

> Avenge o Lord thy slaughtered saints, whose bones
>    Lie scattered on the Alpine mountains cold,
>    Even them who kept thy truth so pure of old
>    When all our fathers worshipped stocks and stones,
> Forget not; in thy book record their groans
>    Who were thy sheep and in their ancient fold
>    Slain by the bloody Piedmontese that rolled
>    Mother with infant down the rocks. Their moans
> The vales redoubled to the hills and they
>    To heaven. Their martyred blood and ashes sow
>    O'er all the Italian fields where still doth sway
> The triple Tyrant, that from these may grow
>    A hundredfold, who having learnt thy way
>    Early may fly the Babylonian woe.

Here we find the bold onward sweep (the tone is prophetic and Biblical), the sentences that ignore line divisions and the customary divisions of the sonnet (most powerfully in line 7 where 'rolled' is placed precipitously at the end of a line, the enjambement with its brief pause enacting the thrusting down of mother and child), the resulting muscularity. There are numerous inversions of which the most powerful is the wrenching back of the imperative 'Forget not'; the reader is lured into taking the clause 'Even them . . . stones' as in apposition to 'saints', only to have a rude awakening with the shock of 'Forget not', which forces him to an unsettling readjustment in his understanding of the syntax. We have already seen how Milton's carefully metaphrastic rendering of Horace's Pyrrha Ode is alert to just these features of the Latin: the sentences that cut across lines and stanzas, the carefully constructed periods, the inversions and the expressive word order. In *Paradise Lost* IV. 381–2 'hell shall unfold / To entertain you two, her widest gates', the entertainment of Adam and Eve is placed, mimetically, within the gates of hell; the word order enacts the meaning.[19] Such effects are easier to obtain in Latin poetry because of the greater freedoms allowed by a more fully inflected language. There was, it will be recalled, just such an example of mimetic syntax in the first line of the Pyrrha Ode. In such writing Milton owes a general debt to Latin poetry and the Latin language, as much as a particular debt to Virgil.

Because English has fewer inflections than Latin, it has to be put under greater strain to achieve similar effects. As a result, Milton's syntax becomes looser than that of any Latin poet, even Virgil, whose syntax, while often experimental, seldom threatens to dissolve completely. By contrast, in a passage that has become something of a *locus conclamatus* for its doubtful syntax, Milton can write (III. 344–9):

> No sooner had the almighty ceased, but all
> The multitude of angels with a shout
> Loud as from numbers without number, sweet
> As from blessed voices, uttering joy, heaven rung
> With jubilee and loud hosannas filled
> The eternal regions.

The classical scholar Bentley vigorously resorted to emendation, changing 'with' (345) to 'gave', reducing the sentence to orderliness and ordinariness. Retaining 'with', one could regard 'The multitude of angels . . . uttering joy' as an extended absolute phrase (such absolute constructions are much commoner in Latin than in English). Alternatively 'The multitude of angels' could be regarded as subject and 'heaven' the object of 'rung' understood transitively.[20] These syntactic uncertainties do not prevent the sentence from attaining its expressive effect, rather the reverse. As Carey has it, 'The shout hangs in the air, re-echoing, passing into clamorous Hosannas. Milton is thinning his grammar like paint, and paints the shout.'[21] Similarly in the opening lines of Book V, 'Now Morn her rosy steps in the eastern clime / Advancing, sowed the earth with orient pearl', 'Advancing' operates with a characteristic looseness and ambivalence: it could act as the participle of a transitive verb with 'steps' as its object, but might instead be taken intransitively in an absolute phrase in agreement with 'steps'. The syntax is not so much manipulative, as K.W. Gransden would have it [22] — controlling and directing the reader's response by its grammatical dislocations — as painterly, delicately building up a picture full and rich. C.S. Lewis gives another telling example:

> . . . heaven opened wide
> Her ever-during gates, harmonious sound
> On golden hinges moving.   (VII, 205)

*Moving* might be a transitive participle agreeing with *gates* and governing *sound*; or again the whole phrase from *harmonious* to *moving* might be an ablative absolute. The effect of the passage, however, is the same whichever we choose. An extreme modern might have attempted to reach it with

> Gates open wide. Glide
> On golden hinges . . .
> Moving . . .
> Harmonious sound.

This melting down of the ordinary units of speech, this plunge back into something more like the indivisible, flowing quality of immediate experience, Milton also achieves. But by his appearance of a carpentered structure he avoids the suggestion of fever, preserves the sense of dignity, and does not irritate the mind to ask questions.[23]

Though Milton's writing is in this respect looser than Virgil's, in other ways it aims at greater precision. W.F. Jackson-Knight has well observed that Virgil likes to exploit 'the empty spaces' which many Latin words seem to have in them ('res', 'thing', is an example, and one from which Virgil spins much verbal magic).[24] The result is a style that is not in general sharp-edged like much good Latin writing but often opaque, suggestive, blurred. Virgil even avoids clear metaphors (metaphors in which one can state precisely the two elements in the implied comparison) in favour of intimations, possibilities of extra meaning. At times we find a kind of impressionism, like the famous description of Charon's eyes: 'stant lumina flamma' (*Aen.* VI. 300) is literally almost meaningless, 'his eyes (*lumina* perhaps also retains something of its primary meaning 'lights') stand with/in flame' — if, however, we are willing to ponder the phrase it offers a brilliant suggestion of the fixity of Charon's fiery stare. Many of Milton's most striking effects depend rather on clarity in the use of words; in particular he likes to thicken the texture of his verse with puns and word plays. In IV. 264–7 'The birds their choir apply; airs, vernal airs, / Breathing the smell of field and grove, attune / The trembling leaves', 'airs' means 'breezes', but also, in conjunction with 'choir' and 'attune', has the secondary meaning 'melodies'.[25] This is complex but not vague (a pun demands that two or more meanings are *precisely* activated). In IV. 521–2 Satan declares of Adam and Eve that he intends to 'build / Their ruin'. This is the sort of etymological paradox that Milton cannot resist. 'Ruin', always a potent word in Milton,[26] originally meant a 'falling', from Latin *ruere*, a sense usually present in Milton's use of it, and thus clashes with 'builds'. A more suggestive use of such a clash of rising and falling occurs in II. 587–91:

Beyond this flood a frozen continent
Lies dark and wild, beat with perpetual storms
Of whirlwind and dire hail, which on firm land
Thaws not but gathers heap, and ruin seems
Of ancient pile . . .

Here the sense of falling active in 'ruin', alongside its developed meaning of a collapsed building, gives a paradoxical quality to the landscape of hell. Whereas we normally think of deep snow as building up (thus 'heap'), it is here likened to something that is falling down, which, in another sense, the snow is. Effects of the kind are everywhere in Milton — Ricks gives innumerable instances — and in general depend, not so much as in Virgil on opening up penumbras of meaning, but on sharpening our responses to language and thus to the things that language denotes.

Certainly there are analogies in Virgil, as also in Homer. *Aeneid* VIII. 64 'caeruleus Thybris, caelo gratissimus amnis' (sky-blue Tiber, a river most pleasing to the skies) seems to link joyfully the blue waters of the Tiber with the blue of the firmament overhead as two aspects of the divine presence. However this example lacks the hardness of a Miltonic pun or paradox. Closer to Milton is the phrase that Virgil uses about the golden bough which Aeneas has to find to effect entry into the Underworld, 'auri . . . aura' (VI. 204), 'a breathing of gold'. This brilliantly combines word-play and oxymoron to convey the paradoxical feeling of something at once tactile and elusive, both of this world and not of it, sinister yet sacred. Etymological plays on words were in antiquity part of the armoury of the learned poet, an aspect of *doctrina*, and there are some instances in the *Aeneid*. Thus III. 540 'bello armantur equi, bellum haec armenta minantur' (horses are armed for war, war these herds threaten) points towards the supposed derivation of *armentum* from *arma*, as Servius saw. Less certain is the play detected by Eduard Norden on the name of Charon (connected with Greek *chairo*, 'I rejoice') when in VI. 392 Charon declares that he did not rejoice ('nec sum laetatus') at ferrying living heroes across the Styx.[27] Elsewhere there are jingles like 'late Latio' (VIII. 14), which are simply matters of sound not sense, like Milton's 'beseeching or besieging' (V. 869). But in general in this aspect of his style Milton resembles Horace or the poets of the Silver Age, in particular Lucan, as much as Virgil.

## Similes

One of the most familiar features of classical epic is the extended simile. Some of Milton's similes derive from the *Aeneid*, but since in his similes Virgil is often imitating Homer, Virgil and Homer tend to come to Milton in combination. Nevertheless it is possible to ask whether Milton's deployment of his similes is closer to Virgil's practice or to Homer's. The standard modern view is that, whereas in Homer's similes there is generally only a single point of correspondence with the narrative, Milton's are marked by multiple correspondence. As James Whaler puts it in an influential article, 'The key to fundamental difference between complex simile as found in Homer and in Milton lies in Milton's predominant method of exact homologation'.[28] Since classical scholars have established that detailed homologation is characteristic of Virgil's similes it would seem to follow that in this respect at least Milton is a Virgilian. The matter, however, is more complex, and will require a careful look at both the Homeric and the Virgilian simile.

Scholars often write as if Homer's normal procedure was to think of an initial comparison (a warrior is like a lion or whatever), and then develop a picture of the subject of the simile that for all its vividness is basically irrelevant or digressive (the word 'ornamental' usually makes an appearance). Thus David West talks of similes 'which have *one* point of comparison with the narrative and a large ornamental development', while M.D. Reeve can speak of 'a conclusion that few people would wish to dispute: Homer elaborates his similes without regard to the narrative'.[29] The debate

about whether Homer's similes are normally based on a single point
of resemblance or on more than one is of long standing. In his
commentary on the bee simile in *Iliad* II. 87ff Chapman, criticising
Spondanus, argues that Homeric similes 'answer in all parts . . . For
who . . . will not conceive it absurd to make a simile which serves to
the illustration and ornament of a poem lame of a foot and idle?'[30]
Certainly Homer's practice is more varied and complex than such
formulations as West's imply, as an example should make clear
(*Iliad* XI. 555–64, Lattimore):

> so Aias, disappointed at heart, drew back from the Trojans
> much unwilling, but feared for the ships of the Achaians. As
> when a donkey, stubborn and hard to move, goes into a cornfield
> in despite of boys, and many sticks have been broken upon him,
> but he gets in and goes on eating the deep grain, and the children
> beat him with sticks, but their strength is infantile; yet at last
> by hard work they drive him out when he is glutted with eating;
> so the high-hearted Trojans and companions in arms gathered
> from far places kept after great Aias, the son of Telamon,
> stabbing always with their spears at the centre of the great shield.

The simile is apt for the stalwart Ajax beating a stubborn retreat. It
should be obvious that Ajax is not just like a donkey (the simile
could not have stopped at the initial comparison), but like a donkey
beaten out of a cornfield by small boys (the boys are not really
'ornamental' either, since the donkey would have retreated more
rapidly before grown men). In other words there is an interaction
between the narrative and the *whole* of the simile. That is not to say
that we should list a series of exact correspondences (donkey =
Ajax: boys = Trojans; sticks = spears; eating = killing, etc.; no
listener or reader is normally tempted to do that), simply that this
simile is relevant as a whole.

In many of Homer's similes there is more than one point of
correspondence. In *Iliad* III the old men of Troy are compared to
cicadas (149–53, Lattimore):

> these were seated by the Skaian gates, elders of the people.
> Now through old age these fought no longer, yet were they
> excellent speakers still, and clear, as cicadas who through the forest
> settle on trees, to issue their delicate voice of singing.

Such were they who sat on the tower, chief men of the Trojans.

The immediate ground of comparison is the sound made by the elders, but it is difficult to believe that a visual point is not also intended. The old men up on the tower look like cicadas in a tree. In a number of similes dual correspondence is actually spelled out by the poet (e.g. VIII. 306ff and XIII. 136ff, or XII 146ff where we enter the simile on one point of comparison and leave it on another).

Allied to the view that Homer's similes are digressive is the notion that their function is primarily to provide relief. J.B. Broadbent says of Milton's similes that they do not merely relieve, but they 'intensify and complicate still more'.[31] This I believe to be true of many of Homer's similes too. In *Iliad* XV Apollo kicks over the wall that the Achaeans have laboured so long to build (361–6, Lattimore):

> and wrecked the bastions of the Achaians
> easily, as when a little boy piles sand by the sea-shore
> when in his innocent play he makes sand towers to amuse him
> and then, still playing, with hands and feet ruins them and wrecks
>    them.
> So you, lord Apollo, piled in confusion much hard work
> and painful done by the Argives.

The simile is obviously pathetic in its effect (in a slightly whimsical way). The endeavours of men are as nought when faced with divine might. The simile hints too at an important characteristic of Homeric gods (Zeus apart), namely their fundamental irresponsibility which is somehow still not seen as culpable. The simile of the child and the sandcastles is lovely in itself, but it is also superbly tailored to its context. Homeric similes do provide relief, but that is not all they do.

Addison contrasts the epic simile with 'the quaint similes and little turns of wit, which are so much in vogue among modern poets', and thought that the former did not need to show 'any surprising point of likeness'.[32] Certainly many of the similes in the *Iliad* have a quality of relaxed inevitability; the poet does not generally seem to strive for effect, and there is the extraordinary sense that this is how the world is which Auden notes in 'Memorial for The City'. By contrast some of the similes in the *Odyssey* are more self-conscious, more artful in their deployment; the simile may lack any obvious rightness, but we can applaud the poet's wit in choosing it. For example in VIII. 521ff Odysseus weeps when Demodocus sings of the Trojan war; a simile compares his weeping with that of a woman who has lost her husband in battle, and is being taken into slavery (we may think of Andromache in the *Iliad*). Both the material, which would have been part of the main narrative of the *Iliad* and not of a simile, and the odd juxtaposing of two very different griefs, a bitter-sweet recalling of the past tinged with sentimentality on the one hand and an urgent and desperate tragedy on the other, give the simile a highly distinctive flavour which is not quite Iliadic. Similarly in *Odyssey* XVI. 11ff Eumaeus, in the presence of the disguised Odysseus, welcomes Telemachus on his return from the mainland, and is likened to a father greeting a son who is coming home after ten years. The simile underlines the bond of affection between the old pig-man and the young prince, but in context there is also a strong flavour of irony. The simile is a curious inverted prolepsis of the re-union of Odysseus and Telemachus; it is the father returning home after ten years of war and ten of wandering who is welcomed by the son. Again the ingenuity of this seems un-Iliadic. (An exception, from a book often described as Odyssean in style, is the simile in *Iliad* XXIV. 480–4 in which — in what appears a deliberate reversal — Priam when he comes to appeal to Achilles is compared to an exiled killer making supplications abroad.) In both cases there is a lack of correspondence between simile and narrative, but it is not one that can properly be described as digressive.

David West has convincingly shown that the similes of the *Aeneid* are marked by multiple correspondence with the enclosing narrative. In order to integrate his similes as carefully as possible in the texture of his poem Virgil resorted to a mosaic of contrived verbal correspondences. In *Aeneid* VI Virgil compares Aeneas' journey through the Underworld to a journey through a wood by night (268–72):

Ibant obscuri sola sub nocte per umbram
perque domos Ditis vacuas et inania regna;
quale per incertam lunam sub luce maligna
est iter in silvis, ubi caelum condidit umbra
Iuppiter, et rebus nox abstulit atra colorem.

(They were going dim under the lonely night through the shadow and through the blank dwellings of Dis and the insubstantial realms, just as by an uncertain moon under its mean light there is a journey in the woods, when Jupiter has buried the sky in shadow, and black night has stolen the colour from things.

Or less prosaically (in one of the few nearly successful imitations of quantitative metre in English):

They wer' amid the shadows by night in loneliness obscure
Walking forth i' the void and vasty dominyon of Ades;
As by an uncertain moonray secretly illumin'd
One goeth in the forest, when heaven is gloomily clouded,
And black night hath robbed the colours and beauty from all
      things.

(Robert Bridges, *Ibant Obscuri*, 1916)

West has shown that the verbal correspondences here are very exact. 'There is a journey' ('est iter') answers 'they were going' ('ibant'), 'under its mean light' ('sub luce maligna') answers 'under the night' ('sub nocte'), 'condidit umbra' ('has buried in shadow') 'through the shadow' ('per umbram'), while Jupiter and the sky correspond to Dis and the abodes of the Underworld. The word 'lonely' in the narrative suggests that the journey in the simile is also solitary (West calls this effect 'unilateral correspondence').[33] Few would deny that the simile is a haunting one (Virgil is good at depicting moonlight).

It should be stressed that West is concerned with description of Virgil's technique, not with evaluation. He nowhere implies that Virgil's similes are better than Homer's. Others, however, have not been slow to argue for Virgil's superiority. A single characteristic example should make the issues clear. Aeneas surveys the now burning city of Troy (II. 298–308):

Diverso interea miscentur moenia luctu,
et magis atque magis, quamquam secreta parentis
Anchisae domus arboribusque obtecta recessit,
clarescunt sonitus armorumque ingruit horror.
excutior somno et summi fastigia tecti
ascensu supero atque arrectis auribus adsto;
in segetem veluti cum flamma furentibus Austris

incidit, aut rapidus montano flumine torrens
sternit agros, sternit sata laeta boumque labores
praecipitesque trahit silvas — stupet inscius alto
accipiens sonitum saxi de vertice pastor.

(Meanwhile the city is confused everywhere with grief, and more
and more, although my father Anchises' house was set back,
withdrawn and screened by trees, the sounds grow clear and the
shiver of arms menaces. I shake myself from sleep and climb up
on to the roof of the house, and stand with ears pricked-up. Just
as when fire falls on a cornfield as the south winds rage, or a
whirling mountain-streaming torrent lays low the fields, lays low
the happy crops and the work of the óxen and drags woods
headlong; a shepherd hearing the sound from a rock's high peak
is bewildered and stunned.)

I quote the interesting note in R.G. Austin's edition:

The simile is very carefully worked out in its applicability to
Aeneas: he is compared to a shepherd (as he was, of the
Trojans), horrified (as he was) at catching from a high rock
(Aeneas was on the roof of the house) the roar of flames or of a
flood (such as was now swallowing Troy), barely realizing (like
Aeneas, fresh from sleep) that his world of crops and ploughland
was being swept away (as Aeneas' world was being swept to
ruin). No doubt Virgil had in mind various passages of Homer, in
particular *Iliad* IV. 452ff:
> As when rivers in winter spate running down from the
> mountains
> throw together at the meeting of streams the weight of their
> water
> out of the great springs behind in the hollow stream-bed,
> and far away in the mountains the shepherd hears their
> thunder;
> such, from the coming together of men, was the shock and the
> shouting.

But the drama is all his own, and the pity: Homer's floods and
fires are *loci communes*, as it were, but Virgil has made a
personal disaster out of a general comparison, and his shepherd
is no casual passer-by but himself the man most affected.[34]

Austin's description of Virgil's technique here seems to me admirable, his critical assumptions more dubious. The absence of exact correspondence in Homer's simile hardly makes it a set of commonplaces. The figure of the shepherd is curiously effective *because* he does not correspond to anything in the narrative (I shall return to him later). One can easily turn Austin's criticisms on their head; Homer's simile has a freshness that Virgil's lacks; Virgil by acting not only as deviser but also in a sense as interpreter of his simile restricts the free play of the reader's imagination; the result is too contrived, too diagrammatic. I am not saying that these criticisms necessarily contain the whole truth, only that they are as plausible as Austin's implied denigration of Homer. West's conclusion is interesting in this respect: Virgil is 'a miniaturist, he worked with words singly, polishing them for their immediate settings'. This comment raises an important critical issue. The trouble with the *Aeneid* may be not that it responds badly to the sort of detailed verbal analysis favoured by the 'New Criticism', but that it responds too well. An epic poem after all is a very different thing from a lyric: to call an epic poet 'a miniaturist' is a paradox. One of the virtues of Homer's style is its functionalism: narrative momentum is effortlessly maintained. In many ways Milton is better than Virgil in maintaining the true epic sweep. Virgil's similes suggest that there may be some truth in the criticism that the *Aeneid* is smothered by over-careful art, leading to imaginative impoverishment.

However this may be, Virgil certainly closes the gap between tenor and vehicle, and sometimes even blurs the distinction between narrative and simile. An example is the double simile describing the dying Euryalus (*Aen.* IX. 433–6):

volvitur Euryalus leto, pulchrosque per artus
it cruor inque umeros cervix conlapsa recumbit;
purpureus veluti cum flos succisus aratro
languescit moriens, lassove papavera collo
demisere caput pluvia cum forte gravantur.

(Euryalus rolls over in death, and over his lovely limbs the blood runs, and his neck sinks and collapses onto his shoulders; as when a shining flower cut at the base by the plough droops as it dies, or poppies with tired necks lower their heads, when they are weighed down by a random shower.)

Some of the vocabulary used about the flowers ('languescit moriens', 'lasso collo', 'demisere caput') could with equal appropriateness be applied to a human being at the moment of death. The picture of the dying youth and the flowers are as it were superimposed, and coalesce into one languid image, which detracts from the sharpness with which each is separately perceived and produces what might be called a 'soft focus' (Virgil's two 'sources' here, *Iliad* VIII. 306–8 and Catullus 11. 21–4, are sharper and fresher). The passage, though achingly lovely, is perhaps self-indulgent, and the blending of aesthetic and erotic sensibility with blood, pain and death is a long way from the unsentimental pathos of superficially similar passages in Homer.

Another instance of such blurring occurs when the lovesick Dido is compared to a wounded deer (IV. 68–73):

uritur infelix Dido totaque vagatur
urbe furens, qualis coniecta cerva sagitta,
quam procul incautam nemora inter Cresia fixit
pastor agens telis liquitque volatile ferrum
nescius; illa fuga silvas saltusque peragrat
Dictaeas; haeret lateri letalis harundo.

(Unhappy Dido burns and wanders throughout the city in frenzy, like a deer shot by an arrow which from afar a shepherd sending his shafts has hit and left the flying weapon, unknowing; she in flight goes through the woods and glades of Crete; the fatal arrow clings to her side.)

The simile, like a number of Milton's, refers beyond the immediate context to the wider action of the poem, proleptically. The wounded doe anticipates the shooting of the stag of Silvia in VII. 483ff, and perhaps glances back at Aeneas' first action on his arrival in North Africa in shooting seven deer (I. 184ff). The image complex suggests how Aeneas and his followers, against their will, bring death and suffering to those they encounter. One detail is puzzling: why should the shepherd who wounds the deer be 'unknowing'? La Cerda, following one of the interpretations offered by Servius, supposed that 'nescius' was used in a passive sense 'unnoticed' (that is, by the deer), but this is scarcely possible and 'incautam' would then be otiose. Perhaps the shepherd thinks that he has missed, and does not see that the fleeing deer has a wound. More probably

126

'nescius' is chosen not because of the situation in the simile, but because of the situation in the narrative. Aeneas does not know the damage that he has done, and will do, to Dido; just as Ascanius will not understand what he is about when he shoots Silvia's stag — the theme of the *unwitting* inflicting of suffering is of prime significance in the *Aeneid*. Aeneas has as it were strayed into the simile, and the result is a slight but suggestive irrationality in the details of the simile itself.

I have tried to show that Homer's similes, even when there is less homologation than with Virgil's, cannot be described as merely digressive or ornamental. Likewise it seems to me that some critics have exaggerated the degree of precise homologation in the relation between the narrative and similes of *Paradise Lost* (the eighteenth-century critics are a useful corrective here). I shall take as an initial example a simile (III. 430–41) that has been ingeniously analysed by Laurence Lerner,[35] an analysis supported and extended by Ricks and Fowler:

> Here walked the fiend at large in spacious field.
> As when a vulture on Imaus bred,
> Whose snowy ridge the roving Tartar bounds,
> Dislodging from a region scarce of prey
> To gorge the flesh of lambs or yeanling kids
> On hills where flocks are fed, flies toward the springs
> Of Ganges or Hydaspes, Indian streams;
> But in his way lights on the barren plains
> Of Sericana, where Chineses drive
> With sails and wind their cany wagons light;
> So on this windy sea of land, the fiend
> Walked up and down alone bent on his prey.

The general propriety of comparing Satan to a bird of prey resting on its travels in search of new victims is obvious; the vulture like Satan journeys from a waste land to one richer in plunder. Less obviously the similarity between the site of the Limbo of Vanity and the wagons on the plains of Sericana (both involve confusion of the elements, as Fowler notes) is established by careful verbal responsion of a Virgilian kind, 'so on this windy sea of land' answering 'drive with sails and wind their cany wagons light'. Other details are more problematic. Fowler apparently sees an allusion to the Last Judgement in the mention of lambs and kids. I find it difficult to read the lines in this way: the actual words sheep and goats might seem required to trigger off the association (moreover the sheep of the Last Judgement are not gorged by Satan). Again it is hard to follow Ricks, when he argues that Tartar suggests Tartarus (Milton was an inveterate punster, but this one seems unduly far-fetched). At all events what gives the simile its life is not the correspondence of detail but the romance of geography that so powerfully engaged Milton.

In this case it is clear that there are more exact correspondences than one. A still more beautiful simile has proved puzzling. Satan sees the gate of Heaven (III. 501–15):

> far distant he descries,
> Ascending by degrees magnificent
> Up to the wall of heaven a structure high,
> At top whereof, but far more rich appeared
> The work as of a kingly palace gate
> With frontispiece of diamond and gold
> Embellished; thick with sparkling orient gems
> The portal shone, inimitable on earth
> By model, or by shading pencil drawn.
> The stairs were such as whereon Jacob saw
> Angels ascending and descending, bands
> Of guardians bright, when he from Esau fled
> To Padan-Aram in the field of Luz,
> Dreaming by night under the open sky,
> And waking cried, 'This is the gate of heaven.'

Ricks has an interesting paragraph on this simile:

Here Satan is compared to Jacob when he too saw the gate of Heaven. And the alternatives are inexorable: either Milton is interested in the gigantic differences between Satan and Jacob, or he is not. If he is not interested, then to devote more than five lines to Jacob is strangely wasteful. Surely the length of the allusion and its beauty . . . press us into thinking that Milton was concerned more than casually with Jacob. And his point here is a simple though implicit one: Satan as he sees the gate of Heaven is compared to Jacob doing likewise — but with what different effects, in what different situations; Satan is the arch-enemy of God, Jacob was the chosen hand of God. If a contrast of this kind is not present, then we ought to deprecate the passage (however beautiful), since it would seem to suggest either than Satan was good, or that Jacob was bad. The length and power of the allusion forces us to choose between damaging irrelevance, or likeness turning grimly into disparity.[36]

Even if we leave aside the correctness or otherwise of Ricks' conclusion, there is surely something to quarrel with in the underlying assumptions. The passage reveals a combination of Johnsonian stone-kicking ('either Milton is interested in the gigantic differences between Satan and Jacob, or he is not': is the process of creativity necessarily quite so straightforward?) and what I can only call a kind of puritanism ('then we ought to deprecate the passage (however beautiful)'). If you believe as I do that these are among the most perfectly phrased lines in seventeenth-century poetry — and how far from the orotundity of Miltonic diction as diagnosed by the anti-Miltonists — then it would be perverse to wish them out of the poem even if the passage were more irrelevant than on *any* interpretation it is. After all in Milton's view Satan and Jacob really saw the same gate: Jacob's ladder was the great Biblical *locus* for the gate of Heaven. Ricks earlier seems to concede the point,[37] but here apparently goes back on his concession.

Isabel MacCaffrey adopts a different stance: 'This passage begins as the vehicle of a greater tenor in the foreground; but it soon usurps the foreground itself and assumes its place in Milton's pattern as a relevant fragment of history.'[38] This is well said, yet one can imagine the impatient response of a critic like A.J.A. Waldock: if the whole of history is Milton's subject (as in a sense one may grant that it is), it is difficult to see how anything he wrote could be irrelevant. MacCaffrey says nothing of the particular treatment Milton accords his 'fragment of history'. Milton has after all not simply recorded the Bible story (Genesis 28), he has re-shaped it by selection and re-emphasis. Much that is important in the Bible account is simply omitted (in particular God's long promise to Jacob in his dream). The wonder and longing conveyed by Jacob's eager exclamation in Milton is rather different from the effect of the same words in the Bible verse from which they are taken: 'And he was afraid, and said, How dreadful is this place! This is none other but the house of God, and this is the gate of heaven' (17). 'Dreaming by night under the open sky' is romantic, where the Bible verse characteristically records without implying an attitude: 'And he lighted upon a certain place, and tarried there all night, because the sun was set; and he took of the stones of that place, and put them for his pillows, and lay down in that place to sleep' (11). Consideration of Milton's treatment of the story suggests an analysis alternative to Ricks'. We need not ask whether Satan is to be clearly identified with Jacob or sharply differentiated from him. The links are emotional rather than diagrammatic. The simile as a whole induces a sense of wonder and yearning. Satan looks up to the heaven from which he has only recently been expelled, and in effect the exclamation 'This is the gate of heaven' becomes as much his as it is later to be Jacob's.

Another well-known simile certainly avoids obvious homologation (I. 777–90):

> Behold a wonder! they but now who seemed
> In bigness to surpass Earth's giant sons
> Now less than smallest dwarfs in narrow room
> Throng numberless, like that pygmean race
> Beyond the Indian mount, or faerie elves,
> Whose midnight revels, by a forest side
> Or fountain some belated peasant sees,
> Or dreams he sees, while overhead the moon
> Sits arbitress, and nearer to the earth
> Wheels her pale course; they on their mirth and dance
> Intent, with jocund music charm his ear;
> At once with joy and fear his heart rebounds.
> Thus incorporeal spirits to smallest forms
> Reduced their shapes immense, and were at large.

Critics point out that the purpose of this simile is to deflate the epic pretensions of Satan and his crew by comparing them with something so small (fairies moreover are sometimes regarded as fallen angels).[39] Certainly Milton is playing tricks with perspective, although the purpose is more than simple mockery. The fairies are not just small, they are magical, frightening, spell-binding. Once again one senses that Milton is peculiarly engaged poetically. It is a commonplace of Milton criticism to say that in order to write his epics Milton had to suppress a large part of himself. The student of Spenser and Shakespeare gradually gave way before the austerely disciplined imitator of the ancients. By the time of the composition of *Paradise Regained* the ghost of Milton's past had been all but exorcised. In *Paradise Lost* by contrast the battle is still being fought, and the tensions that result are a great source of poetic strength. The similes are one of the places where the old Milton is most apt to re-appear: 'naturam expellas furca, tamen usque recurret'. It is significant that in this passage Milton should again echo *A Midsummer Night's Dream*, earlier a favourite quarry for *Comus* (the whole simile is in fact suffused with the sort of lyricism and melancholy that one associates with Shakespeare's romantic comedies). This simile thus contributes to an enlargement of the poem. In this it is Homeric, as also in its freedom from precise correspondence and verbal responsion: nobody, so far as I know, has tried to interpret exactly all the details of this simile. Of course, it is more literary than a Homeric simile; the allusion to *Aeneid* VI. 451–4, where Aeneas, when he catches sight of Dido in the darkness of the underworld, is compared to someone who sees or thinks he has seen — 'aut videt aut vidisse putat' — the new moon rising in the clouds, is particularly effective for those who know the original, although Milton's lines are more wry, less melancholy than Virgil's. Homeric too is the figure of the peasant whose responses to the fairies constitute so important a part of the simile. In a number of Homeric similes dealing with natural phenomena the figure of a shepherd appears (for example the simile from *Iliad* IV discussed above), apparently irrelevant to the comparison, but actually serving to relate the objective world to the subjective, human consciousness. As Kirk in his interesting discussion of the *Iliad* simile observes, 'the distant shepherd not only emphasizes the strength and solitude of these mountain torrents, he also connects the phenomena of nature with the feelings and experiences of men'.[40] Milton's peasant has a somewhat similar effect.

We may now return to the original question of whether in general Milton's similes are more Virgilian than Homeric. In some respects they are like Virgil's. They are obviously literary; there is more homologation than in Homer, though less than in Virgil. Several of them are proleptic (though I have given an example of prolepsis from the *Odyssey*), or have a moral dimension that Homer's lack.[41] For example a pair of balanced similes in *Aeneid* XII (684ff; 701ff) is designed to show the moral differences between Aeneas and Turnus; Turnus is a rolling stone, Aeneas a mountain which he resembles in strength and fixity (in the *Iliad* both similes are used of Hector). In an earlier pair of similes we have water boiling in a cauldron for Turnus, light reflected from the ruffled surface of water in a basin for Aeneas (VII. 462ff; VIII. 18ff). Similarly the Leviathan simile in *Paradise Lost* I. 192ff is not just about size, but points to Satan's deceitfulness and the danger of relying on appearances where he is concerned.

At another level Milton's similes often seem to me closer to Homer's, particularly those of the *Iliad*. As a group the Iliadic similes constitute an essential element in the poem: remove them and you shift the whole balance of the work, impoverishing it beyond measure. This appears to me equally true of the similes of *Paradise Lost* as a group, much less true of those in the *Odyssey* and *Aeneid*. The reason is not hard to find. In the *Iliad* Homer concentrates on war, while the everyday world familiar to the poem's original listeners is described principally in the similes (and the description of the shield of Achilles which acts as a kind of extended simile). Likewise Milton's similes deal with much that was immediately familiar to the seventeenth-century reader both in books and in life, while, as Johnson observed, the main action of the poem is in a certain sense remote. (That is perhaps to put the point in too negative a way. *Paradise Lost* is, *inter alia*, concerned with accounting for the nature of the post-lapsarian world; the similes are one of a number of ways in which the world as we know it is brought into the poem.) In the *Odyssey* and *Aeneid* the difference between the material of the similes and of the narrative is much less strong, since the stories are of a different kind and less in need of the contrast that similes can provide. Much that appears in the *Iliad* only in the similes is found in the main action of the *Odyssey* (which has in fact many fewer similes), while the war scenes of the *Aeneid* are set in an Italian landscape familiar to the Roman reader. Above all Milton's similes have something of the imaginative freedom that Virgil's (perhaps through excess of verbal correspondence) sometimes seem to lack: for all their studied artistry they have paradoxically a freshness that can be called Homeric. Johnson writes well of how much they increase the poem's scope: 'his great excellence is amplitude, and he expands the adventitious image beyond the dimensions which the occasion required. Thus, comparing the shield of Satan to the orb of the moon, he crowds the imagination with the discovery of the telescope and all the wonders which the telescope discovers.'[42] If Johnson here misses the full resonance of this particular simile, he also has a larger sense than most moderns of that crowding of the imagination which is the principal characteristic of the Miltonic simile.

132

*Virgil*

## Imitations

None of this is to deny that Virgil is an important influence on *Paradise Lost*. This is partly a question of structure, including the use of blocks of four books, partly of matters that are hard to quantify, for example mastery of paragraphing and verbal music, and partly of a series of allusions or imitations. In particular, like Dante before him, Milton used *Aeneid* VI — Aeneas' descent into Hades — as a quarry for material suitable for a Christian hell. Dante had based his description of Limbo (*Inferno* IV) in part on Virgil's Elysium (637ff); the righteous pagans were to be given what one of the most righteous of their number had imagined as the best possible lot for the virtuous dead. Milton is less generous. The games in Virgil's Elysium lie behind the passage describing the devils relaxing or at play after their great consult (II. 521ff). In VIII. 240–4 Raphael describes how he and a squadron of angels were sent on a mission to the gates of hell; they found all shut and heard groans and torture within. This recalls the powerful moment when Aeneas turns to see Tartarus and hears with dread the sounds of torment (548ff), but it does not match its power — there is little of shock or terror, and the reader is unlikely to be involved with the pointless mission of Raphael as he is with the arduous and momentous journey of Aeneas.

Indeed in general — with one or two notable exceptions, in particular the Vallombrosa simile — these imitations of Virgil do not show Milton quite at his best. Addison thought that the convulsions in nature after the Fall (IX. 780–4, 1000–4) were derived from the storm that accompanies the union of Dido and Aeneas in the cave.[43] The passage is one of the most imaginative in the *Aeneid*; various features of a Roman wedding are reproduced at a cosmic level. Juno acts as *pronuba*, the matron who took the bride to the bridal chamber, the lightning corresponds to the wedding torches, the air is witness, while the shout of the nymphs is both a ritual cry and a cry of woe foreshadowing the disastrous consequences of the consummation (IV. 166–8):

> prima et Tellus et pronuba Iuno
> dant signum; fulsere ignes et conscius aether
> conubiis, summoque ulularunt vertice Nymphae.

133

(primeval earth and Juno as *pronuba* give the signal; the lightning fires blazed out and heaven witness to the bridal, and on the mountain peaks the nymphs cried out.)

Byron gets something of the effect — though without the ominous undertones — when he describes the lovemaking of Juan and Haidée in a natural 'marriage' free from the corruptions of civilisation:

> And now 'twas done — on the lone shore were plighted
>> Their hearts; the stars, their nuptial torches, shed
> Beauty upon the beautiful they lighted;
>> Ocean their witness, and the cave their bed,
> By their own feelings hallowed and united,
>> Their priest was Solitude, and they were wed.
>
> *(Don Juan* II. 204)

In Milton the idea of nature feeling woe at the Fall is a telling one, not least because we are dealing not with a pathetic fallacy but with genuine cosmic repercussion, but there is no especial distinction to the language or grandeur in the imagery.

Similarly in XII. 644 the 'dreadful faces' of the cherubim posted to keep Adam and Eve out of Eden recall but inevitably cannot match the fearful epiphany that Aeneas sees in Troy (II. 622–3): 'apparent dirae facies inimicaeque Troiae / numina magna deum' (dreadful shapes appear and hostile to Troy the mighty powers of the gods). This is perhaps the supreme moment of terror in the *Aeneid*. Venus takes the cloud from Aeneas' sight, and he can witness the gods taking part in the destruction of Troy like a very apocalypse of devils.[44] At such a moment the sense of divine providence falters, as does the verse (line 624 is one of the most effective half-lines in the poem), and the reader, at least momentarily, may entertain the idea that the universe and the gods might be evil. Milton could afford only the ghost of an echo.

Three more examples tell something of the same story. In *Aeneid* II. 203ff the pair of snakes that are to destroy Laocöon and his children are seen by the Trojans moving towards the shore breasting the sea with huge coils, their crested heads raised above the waves. These fine lines lie behind the description of Satan in I. 193–5, his head above water 'his other parts besides / Prone on the flood'. Milton can write as well as anyone about the sinuous movement of snakes, but since Satan is stationary at this point, the trick is not there for the taking, and the echo falls flat. In *Aeneid* VI, when Aeneas climbs on to Charon's boat, it groans under his weight and takes in water through its chinks (413–14). This is effective because of the precision of the detail and because of the notion of a living man climbing aboard a craft designed for the weightless souls of the dead — we are made to feel the solidity and size of Aeneas in a world of shadows. By contrast the moment when Satan takes flight 'incumbent on the dusky air / That felt unusual weight' (I. 226–7) is comparatively tame, partly because this must be the first time that this air has felt any weight at all, and partly because we are inured to the size of Satan on which Milton has been insisting from the first, and are not jolted into any fresh perception of it.[45]

For his account of Eden (IV. 131ff) Milton remembered the famous set-piece description of the place of Aeneas' first landfall in Africa (I. 159ff), which delicately counterpoints the awesome — the rearing cliffs, the threatening peaks, the dark trees, the hanging rocks, the silence — with the hope of rest — sweet waters and seats of living rock within, the home of the nymphs. Milton takes one detail, the baroque image of the 'theatre' of trees ('scaena' 164), but has no use for the most Virgilian touches in the passage, the mysterious stillness, the word 'hanging' ('pendentibus', 166), a special favourite of Virgil's and one he uses to notable effect.[46] However Milton's lines are also fine in their different way. The trees are envisaged as like the ranks of seats of a theatre going up endlessly, shade upon shade. The involved sentence takes the reader from one feature to the next in a way that blurs the visual picture, but gives an impression of a magnificent wild lushness that is yet artistic; hence the comparison with a theatre and the word 'grotesque' (136), a term of architecture and garden design (the word derives from 'grotto').

The comparative unsuccess of a number of these imitations of Virgil — in comparison, say, with the fine series of Ovidian moments in *Paradise Lost* — may merely demonstrate, to adapt what Virgil himself is supposed to have said about Homer, that taking a line from the *Aeneid* is as difficult as stealing the club of Hercules; but it might also suggest some underlying difference in the sensibility of the two poets. Against this could be urged at least two occasions where Milton uses an epic motif found in both Virgil and Homer, but where it is Virgil's influence that is stronger. At the end of *Paradise Lost* I the fallen angels as they throng

Pandaemonium are compared to bees (768–75):

> As bees
> In spring time, when the sun with Taurus rides,
> Pour forth their populous youth about the hive
> In clusters; they among fresh dews and flowers
> Fly to and fro, or on the smoothed plank,
> The suburb of their straw-built citadel,
> New rubbed with balm, expatiate and confer
> Their state affairs.

There are bee similes in Homer (*Iliad* II. 87–90, of the Greeks gathering for assembly — 'in clusters' translates Homer's 'botrudon' which also begins a line) and in Virgil (*Aen.* I. 430–6, of the Carthaginians at work, and VI. 706–9, of the dead awaiting re-incarnation); Vida had already compared his devils to bees engaging in combat over rival bee 'kings' (*Christiad* I. 229–33). In Milton the initial point of comparison is the enormous number of densely packed beings, but the feeling of the lines is startlingly contrasted with the surrounding context. There is an atmosphere of bustle and business (the previous sentence already gives a sense of swarming, hissing and rustling, 'brushed with the hiss of rustling wings', 768), of pleasant warmth, of orderly community. It is difficult to be sure why Milton contrived a scene of such cheerful lyricism (though giddy changes of mood are frequent in these early books), particularly given the fact that bees were traditionally associated with order and civic virtue. The belief that the head of the hive was a king meant that the organisation of the bee community became a traditional argument for monarchy; Milton had touched on this point in his reply to his opponent Salmasius, upholder of monarchy.[47] Thus it could be that there is a latent ideological point in Milton's association of bees with the devils whose leader is presented in a number of passages as a kind of oriental potentate. More clearly the simile contributes to the series of shifts in perspective at the close of this book; the fallen angels, previously gigantic forms, are compared with small creatures before they become small in actuality (777ff). Moreover the simile has a comic dimension in the portentousness with which the bees 'expatiate and confer / Their state affairs'.

There can be little doubt that behind the simile lies Virgil's treatment of bees in the first half of *Georgics* IV, where the language constantly associates the bees with human communities and specifically the Roman people (at line 201 they are termed 'Quirites', Roman citizens). Classical scholars are apt to take the analogy rather seriously, and treat this whole section of the poem as an extended allegory about the proper organisation of Rome, but this is to miss the tone of Virgil's treatment and its delicate humour — significantly the opening lines are echoed by Pope at the beginning of 'The Rape of the Lock'. Virgil here approaches a mock-heroic manner, which allows for humour, whimsy, sympathy and pathos. He shows both an amused superiority and a readiness to come down to the bees' level. When he describes bees wetted, he uses the epic metonymy for sea, 'Neptune' (29), for the stream; this is humorously grandiose, but it also allows us to see the matter from the angle of the bees. In other words Virgil presents us with a miniature world, but also reminds us that size is a relative matter; the full effect of this thus depends on our willingness to co-operate with the changed perspectives offered by the poet. The most extreme and dazzling example of the technique occurs when the bees at work are compared to the giant Cyclopes busy at their forges (170ff). There is playfulness evident here, even laughter, but not only that; the bees command respect for their heroic commitment and energy. Similarly after describing, with epic pomp, a battle of the bees Virgil concludes 'these mighty struggles by the throwing of a little dust are checked and vanish' (86–7), and laughter gives place to sadness as we reflect on human insubstantiality. Something of all this (though not the elegiac undertone) has found its way into Milton's simile. Milton seems to have liked this part of the *Georgics*, for in his description of the emmet (VII. 486) he almost translates a line from it 'in small room large heart enclosed' (cf. *Georgics* IV. 83 'ingentes animos angusto in pectore').[48]

As Milton draws close to Virgil in this simile so he moves away from Homer. Homer is remarkably fair to animals, showing how they have their own interests which frequently run counter to those of human beings. Thus *Iliad* XVII. 570–2 does justice to the persistence and courage of an insect as it repeatedly tries to bite a man. In XVI. 259–65 the Myrmidons are compared to a hoard of wasps who fly out to harry a traveller:

The Myrmidons came streaming out like wasps at the wayside
when little boys have got into the habit of making them angry
by always teasing them as they live in their house by the roadside;

silly boys, they do something that hurts many people;
and if some man who travels on the road happens to pass them
and stirs them unintentionally, they in fury of heart
come swarming out each one from his place to fight for his
   children.

(Lattimore)

Christopher Logue's rendering of this fine simile, conveying only a
sickened disgust, helps to highlight the cool, unhysterical sympathy
and humanity of Homer:

Hornets occasionally build their nests near roads.
In the late Spring they breed; feeding their grubs
And feeding off the sticky spit the grubs exude.
Now and again a child pokes a stick into the nest
And stirs. The hornets swarm. Jab, jabbing their
Insect poison in its eyes and flesh.
Often the swollen child dies that night. Sometimes
They menace passers-by instead.

The *Odyssey* introduces a sweeter, softer pathos in the treatment of
animals, in the episode of the dog Argus who dies having seen his
master return after 20 years (XVII. 290ff), a scene that is always
popular with English readers. (It is true that Achilles' horses weep
for Patroclus in *Iliad* XVII. 426ff, but they are a special case,
because they are immortal, a gift to Peleus from the gods, and have
on occasion the power of speech, XIX. 404ff). Virgil too is rightly
praised for his sympathy for animals, particularly in the *Georgics*,
but the anthropomorphism is more evident, and with the sympathy
there is often a mixture of the humorous or patronising. For
example in *Georgics* III 209ff two bulls compete for the hand of a
fair heifer, and the defeated bull goes into a lovesick exile; the
language constantly suggests human emotions and human activi-
ties. Tiny creatures in particular, like the little mouse, 'exiguus mus'
(*Georgics* I. 181), aroused in Virgil an amused interest. Bees who
'expatiate and confer' thus belong more to Virgil's world than to
Homer's.

   The descent of Raphael to warn Adam and Eve of Satan's wiles
(V. 247ff) is Milton's version of a typical epic sequence.[49] In
*Odyssey* V. 28ff Zeus sends Hermes to tell Calypso to allow
Odysseus to return home. Virgil, following closely in Homer's

footsteps, has Jupiter despatch Mercury to order Aeneas to leave
Carthage and continue his quest (*Aen.* IV. 219ff). Milton carefully
indicates his allegiance when he compares Raphael with Hermes/
Mercury (285–6): 'like Maia's son he stood / And shook his plumes'.
Virgil's reworking of the Homeric material shows a characteristic
increase in mystery and linguistic richness. He uses the more
picturesque details in Homer (Hermes' wand, the comparison of
Hermes to a sea-bird), but has no use for the more homely
elements, as when Hermes and Calypso share a meal before
Hermes delivers, adroitly and tactfully, the message from Zeus. By
contrast Virgil's Mercury appears suddenly, delivers his uncom-
promising message abruptly, and then disappears vanishing into
thin air, leaving an awestruck Aeneas. Virgil also makes more than
Homer of the element of miraculous flight; we follow in detail
Mercury's descent as he flies down towards Mount Atlas and then
launches himself over the waves.

Milton, more opulent and baroque still, further increases the
buoyancy and glamour in a *tour de force* of angelic vision and flight.
Raphael looks down from Heaven's gate and sees the heavenly
bodies, and earth a small one among many. This angel's-eye view is
aided by the giddily abrupt syntax in lines 257ff:

> From hence no cloud or, to obstruct his sight,
> Star interposed, however small he sees,
> Not unconform to other shining globes,
> Earth and the garden of God, with cedars crowned
> Above all hills.

Earth and Eden are kept back until last so that we can follow
Raphael's eye as it ranges over space until finding the crucial spot,
as if focusing a telescope — it may even be implied that his clear
vision sees the cedars of Eden. This leads to the simile about Galileo
which brilliantly reverses the viewpoint as a man tries, less
successfully, to see the heavens. The clarity is further blurred in the
second simile, with its romantic setting among Greek islands where
a ship's pilot peers out at a cloudy spot on the horizon. Almost
dizzied by these efforts at long sight we now marvellously see
Raphael sailing 'between worlds and worlds', and then we are given
a curious upward bird's-eye view of him just within range of eagles,
seen by birds lower down as a phoenix, a great golden, avian object,
a rare and wondrous sight. Thus Milton is lusher and grander even

than Virgil, leaving Homer still further behind him. (However the note of homeliness in Homer which Virgil suppressed is retained when Raphael is subsequently given lunch by Adam and Eve.) In such a passage as this it is proper to see Milton as a Virgilian, striving to outdo his master.[50]

## Time

Virgil is usually and rightly regarded as one of the great poets of time and historical process.[51] The numinous sense of the past in the *Aeneid* has often been remarked on, never more seductively than by C.S. Lewis. After noting the importance of prophecy and time future in the poem Lewis continues:

> If I am not mistaken it is almost the first poem which carries a real sense of the 'abysm of time'. *Priscus, vetus,* and *antiquus* are key-words in Virgil. In Books VI to VIII — the true heart of the poem — we are never allowed to forget that Latium — *Lurkwood*, the hiding place of aged Saturn — has been waiting for the Trojans from the beginning of the world. The palace of King Latinus is very unlike any house in Homer: 'Awful with woods and piety of elder days' . . . There is a poetry that reiterated readings cannot exhaust in all these early Italian scenes; in the first sight of the Tiber, the lonely prayer to that unknown river, and the long river journey on which the ships startle those hitherto unviolated forests. I do not know a better example of imagination, in the highest sense, than when Charon wonders at the Golden Bough 'so long unseen'; dark centuries of that unhistoried lower world are conjured up in half a line (VI, 409).[52]

This pervading sense of time has often been seen as an important — even the most important — difference between the *Aeneid* and the Homeric epics. In the first section of his poem 'Memorial for The City' Auden presents 'Homer's world' as alien to us because it is a vision of an unchanging reality, 'a space where time has no place':

> That is the way things happen; for ever and ever
> Plum-blossom falls on the dead, the roar of the waterfall covers
> The cries of the whipped and the sighs of the lovers

And the hard bright light composes
A meaningless moment into an eternal fact
Which a whistling messenger disappears with into a defile:
One enjoys glory, one endures shame;
He may, she must. There is no one to blame.

A world without time is a world that cannot be redeemed, and therefore a world ultimately without meaning (this is a characteristic post-Christian perception, but Homer has in fact his own values, however little they may be ours). By contrast, it is implied, Virgil presents us with the possibility of change and therefore of improvement, even of redemption; an example would be when time brings the saviour god Hercules to rid the world of the monster Cacus (VIII. 200–1). In an evocative passage at the end of *Georgics* I. (493ff) Virgil imagines the day when the countryman will dig up the rusty weapons and giant bones left from the battles of the civil wars. The lines movingly counterpoint a sense of degeneration — men are getting smaller — with the healing changes that time brings as the sword gives way to the ploughshare. This is part of one of the most anguished passages in the poem as Virgil laments the havoc wrought by civil war, yet the horror is also offset by a sense of wonder ('mirabitur' in line 497 is a key word), just as it is in the passage where Aeneas views dolorous scenes from the Trojan war on Juno's temple gates at Carthage (I. 494–5).

This contrast between Homer poet of an unchanging reality and Virgil poet of time and history contains truth, but it is not the whole truth. There are occasions on which Homer changes the temporal perspective most movingly; for example, Helen, with a curious detachment, seems to see herself and the events through which she is living almost with the eyes of future generations (*Iliad* III. 125–8; VI. 357–8). More importantly Virgil's whole procedure is an expansion of an essential feature of the *structure* of the Homeric epics which had been brilliantly analysed by Aristotle (*Poetics* ch. 8). Aristotle observes that most epic poets supposed that a unified poem would result if they recounted all the deeds of one man. Homer, aided by art or nature, perceived the need for a unified action. The *Iliad* is not an account of all that happened at Troy, nor a life of Achilles, it deals with the wrath of Achilles and its consequences; the *Odyssey* is not the story of Odysseus but of his return to Ithaca. In each case the *in medias res* opening means that the reader (or listener) is presented with what is in one sense an excerpt from a longer story, and will bring to bear his knowledge of events before and after the action of the poem. Homer does not rely on the listener's knowledge alone; he employs a deliberate technique of recalling past events and foreshadowing future ones. This is most obvious in the *Odyssey* with its more evident sophistication of structure; the poem looks back to events before the Trojan War and forward to Odysseus' mysterious death. It also employs — and made canonical for future epics, including Milton's — the technique of flashback narrative when Odysseus tells the Phaeacians the tale of his previous wanderings.

The *Iliad*, although it does not employ flashback, is similarly constructed, if anything with more subtle art. The shadow of the future — Achilles' death, the eventual destruction of Troy — lies heavy on the later books. Achilles' fate is prophesied directly by his horse Xanthus (XIX. 404ff) and by Hector at point of death (XXII. 355ff), and is also more obliquely suggested. The opening of Thetis' lament for Patroclus sounds like a threnody for her own son (XVIII. 52ff); when Achilles lies in the dust in helpless grief Homer employs a formula most naturally used to describe a dead man, so that we see, proleptically, Achilles' corpse (XVIII. 26–7). Our sense that Achilles has not long to live makes tolerable the nihilistic savagery of his actions as he seeks to assuage his sense of guilt for his friend's death. Hector's fate will necessarily lead to doom for Troy, death for his baby son and slavery for his wife and mother. Events before the action of the poem are also evoked. In Book III, when Paris sleeps with Helen, he as it were re-enacts his original seduction of her to which he directly refers (442–6); in Book XXII Homer, with economical pathos, reminds us of the time before the Greeks came, as Hector runs past the now disused washing-places of the Trojan women (153–6). All that Virgil has done is to widen the time-scale involved: the *Aeneid*, whose plot is the coming of Aeneas to Italy, looks back to the sack of Troy and forward to the victories of Augustus in a vast temporal span. The poem is indeed a marvel of organisation, but without the example of Homer before him Virgil could hardly have achieved it.

It is the case nevertheless that Virgil has what we would recognise as a sense of history, even if it is a kind of sacred history, where Homer, for obvious reasons, does not. This sense of history is a powerful informing presence throughout the *Aeneid*, and not only in the great prophetic passages in Books I, VI and VIII. The tragic liaison between Dido and Aeneas is not a romantic interlude, or even just another test of Aeneas' virtue, since behind the human figures we should sense the presence of vast historical forces, the clash of two mighty empires, Rome and Carthage — the theme is so important that it is stated at the outset, I. 12ff. Juno hates Aeneas not only for what has been — the Judgement of Paris — but for what will be — the loss of her favourite city. When Mercury descends to find Aeneas in costly array building towers and houses in Carthage, we should appreciate the *frisson* for a Roman reader: the father of the nation helping to construct the city of the hated enemy (IV. 259ff). The abandoned Dido curses Aeneas and prays for an avenger to harry his descendants with fire and sword; this is a veiled reference to Hannibal and the terrible crisis of the second Punic war (621ff). Again Virgil has Dido stab herself on a pyre, partly to complete a dominant image pattern (at the beginning of the book Dido is, metaphorically, feeding her wound with her life blood and consumed by hidden fire, 'volnus alit venis et caeco carpitur igni', 2), partly no doubt to suit her passionate and theatrical nature, but above all because he intends a prolepsis of the destruction by fire of Carthage in 146 BC at the end of the third Punic war. The point is signalled by a simile that compares the scene with the sack of a city (665–71, Surrey):

The clamour rang unto the palace top,
The brute [noise] ran throughout all the astonied [confounded]
    town.
With wailing great and women's shrill yelling
The roofs gan roar, the air resound with plaint,
As though Carthage or the ancient town of Tyre
With press of entered enemies swarmed full,
Or when the rage of furious flame doth take
The temples' tops and mansions eke of men.

In fact the germ of the idea is in Homer. In *Iliad* XXII. 408ff Priam and the Trojans cry out in anguish at Hector's death 'as if all beetling Troy were utterly burning with fire'. In Homer the point is readily intelligible: Hector's death makes inevitable the fall of Troy. By contrast Virgil's simile is typological; it mysteriously prefigures a distant future. While it suggests the historical dimension, there is no question of historical causation as we would understand it; Dido's death does not cause the destruction of Carthage, rather it is a weird pre-echoing of it across the centuries. In this Virgil is both closer and less close to us than Homer, closer in the sense of historical process that he shares with us, more remote in his apparently symbolic and typological understanding of it.

The function of the historical subtext to *Aeneid* IV is clear enough. Elsewhere historical undercurrents can be less obviously focused. For example in II. 557–8 Priam's corpse is represented as lying on the shore, a headless trunk, a body without a name: 'iacet ingens litore truncus / avolsumque umeris caput et sine nomine corpus.' The picture is a striking one, but the detail is puzzling. Since Priam was killed in his palace, it is unclear why his corpse should lie on the shore. At least part of the answer appears to be that a famous episode from recent Roman history is being recalled. The great general Pompey, defeated by his rival Julius Caesar at Pharsalia, fled to Egypt where he was decapitated on the orders of the boy king Ptolemy, and his headless body left unburied on the Egyptian strand. It is not easy to see why the aged Priam should be compared to Pompey, unless it is that both men had been unusually fortunate but both proved in the end unlucky. The effect of the coalescing of the two deaths is disturbing, slightly phantasmagoric, the underlying meaning elusive and enigmatic, but again it suggests that Virgil saw history in terms of repeated patterns, one event echoing or pre-echoing another. Thus the fighting in the second half of the *Aeneid* is both a re-run of the Trojan War and a foreshadowing of the civil wars at Rome.

Milton owes much to Virgil for the organisation of his epic with respect to time, its incorporation of flashback and prophecy. Thus the opening of Raphael's narrative (V. 563–4), 'High matter thou enjoinest me, o prime of men, / Sad task and hard', gestures gravely towards the words with which Aeneas begins his tearful account of the last hours of Troy (II. 3 'infandum, regina, iubes renovare dolorem'). Since Raphael recounts the victory of good over evil there is no place for the full plangency of the lines echoed, but his words clearly signal the structural debt to Virgil. In general Milton has in this area what one might regard as one advantage over Virgil but also one substantial disadvantage. The advantage is that Milton can exploit an even grander time-scale, all time from Creation and before through to the Last Day and beyond into eternity. This is evident, for example, in the great typological passage that concludes Book VI (analysed in Chapter 1). At such moments Milton can surpass his master if only because the Christian concept of eternity overtops in imaginative splendour Virgil's vision of

empire without end. As we have seen Milton achieves his effect
partly by the manipulation of tenses. There is a similar moment in
Book III when God replies to the Son's offer of the Atonement
(298–302):

> So heavenly love shall outdo hellish hate,
> Giving to death and dying to redeem,
> So dearly to redeem what hellish hate
> So easily destroyed, and still destroys,
> In those who, when they may, accept not grace.

As Fowler observes, the past and present tenses in line 301 give a
jolt, suggesting as they do that the Fall has already taken place and
that men are sinning in a fallen world. This is because, whereas the
human mind can only experience time sequentially, to God all time
is simultaneously present in an eternal moment — the doctrine is
Boethian and allows for the reconciliation of God's foreknowledge
and man's freedom. For one privileged moment we are allowed to
share in the eternal vision of him who 'past, present, future . . .
beholds' (III. 78). Milton is also good at giving a sense of boundless
time. During his voyage through chaos Satan meets 'a vast vacuity'
(II. 932–8):

>         all unawares
> Fluttering his pennons vain plumb down he drops
> Ten thousand fathom deep, and to this hour
> Down had been falling, had not by ill chance
> The strong rebuff of some tumultuous cloud,
> Instinct with fire and nitre, hurried him
> As many miles aloft.

The thought that Satan might still be falling as we read these lines is
dizzying and the whole effect superbly vertiginous — those who
have experienced it may think of the sudden stomach-turning drop
of an aeroplane in certain atmospheric conditions. It is interesting
that Satan's arrival on earth is made to depend on an accident.
Contingency allows for freedom.

Like the advantage the disadvantage to which I have referred
springs from the nature of Milton's subject-matter. The settings of
*Paradise Lost* — hell, heaven and Eden — preclude what we would
normally recognise as the poetry of place, which finds expression

only in an important series of geographical similes. Now in Virgil the sense of time is closely linked with the sense of place. This is not an accident, since it is through place — where the differences and continuities that exist between the past and the present find concrete form — that the abstract notion of time is most readily made available to us. The link is common enough in English letters, for example in Kipling's Puck stories, Housman's 'On Wenlock Edge', or in a well-known poem by John Masefield on the Berkshire Downs:

Up on the downs the red-eyed kestrels hover,
Eyeing the grass.
The field-mouse flits like a shadow into cover
As their shadows pass.

Men are burning the gorse on the down's shoulder;
A drift of smoke
Glitters with fire and hangs, and the skies smoulder,
And the lungs choke.

Once the tribe did thus on the downs, on these downs burning
Men in the frame,
Crying to the gods of the downs till their brains were turning
And the gods came.

And to-day on the downs, in the wind, the hawks, the grasses,
In blood and air,
Something passes me and cries as it passes,
On the chalk downland bare.

Masefield's poem opens with a landscape which emphasises the savagery of nature; then a routine agricultural activity is described in a way that does justice to its impressive and even frightening features. The third stanza moves abruptly to a prehistoric scene, stressing the identity of place and linking the gorse-burning with the very different burning of sacrifice. The final lines return us to the present and to the poet; to the natural features of the opening is added a *frisson* or *numen*. The poem depicts a moment when the past seems to intrude and superimpose itself upon the present. It is unclear whether the poem deals with a certain atmosphere, created by the imagination of someone with a sense of history in relation to place, or rather with something more mysterious: the cry could be the cry of a creature or a sound from the past. Virgil would have liked this poem.

Virgil belonged to a generation of poets who were writing in a somewhat novel way about landscape. His friend Horace was the first European poet who focused his love of nature consistently on those places where he had himself lived and which he for private reasons loved, the area around his Sabine farm and the landscapes of his childhood in southern Italy. Of course the feelings were not new, but it was Horace who firmly put these attachments at the centre of his poetic vision, even linking them with his poetic inspiration, and made them part of the *literary* experience of Europe. His fifth Satire, an account of a journey from Rome to Brindisi, contains such sharply etched details as this description of Terracina: 'subimus / impositum saxis late candentibus Anxur' (we crawl up to Anxur perched on rocks that shine far around). On this Eduard Fraenkel has written well:

> This is not an entry in an itinerary; it is a colourful picture of the lovely town perched on its bright rocks and greeting from afar the travellers as they emerge from the swamps below. Perhaps it was the first time in the history of European poetry that so faithful and so suggestive a picture of a definite piece of landscape was given in a few words. The ability to achieve such a thing, though conspicuous in Horace, is not peculiar to him alone: we should perhaps rather regard it as one of the fresh conquests of the generation of Virgil and Horace. When we read

> > tardis ingens ubi flexibus errat
> > Mincius et tenera praetexit harundine ripas,

> [where large Mincius wanders with slow windings and fringes its banks with tender reeds, *Georgics* III. 14–15]

> we have before our eyes the lake-like stretches of water with which the slow-flowing Mincio surrounds the city of Mantua on three sides so as to make it look like a peninsula.[53]

The most telling instance of the meeting of time and place in the *Aeneid* occurs in Book VIII when Aeneas visits the future site of Rome. Here Virgil superimposes the Rome of his own day on the rustic settlement of Evander and his Arcadians. The contrast

147

between the past and present state of a place is something of a commonplace in Latin poetry, but Virgil surpasses all comers in imagination. The passage brings into prominence one of the essential tensions of the *Aeneid*, that between city and country. Aeneas comes from a great city to make possible the founding of a greater, but the world into which he comes, and which he to some extent destroys, is essentially a rustic world which recalls features of both the *Eclogues* and the *Georgics*, a world where man is in harmony with nature — thus the landscape mourns for the dead Umbro in VII. 759–60 — and which embodies the virtues of hard work and frugality (see IX. 603ff). Evander's idyllic settlement will give place to the splendours of a Rome which Augustus had found brick and left marble, but for the time being cattle browse in what was to be the favoured district of the Carinae (in line 361 Virgil uses the adjective *lautus*, chic or smart, and the word jarringly raises the question of his emotional allegiance). Most breath-taking of all is the moment when Aeneas sees the ruined walls of older cities built by Saturn and Janus, so that yet a third layer is shaded into the other two.

Such effects are necessarily denied to Milton by the limits of his material. Where, however, he can be faulted in comparison with Virgil is in his handling of the element of prophecy, the vision of the future. The three main prophetic passages in the *Aeneid* are skilfully placed and integrated into the narrative, the first a speech by Jupiter, the second a vision in the underworld, the third scenes on a shield (I. 229ff; VI. 756ff; VIII. 626ff). By contrast Milton devotes most of the last two books of *Paradise Lost* to an extended Biblical history, which C.S. Lewis called 'an untransmuted lump of futurity',[54] told in a manner that is comparatively dry and undernourished. Even the admiring Addison, who thought highly of Book XI, regretted the switch from a series of visions to a straightforward narrative by Michael, 'as if an history painter should put in colours one half of his subject, and write down the remaining part of it'. Milton may have intended to introduce some variety, but the effect is rather of a loss of interest, a desire to get the job finished, and as Addison says, 'If Milton's poem flags anywhere, it is in this narration where in some places the author has been so attentive to his divinity that he has neglected his poetry.'[55] It has become fashionable to offer ingenious defences of these books. One could, for example, argue that the tired style is designed to reflect the weariness of the fallen world, but this hardly justifies the reader's weariness — it would be the old problem of the bore in literature. Again Milton may be seen as moving towards the more skeletal stylistic refinements of *Paradise Regained*, adjusting the style to the Biblical subject and avoiding anything reminiscent of the false allures of pagan epic. There may be truth in this too, but if so the price was too heavy. Moreover none of the defences offered really explains why amid the relative dross there gleam from time to time nuggets of purest gold, for example the lines on the loss of Eden in the Flood which are among the finest in the entire work (XI. 829ff), and of course the incomparable ending. But in general of this part at least of *Paradise Lost* one may agree with Johnson: 'No one ever wished it longer than it is.'[56]

## Notes

1. For a cogent critique of these distinctions see G.S. Kirk, *Homer and the Oral Tradition* (Cambridge University Press, 1976), pp. 69–112, especially pp. 85ff.

2. See Edgar H. Riley, 'Milton's Tribute to Virgil', *Studies in Philology*, vol. 26 (1929), pp. 155–65.

3. *The Works of John Milton*, ed. Frank Allen Paterson *et al.* (18 vols and 2 vols index, Columbia University Press, New York, 1931–40), vol. 7, p. 324. (Hereafter *Columbia Milton*.)

4. Edward Gibbon, *Critical Observations on the Sixth Book of the Aeneid* (1770) in Patricia B. Craddock (ed.), *The English Essays of Edward Gibbon* (Oxford University Press, London, 1972), pp. 138–9; *Defensio Prima* in *Columbia Milton*, vol. 7, pp. 324–5. See Howard Erskine-Hill, *The Augustan Idea in English Literature* (Edward Arnold, London, 1983), p. 261.

5. See John S. Coolidge, 'Great Things and Small: The Virgilian Progression', *Comparative Literature*, vol. 17 (1965), pp. 1–16; Richard Neuse, 'Milton and Spenser: The Virgilian Triad Revisited', *ELH*, vol. 45 (1948), pp. 606–39.

6. See Ann Gossman, 'Maia's Son: Milton and the Renaissance Virgil', in Betsy F. Colquitt (ed.), *Studies in Medieval, Renaissance, American Literature: a Festschrift* (Texas Christian University Press, Fort Worth, 1971), pp. 109–19.

7. Charles Hoole, *A New Discovery of the Old Art of Teaching School* (1660; repr. Scolar Press, Menston, 1969), p. 180.

8. *Columbia Milton*, vol. 12, pp. 308–9; vol. 18, pp. 278–9. Certainty is impossible, and Milton must surely have consulted a good number of Virgil commentaries during his life. These may have included a handsome edition published by Plantin in Antwerp in 1575, with notes by Germanus Valens that are rich in the citation of Greek parallels (the volume also contains J.J. Scaliger's commentary on the Virgilian Appendix) and a kind of variorum edition published at Basle in 1613 which includes Servius's commentary and notes by a number of scholars. (Both belong to the tradition of humanist scholarship.) See Jackson Campbell Boswell, *Milton's Library: A Catalogue of the Remains of John Milton's Library and an Annotated Reconstruction of Milton's Library and Ancillary Readings* (Garland Publishing, New York and London, 1975), p. 252.

9. *Columbia Milton*, vol. 3, pp. 303–4.

10. So K.W. Gransden, 'The *Aeneid* and *Paradise Lost*' in Charles Martindale (ed), *Virgil and his Influence: Bimillennial Studies* (Bristol Classical Press, 1984), pp. 95–116 (for an earlier version see *Essays in Criticism*, vol. 17 (1967), pp. 281–303); Janette Richardson, 'Virgil and Milton Once Again', *Comparative Literature*, vol. 14 (1962), pp. 321–31.

11. Di Cesare, 'Advent'rous Song: The Texture of Milton's Epic' in R.D. Emma and J.T. Shawcross (eds), *Language and Style in Milton : A Symposium in Honor of the Tercentenary of Paradise Lost* (Frederick Ungar Publishing Co., New York, 1967), p. 2.

12. So E.M.W. Tillyard, 'Milton and the Classics', *Essays by Divers Hands, being the Transactions of the Royal Society of Literature of the United Kingdom*, vol. 26 (1953), pp. 59–72 (pp. 62–3).

13. Jonathan Swift, *Prose Works*, ed. Herbert Davis (Shakespeare Head Press and Basil Blackwell, Oxford, 1939), vol. 1, p. 157.

14. See the introduction to Emrys Jones's edition (Clarendon Press, Oxford, 1964).

15. G.S. Kirk, 'Verse-Structure and Sentence-Structure in Homer' in *Homer and the Oral Tradition* (Cambridge University Press, 1976), pp. 146–82.

16. Addison, 'Notes upon the Twelve Books of Paradise Lost' (*The Spectator*, 1712): in John T. Shawcross (ed.), *Milton: The Critical Heritage* (Routledge & Kegan Paul, London, 1970), p. 162, and Donald F. Bond (ed.), *The Spectator* (5 vols, Clarendon Press, Oxford, 1965), vol. 3, p. 15.

17. Kirk, *Homer and the Oral Tradition*, pp. 94–7 (96).

18. Ibid., p. 99.

19. For this and other examples in this section I am indebted to M. Di Cesare in Emma and Shawcross (eds), *Language and Style in Milton*, pp. 7–8.

20. See R.M. Adams, *Ikon: John Milton and the Modern Critics* (Cornell University Press, Ithaca, N.Y., 1955), pp. 105–6.

21. John Carey, *Milton* Literature in Perspective Series (Evans Brothers, London, 1969), p. 116.

22. K.W. Gransden, 'The *Aeneid* and *Paradise Lost*' in Martindale (ed.), *Virgil and his Influence*, pp. 110–11.

23. C.S. Lewis, *Preface to Paradise Lost* (Oxford University Press, London, Oxford, New York, 1942), pp. 47–8.

24. W.F. Jackson-Knight, *Roman Vergil* (2nd edn, Faber & Faber, London, 1944), p. 192. Cf. Guy Lee, 'Imitation and the Poetry of Virgil', *Greece and Rome*, vol. 28 (1981), pp. 10–22; Martindale (ed.), *Virgil and his Influence*, pp. 9–11.

25. See Christopher Ricks, *Milton's Grand Style* (Oxford University Press, London, Oxford, New York, 1963), pp. 104–6.

26. For the history of the poetic use of 'ruin' see Owen Barfield, *Poetic Diction: A Study in Meaning* (Faber & Gwyer, London, 1928), pp. 113ff; Barfield is wrong to say that Milton never uses the word in its modern sense (p. 120).

27. For these various points see the commentaries of R.D. Williams (ed.), *Aeneid Book III* (Clarendon Press, Oxford, 1962) and R.G. Austin (ed.), *Aeneid Book VI* (Clarendon Press, Oxford, 1977). For word-play in Homer see C.W. Macleod's edition of *Iliad Book XXIV* (Cambridge University Press, 1982), pp. 50–3.

28. James Whaler, 'The Miltonic Simile', *PMLA*, vol. 46 (1931), p. 1065 (1034–74).

29. David West, 'Multiple-Correspondence Similes in the *Aeneid*', *Journal of Roman Studies*, vol. 59 (1969), p. 40; M.D. Reeve, 'The Language of Achilles', *Classical Quarterly*, n.s., vol. 23 (1973), p. 193. For the opposite extreme see Hermann Fränkel, *Die homerischen Gleichnisse* (Dandenhoed & Ruprecht, Göttingen, 1921).

30. *Chapman's Homer*, vol. 1, p. 70. For similar disputes in antiquity see Robin R. Schlunk, *The Homeric Scholia and the Aeneid: A Study of the Influence of Ancient*

# Virgil

*Homeric Literary Criticism on Vergil* (University of Michigan Press, Ann Arbor, 1974), esp. ch. 3; N.J. Richardson, 'Literary Criticism in the Exegetical Scholia to the *Iliad*: A Sketch', *Classical Quarterly*, vol. 30 (1980), pp. 279–81.

31. J.B.Broadbent, 'Milton and Arnold', *Essays in Criticism*, vol. 6 (1956), p. 409.

32. Addison, 'Notes': in Shawcross (ed.), *Milton*, pp. 172–3, and Bond (ed.), *Spectator*, vol. 3, pp. 90–1.

33. West, 'Multiple-Correspondence Similes', p. 46.

34. R.G. Austin (ed.), *Aeneid Book II* (Clarendon Press, Oxford, 1964), p. 139. I replace the Greek text of Homer with Lattimore's translation.

35. Laurence Lerner, 'The Miltonic Simile', *Essays in Criticism*, vol. 4 (1954), pp. 301–2; Ricks, *Milton's Grand Style*, pp. 126ff.

36. Ricks, *Milton's Grand Style*, p. 128.

37. Ibid., p. 121.

38. Isabel MacCaffery, *Paradise Lost as 'Myth'* (Harvard University Press, Cambridge, Mass., 1959), p. 121. For the stairs see Claes Schaar, *The Full Voic'd Quire Below: Vertical Context Systems in Paradise Lost,* Lund Studies in English 60 (Gleerup, Lund, 1982), pp. 149–61.

39. See Whaler, 'The Miltonic Simile', p. 1055; Schaar, *Full Voic'd Quire*, pp. 79–82.

40. G.S. Kirk, *The Songs of Homer* (Cambridge University Press, 1962), p. 380.

41. See Schlunk, *The Homeric Scholia*, pp. 95–9.

42. 'The Life of Milton' in Samuel Johnson, *Lives of the English Poets*, ed. G.B. Hill (3 vols, Clarendon Press, Oxford, 1905), vol. 1, p. 179.

43. Addison, 'Notes': in Shawcross (ed.), *Milton*, p. 206, and Bond (ed.), *Spectator*, vol. 3, p. 311.

44. See the Introduction to R.G. Austin (ed.), *Aeneid Book II* (Clarendon Press, Oxford, 1964), p. xx and note *ad loc.*

45. So Carey, *Milton*, p. 120.

46. So Stephen Medcalf, 'Virgil at the Turn of Time', in Martindale (ed.), *Virgil and his Influence*, pp. 223–5.

47. *Columbia Milton*, vol. 7, pp. 85–7 (*Defensio Prima*). For bees and monarchy see, for example, Seneca, *De Clementia* 19.

48. For Milton's bee simile see D.P. Harding, 'Milton's Bee-Simile', *Journal of English and Germanic Philology*, vol. 60 (1961), pp. 664–9; Freeman, *Milton and the Martial Muse: Paradise Lost and European Traditions of War* (Princeton University Press, 1980), pp. 186–99; Schaar, *Full Voic'd Quire*, pp. 75–8. For the *Georgics* see Jasper Griffin, 'The Fourth *Georgic*, Virgil and Rome', *Greece and Rome*, vol. 26 (1979), pp. 61–80 and my article 'Sense and Sensibility: The Child and the Man in "The Rape of the Lock" ', *Modern Language Review*, vol. 78 (1983), pp. 278–9.

49. For a full study of this motif see Thomas Greene, *The Descent from Heaven: A Study in Epic Continuity* (Yale University Press, New Haven and London, 1963); cf. Schaar, *Full Voic'd Quire*, pp. 251–8. Raphael corresponds to various instructor figures in the *Aeneid*, including Aeneas himself who tells Dido of his past in Books II and III, and Anchises, the opening of whose Stoic-Platonic discourse about God and the soul in VI. 724ff lies behind Raphael's words to Adam, V. 469ff.

50. For imitations of Virgil in Milton, probable, possible and improbable, see also the *Columbia Milton* index under 'Vergil' and, in addition to other works cited elsewhere, Douglas Bush, 'Virgil and Milton', *Classical Journal*, vol. 47 (1952), pp. 178–82 and 203–4; Elizabeth Nitchie, *Vergil and the English Poets* (Columbia University Press, New York, 1919). Robert J. Edgeworth, 'Milton's "Darkness Visible" and *Aeneid 7*', *Classical Journal*, vol. 79 (1983/4), p. 97, adduces *Aen*. VII. 456–7 *Atro lumine* as a source for Milton's phrase; the parallel for the oxymoron is interesting but not very close and the assumption that there must be a source is questionable.

51. See, for example, the essays by K.W. Gransden, S. Medcalf and A.D. Nuttall ('Virgil and Shakespeare') in Martindale (ed.), *Virgil and his Influence*.

52. Lewis, *Preface to Paradise Lost*, p. 35.

53. Eduard Fraenkel, *Horace* (Clarendon Press, Oxford, 1957), p. 110. There are, however, isolated precedents in Republican poetry, and cf. Niall Rudd, *The Satires of Horace* (Cambridge University Press, 1966), pp. 59–60 (neither of the passages he cites are, however, as vivid as Horace's lines).

54. Lewis, *Preface to Paradise Lost*, p. 129.

55. Addison, 'Notes': in Shawcross (ed.), *Milton*, p. 217, and Bond (ed.), *Spectator*, vol. 3, p. 386.

56. 'The Life of Milton' in Johnson, *Lives of the English Poets*, ed. Hill, vol. 1, p. 183.

# 4
# OVID

## The Renaissance Ovid

The *Metamorphoses* of Ovid is a golden book, a book of stories of the kind that, in words from Sidney's *Apology*, 'holdeth children from play and old men from the chimney corner'. From the twelfth until the seventeenth century its influence on the literature and culture of Western Europe was almost certainly greater than that of any other classical poem. Although of epic dimensions and written in the hexameters proper to epic, it is quite unlike the 'true' epics of Homer and Virgil. Instead of a unified epic theme with a single basic action it offers us a series of stories, ingeniously woven together and contained within a rough chronological sequence which extends from the Creation to the poet's own day (since most of the myths treated cannot be dated, this sequence is more apparent than real).

The poem's curious status — both epic and non-epic — is treated with a characteristic Ovidian lightness of touch and feeling for paradox in the exordium (1–4):

In nova fert animus mutatas dicere formas
corpora; di coeptis — nam vos mutastis et illas —
adspirate meis primaque ab origine mundi
ad mea perpetuum deducite tempora carmen

(My mind leads me to tell of shapes changed into new bodies;
gods — for you also changed them — breathe on my enterprise
and bring down an unbroken song from the beginnings of the
world to my own times)

We have seen that Callimachus had condemned the writing of long epics after the example of Homer, favouring shorter, more highly-wrought forms and recherché subject-matter. Ovid both keeps and breaks these influential admonitions. The first two words ('in nova') hint at the novelty of his enterprise; 'deducite' implies that his song is *deductum* (fine-spun) as Callimachus had

recommended (cf. Virgil, *Eclogue* VI. 5), while the subject-matter
— metamorphosis and love — is also of an Alexandrian kind. But
Ovid does tell a continuous story ('perpetuum carmen') of
authentically epic length, even if it is broken down into shorter,
largely self-contained units.[1]

The title of the poem should, despite many modern scholars, be
taken seriously, for the constant changes mirror a world of flux, for
which the speech of Pythagoras in XV. 143ff supplies a
philosophical basis. Only poetry, as the proud epilogue proclaims,
can hope for a conquest of time and a transcendence of change (XV.
871–9). A critic who argues thus admittedly runs the risk of
sounding heavy-footed, of attributing an undeserved solemnity to
the poem. For with Ovid, as with Johnson's friend Oliver Edwards,
cheerfulness is always breaking in. Quintilian (X. 1. 88) rightly
identified *lascivia*, a sort of playful exuberance or exuberant
playfulness, as a key Ovidian characteristic. Most of the stories are
told wittily and a number are outrageously funny. Moreover to a
large extent — in this too unlike Homer and Virgil — Ovid creates a
world that is self-sustaining and self-referring, an escape from drab
normality. No one has put the point better than Gilbert Murray:

> He was a poet utterly in love with poetry: not perhaps with the
> soul of poetry — to be in love with souls is a feeble and somewhat
> morbid condition — but with the real face and voice and body
> and clothes and accessories of poetry . . . He strikes one as having
> been rather innocent and almost entirely useless in this dull world
> which he had not made and for which he was not responsible,
> while he moved triumphant and effective through his own
> inexhaustible realm of legend . . . What a world it is that he has
> created in the *Metamorphoses*! . . . A world of wonderful
> children where nobody is really cross or wicked except the
> grown-ups; Juno, for instance, and people's parents, and of
> course a certain number of Furies and Witches. I think among all
> the poets who take rank merely as story-tellers and creators of
> mimic worlds, Ovid still stands supreme. His criticism of life is
> very slight; it is the criticism passed by a child, playing alone and
> peopling the summer evening with delightful shapes, upon the
> stupid nurse who drags it off to bed.[2]

Yet I would baulk at the last sentence quoted, for, as I have already
implied, the poem does offer a kind of oblique vision of reality,

however different from that found in the *Aeneid*, and one which in some respects our own age is particularly well placed to appreciate. While the structure of the *Aeneid* reflects a teleological view of human history, one which can, without too much strain, be put at the service of Christianity, the constant turns of the *Metamorphoses* allow for no fixity; the only still point in Ovid's turning world resides in poetic creation itself.

Ovid's *Metamorphoses* was apparently Milton's favoured Latin reading, at least in old age.[3] This choice might be felt an unexpected one for the ageing, blind, puritan poet, surrounded by the worldliness of Restoration England. But perhaps we might have expected it. Milton's favourite English poets were also Ovidians: Spenser, who in the *Faerie Queene* put scenes from the *Metamorphoses* to more sage and serious use, and Shakespeare, who had been regarded by contemporaries as a kind of Ovid redivivus — as Francis Meres put it in 1598: 'As the soul of Euphorbus was thought to live in Pythagoras, so the sweet, witty soul of Ovid lives in mellifluous and honey-tongued Shakespeare, witness his *Venus and Adonis*, his *Lucrece*, his sugared sonnets.'[4] Milton's fondness for Ovid, which marks him as a true son of the English Renaissance, might already have appeared old-fashioned in the last decades of the seventeenth century. In his critical writings Dryden begins to shadow forth the new attitudes of a nascent Neoclassicism. He partly modified, at least in theory, an early enthusiasm for Ovid in favour of the supposed stylistic purity of more restrained authors, especially Virgil and Horace. In 1667 he had praised Ovid for 'invention' and 'fancy', and found his representation of female passion superior to Virgil's: 'Ovid has touched those tender strokes more delicately than Virgil could.' But by 1685 he was criticising Ovid's lack of 'majesty' and metrical variety ('he is always . . . upon the hand-gallop, and his verse runs upon carpet ground'), while in 1700, comparing Ovid with Chaucer, he was more severe: Ovid's conceits are 'glittering trifles' that 'in a serious poem . . . are nauseous, because they are unnatural'. We may compare his changed attitude to du Bartas, who was, as we have seen, another Miltonic and early seventeenth-century favourite:

I remember, when I was a boy, I thought inimitable Spenser a mean poet in comparison of Sylvester's *du Bartas*, and was rapt into an ecstasy when I read these lines:

Now, when the winter's keener breath began
To crystallize the Baltic Ocean,
To glaze the lakes, to bridle up the floods,
And periwig with snow the bald-pate woods.

I am much deceived if this be not abominable fustian, that is, thoughts and worlds ill sorted, and without the least relation to each other.[5]

In fact Dryden never wholly lost his admiration for Ovid, as the brilliant translations for the *Fables* show, and it would be wrong to force undue consistency on his vacillating critical pronouncements. Nevertheless he shows an increasing willingness to criticise Ovid for his failure to live up to a neoclassical sense of decorum, picking up and developing the criticisms made in antiquity by Quintilian and others. Today Milton's preference should appear less surprising, for a sense of Ovid's greatness and place in European culture is gradually being recovered. The poet and critic Charles Tomlinson even makes Ovid a presiding genius of literary Modernism, exploring his influence on Eliot and Pound. One of the most delicate and moving allusions to the Ovidian theme of metamorphosis occurs at the end of Part I of *Finnegans Wake*: 'My foos won't moos. I feel as old as yonder elm . . . My ho head halls. I feel as heavy as yonder stone.' Joyce gives his washerwomen something of the tenderness that Ovid shows his Philemon and Baucis.[6]

Before I attempt to sketch some of the reasons that may have drawn Milton to Ovid, and to describe the nature of the Ovidian presence in *Paradise Lost*, I would make some initial caveats. First, as with Homer and Virgil, it is important to remember that Milton's Ovid is not quite today's Ovid; the texts that Milton used differed in some respects from ours, and different emphases were laid in the Renaissance commentaries that he read, and in the way that Ovid was taught in school. David Harding, author of the fundamental study of Milton's use of Ovid, gives an instance of what can be missed if this point is ignored. In *Metamorphoses* II. 2 the Palace of the Sun is described as 'clara micante auro flammasque imitante pyropo' (bright with sparkling gold and pyropum that imitates flames). *Pyropum* probably signifies an alloy of gold and bronze, but in the Renaissance it was usually taken to mean 'carbuncle'. Milton, with Ovid in mind, mentions carbuncle in his description of the Sun (*PL*. III. 596). The tiny reference passed unnoticed among commentators well versed in Ovid, but unfamiliar with the Renaissance usage.[7] A failure to differentiate the Renaissance from the modern Ovid vitiates Louis Martz's otherwise attractive treatment of Ovid and Milton in *Poet of Exile*, so that some of his observations are attended by a strong whiff of anachronism.[8] For example, noting that modern critics have detected a slackening in the writing in the later books of the *Metamorphoses*, and also in *Paradise Lost* XI and XII, Martz suggests that Milton may deliberately be reproducing an Ovidian effect in the altered manner. But Martz does not stop to ask whether seventeenth-century readers shared the modern view of the closing four books of the *Metamorphoses*, or agreed that the writing in them was less lively. In fact it seems probable that they did not, since the last books were generally much more admired in the Renaissance than in the twentieth century. Mirandula's quotation book is particularly rich in citations from Book XV, a book which Shakespeare frequently echoes in the sonnets.[9] Dryden thought it worth his while to translate the whole of Book XII, praising especially the House of Fame, the fight between Achilles and Cygnus and the battle of the Lapiths and Centaurs, including what he describes as the 'wonderfully moving' 'loves and death' of the centaurs Cyllarus and Hylonome (393ff), a passage that many today would be tempted to see as kitsch, or as parodic rather than authentic pathos. Likewise Dryden though the lines on Pythagoras' philosophy in *Metamorphoses* XV 'the most learned and beautiful' section of the poem (headnotes from *Fables Ancient and Modern*, 1700). I know of no evidence that earlier readers detected a substantial change of stylistic direction in Ovid's closing books; by contrast worries were early expressed, by Addison and others, about the flatness of the writing towards the end of *Paradise Lost*. Martz also argues that the structure of the *Metamorphoses* was imitated by Milton. He accepts the contentious and (in my view) implausible structural analyses of the *Metamorphoses* in terms of balancing 'panels', and finds analogies for these panels in *Paradise Lost*. However it seems obvious that *Paradise Lost* recalls the epic structure (with its teleological implications) of the *Aeneid*, and not the fluid and episodic form (or perhaps rather non-form) of the anti-classical *Metamorphoses*.

However, in avoiding the Scylla of anachronism, we must not sail into a Charybdis of crude historicism. Equally unconvincing would be the assumption that Renaissance responses to Ovid were restricted to the kinds of observation made in the commentaries. At a time when literary criticism was in its infancy, much that was felt would not find ready expression, or would find expression only in direct imitation. Thus, earlier, Chaucer had obviously understood Ovid's sly humour, despite the fact that medieval commentaries largely ignore this aspect of the *Metamorphoses*, concentrating on moral and allegorical exegesis. Ovid was Chaucer's true master among the ancients; even when adapting the story of Dido and Aeneas out of *Aeneid* IV Chaucer recalls the manner of Ovid. The royal pair take refuge in the cave, where their love is to be consummated, and Chaucer cheekily observes in *The Legend of Good Woman* (1225–8):

> She fledde hireself into a litel cave,
> And with hire wente this Eneas also.
> I not [know not], with hem if there wente any mo [more];
> The autour maketh of it no mencioun.

Similarly Marlowe's understanding of Ovid, whether or not he could have articulated it in prose, is expressed in *Hero and Leander*. George Sandys, whose translation of the *Metamorphoses* quickly supplanted the version by Arthur Golding which Shakespeare and the Elizabethans had used, while he seldom enlarges on Ovid's wit in his commentary, can show a perfect appreciation of it in his translation. For example, for Ovid's jesting comparison of the palaces of Jupiter and Augustus (I. 175–6)

> hic locus est quem, si verbis audacia detur,
> haud timeam magni dixisse Palatia caeli

Sandys gives:

> This glorious roof I would not doubt to call,
> Had I but boldness lent me, heaven's Whitehall.

In the case of Milton, whose feeling for classical literature was clearly exceptional, it would be wrong to assume that his Ovid is merely the Ovid of the commentators.

A second general difficulty is the problem of determining whether Ovid is in fact the source for particular passages in *Paradise Lost*. Many of the likely Ovidian allusions are to stories in the *Metamorphoses*, and most of these stories would have been familiar to Milton from other sources as well as from Ovid. In Book II at their games the devils tear up rocks and hills amid 'wild uproar' (542–6):

As when Alcides from Oechalia crowned
With conquest felt the envenomed robe, and tore
Through pain up by the roots Thessalian pines,
And Lichas from the top of Oeta threw
Into the Euboic sea.[10]

Milton would have known the story of Hercules' death from the *Trachiniae* and the *Hercules Oetaeus* as well as from Ovid, and doubtless numerous commentaries and handbooks. Certain verbal details, together with the fact that Ovid (unlike Sophocles and Seneca) places the scene in Thessaly, suggest that the *Metamorphoses* (IX. 134ff) is the main source. Yet even if this is so, the passage is not especially Ovidian in feeling. The baroque muscularity (to use Ricks's word) of the writing, in particular the separation of 'tore' from 'up', creating an effect of violent dislocation, and the dizzy pause that results from the placement of 'threw' at the end of the line so that we can see the moment when Lichas topples over the edge, recalls the epic manner of Virgil. Admittedly in his account of Hercules Ovid is writing more 'epically' than usual: in particular he imitates Virgil's emphatic positioning of verbs at the beginning and ends of lines (212, 217) and striking use of enjambement ('terque quarterque rotatum / mittit in Euboicas tormento fortius undas', whirling him repeatedly he throws him into the Euboean sea more strongly than a catapult, 217–18). However it was not primarily from Ovid that Milton learned such effects.

Thirdly, we must be careful not to restrict Ovid's influence on Milton to supposed verbal 'allusions' or imitations. Rather it may on occasion be felt in the manner of writing. For example there was nothing in the spare Biblical narrative of Genesis to help Milton when he set himself to describe Adam and Eve, and it seems that Ovid's Deucalion and Pyrrha, who recreate the human race after the Flood, came into his mind (in Book XI he directly compares the two couples). Ovid uses carefully balanced phrasing suggestive of the mutuality and mutual dignity of his lone man and woman (this particular rhetorical device, a kind of verbal echoing, is more characteristic of Ovid than, say, Virgil or Horace):

et superesse virum de tot modo milibus unum,
et superesse videt de tot modo milibus unam,
innocuos ambo, cultores numinis ambo.   (I. 325–7)

(Jupiter sees that one man is left from so many thousands, that one woman is left from so many thousands, innocent both, worshippers of divinity both.)

Milton employs comparable procedures throughout his initial description of Adam and Eve (IV. 297–8, 323–4):

For contemplation he and valour formed,
For softness she and sweet attractive grace . . .

Adam the goodliest man of men since born
His sons, the fairest of her daughters Eve.

The context within which Milton read the *Metamorphoses* must now be briefly sketched.[11] Broadly, there were four aspects to the Renaissance Ovid, even four different Ovids, available for Milton's use. First, we have 'moral' or 'exemplary' Ovid: each Ovidian story could be read as pointing an improving moral. There was precedent for such an approach in antiquity. In *De Providentia* V. 9–11 Seneca uses the opening of the tale of Phaethon who asks to borrow the chariot of his father, the Sun-god Apollo, to illustrate a proper ardour for the challenges and difficulties of the virtuous life. This is an odd reading in view of the disastrous sequel when Phaethon loses control of the chariot and crashes to his death, and the Renaissance more plausibly rather saw an example of youthful folly and, in George Sandys's phrase, 'ruining ambition'.[12] Humanists, who emphasised the educational value of classical poetry, and the conjunction in it of profit and pleasure, favoured exemplary readings. Some doubted whether Ovid was the most suitable author for such purposes, including Thomas Elyot, who expressed his preference for Horace as an author for children:

I would set next unto him [Virgil] two books of Ovid, the one called *Metamorphoses* . . . the other is entitled *De Fastis* . . . both right necessary for the understanding of other poets. But because there is little other learning in them concerning either virtuous manners or policy, I suppose it were better that as fables and ceremonies happen to come in a lesson it were declared abundantly by the master than that in the said two books a long time should be spent and almost lost; which might be better employed on such authors that do minister both eloquence, civil policy and exhortations to virtue. Wherefore in his place let us bring in Horace, in whom is contained much variety of learning and quickness of sentence.[13]

However, Raphael Regius, whose humanist edition of the *Metamorphoses*, first published in Venice in 1492, was immensely popular throughout the sixteenth century, lent his authority to the moralisers, as in this passage from the preface (here translated by Sandys):

There is nothing appertaining to the knowledge and glory of war, whereof we have not famous examples in the *Metamorphoses* of Ovid — not to speak of stratagems nor the orations of commanders — described with such efficacy and eloquence that often in reading you will imagine yourself embroiled in their conflicts. Neither shall you find any author from whom a civil life may gather better instructions.

For Regius Jupiter's transformation of the evil Lycaon into a wolf illustrates the penalties assigned to robbers, while the story of Daphne who escapes the amorous pursuit of Apollo by her metamorphosis into a laurel exemplifies the virtue of chastity and its rewards.

Golding's translation of the *Metamorphoses* (1567), which nourished the imagination of an age, includes an 'Epistle' and 'Preface' which can largely be assigned to this tradition.[14] Golding defines the general use of his book thus ('Epistle', 569–73):

The use of this same book therefore is this: that every man,
Endeavouring for to know himself as nearly as he can,
As though he in a chariot sat well ordered, should direct
His mind by reason in the way of virtue, and correct
His fierce affections with the bit of temperance . . .

He offers exemplary readings of most of the stories, finding in them 'pithy, apt and plain / Instructions' (64–5). For example, 'Narcissus is of scornfulness and pride a mirror clear, / Where beauty's fading

vanity most plainly may appear' (105–6). It was how to understand
the gods that caused Golding most trouble. In the Epistle he toys
with the euhemeristic view whereby the gods are 'noblemen, who
for their virtues be . . . canonized . . . by heathen men' (18–19). In
the Preface they are interpreted as standing for different sorts of
men, virtuous or vicious (57ff). Golding also saw glimmerings of a
deeper understanding. 'Little seeds and sparks of heavenly light'
were operative even in pagans (Preface, 5–7). Although their
writings 'nothing may in worthiness with holy writ compare'
(Epistle, 334), yet they contain glimpses of the truth (306ff). Ovid
may have read Genesis (338ff), and mystic senses can be assigned to
some details: for example Prometheus in the Creation story may
stand for the Word of God (453).

Golding's occasional forays into Christian allegory bring us to the
second Ovid, the allegorical Ovid, the Ovid of the High Middle
Ages. In the exemplary approach each story *as a whole* yielded a
moral, which was at least fairly plausible and to some extent suited
it. However in the allegorising commentaries of the Middle Ages
multiple inconsistent readings were offered for each story, and also
the details of the story were given allegorical significance, in a way
that often quite lacks any superficial plausibility (the multiple
allegories might include exemplary moral allegory of the kind
already discussed). Two points should be underlined. First, the
essential impulse was not a desire to bowdlerise unsuitable material,
but rather to make Ovid relevant to contemporary concerns.[15]
Secondly, there were so many versions that there was no agreement
about the meanings of the stories, and hence no readily available
fixed code of meanings for poets to exploit. It is rather a question of
habits of mind. It is usually said that the Renaissance saw the
development of a more historically aware attitude to the classics.
There is much truth in this: for example Regius' edition of the
*Metamorphoses* is devoted to correcting the text and explaining
Ovid's words, ignoring allegorical exegesis, although it should be
remembered that Regius' notes were often combined with a
Christian interpretation of the first book by Lavinius. Nevertheless
the old approaches continued. Sandys's extensive commentary
accompanying his translation in the 1632 edition contains much
traditional allegorical lore. Alexander Ross's *Mystagogus Poeticus
or the Muses' Interpreter* of 1647 continued in use until the end of the
seventeenth century, to familiarise English schoolboys with many of
the allegorisations. For example, Ross interprets Ceres as a type of

God's Church and of Christ, who 'is truly Ceres, which having lost mankind, being carried away by the Devil, he came, and with the torch of his word, found him out; and . . . went down to Hell, and rescued us from thence'.[16] Similarly in Giles Fletcher's *Christ's Victory and Triumph in Heaven and Earth, Over and After Death* (1610) we find some of the traditional connections between Scripture and pagan mythology ('Christ's Triumph Over Death', stanza 7):

> Who doth not see drowned in Deucalion's name,
> (When earth his men, and sea had lost his shore)
> Old Noah, and in Nisus' lock the fame
> Of Samson yet alive? And long before
> In Phaethon's mine own fall I deplore;
>    But he that conquered hell, to fetch again
>    His virgin widow, by a serpent slain,
> Another Orpheus was than dreaming poets feign.

Indeed Fletcher moves so easily in this world of classical analogues that he can, without apology, compare the Ascension with the homosexual rape of Ganymede by Jupiter, a comparison that Milton, with his far stronger sense of what separated Christianity and paganism, would never have attempted ('Christ's Triumph After Death', stanza 14). It would in fact be wrong to make an absolute distinction between a humanist exemplary Ovid and a medieval allegorical Ovid. In 1555 Georgius Sabinus, son-in-law of the reformer Melanchthon, produced a commentary on the *Metamorphoses* containing *interpretatio, ethica, physica et historica*, which was widely used and which marks a kind of compromise between the two approaches.

Despite the efforts of Sandys, Ross and others, the tide was turning for the allegorisers. The urbane Addison, who translated a number of Ovidian tales, was able to represent such interpretations as merely silly:

> There are few books that have had worse commentators on them than Ovid's *Metamorphoses*. Those of the graver sort have been wholly taken up in the mythologies, and think they have appeared very judicious if they have shown us out of an old author that Ovid is mistaken in a pedigree, or has turned such a person into a wolf that ought to have been made a tiger. Others

have employed themselves on what never entered into the poet's thoughts, in adapting a dull moral to every story, and making the persons of his poems to be only nicknames for such virtues or vices; particularly the pious commentator Alexander Ross has dived deeper into our author's design than any of the rest; for he discovers in him the greatest mysteries of the Christian religion, and finds almost in every page some typical representation of the world, the flesh and the devil . . . I shall, therefore, only consider Ovid under the character of a poet . . .[17]

So, with the lightest of sneers, Addison taught the rest to sneer. Likewise he was opposed to the use of classical fables in modern poetry in general (*Spectator*, 523), and objected to some of the mythological embellishments in *Paradise Lost*.

The remaining two Ovids bring us closer to twentieth-century perceptions. First, there is the 'rhetorical' Ovid, 'poetarum elegantissimus,' most elegant of poets, as Milton called him,[18] master of artifice and of all the ornaments of rhetoric. At St Paul's School Milton will have been taught to dissect this aspect of Ovid's art in the minutest detail. Ann Moss has demonstrated that in France there was a shift in editions of Ovid during the sixteenth century towards rhetorical comment and away from allegory.[19] A similar story could doubtless be told of England, even if it is arguable that the Renaissance in this country was a late and sickly growth. Shakespeare's Holofernes, that doyen of Elizabethan schoolmasters, puts the point with heavy pedagogic humour, punning on Ovid's cognomen Naso (connected with the Latin word for nose): 'Ovidius Naso was the man [viz. 'for the elegancy, facility and golden cadence of poesy']: and why, indeed, *Naso*, but for smelling out the odoriferous flowers of fancy, the jerks of invention' (*Love's Labour's Lost* IV. ii. 118ff). We have seen that Ovid's exuberant rhetoric began to diminish in appeal after the Restoration, and it is possible that Milton may have listened, to some degree, to the criticisms. Some frivolous details in Ovid's description of the Flood had been condemned by Seneca (*Naturales Quaestiones* III. 27.13). Seneca is specifically commenting on line 304, 'nat lupus inter oves, fulvos vehit unda leones' (the wolf swims among the sheep, the water carries tawny lions). Sandys sensibly comments: 'Seneca reproves this part of the description, as too light for so sad an argument, herein perhaps a better philosopher than a poet.' But it may be significant that Milton's account of the Flood

(XI. 738ff), while picking up the theme, tones down Ovid's
excesses, so that the resulting description becomes more Virgilian
(750–2):

> . . . and in their palaces
> Where luxury late reigned, sea monsters whelped
> And stabled . . .

Milton's restraint was to receive its due reward in Addison's
discussion of the passage:

> As it is visible that the poet had his eye upon Ovid's account of
> the universal deluge, the reader may observe with how much
> judgement he has avoided everything that is redundant or puerile
> in the Latin poet. We do not here see the wolf swimming among
> the sheep, nor any of those wanton imaginations which Seneca
> found fault with as unbecoming the great catastrophe of nature.[20]

In fact it is Dryden who best reproduces these wanton imaginations
that are so conspicuous a part of Ovid's sensibility, both in his
translations of Ovid and in some of his original poetry, including
*Annus Mirabilis*.

Finally, there is what may be dubbed the 'amoral' Ovid. In the
1590s there was a fashion for short narrative poems, usually of a
strongly erotic character, influenced by Ovid but not by the
allegorical and moral commentary upon him.[21] The wit, humour (at
times approaching farce), grotesqueness, brittle pathos, lyricism
and elegance of Ovid's narratives were reproduced in poems which
might be seen as the literary analogues of Titian's mythological
paintings, like the 'Bacchus and Ariadne' that can be seen in the
National Gallery in London or 'The Rape of Europa', now in
Boston.[22] Marlowe in particular showed considerable sensitivity to
various aspects of his master's art. For example in the story of
Hermaphroditus beloved by the nymph Salmacis, Ovid plays
cleverly on the dual nature of Salmacis, partly a pool, partly a water
nymph; thus, when Salmacis embraces Hermaphroditus the word
*circumfunditur* (IV. 360) — 'is poured round' — is appropriate both
to a human embrace and to the movement of water around a body
(the trick, though often enough found in ancient literature, is a
particular favourite of Ovid's). Similarly in *Hero and Leander*,
when Neptune attempts to seduce Leander, he is both the

anthropomorphic god of the sea and the waters of the Hellespont, and on one level the passage is perhaps the most *accurate* and sensuous description of swimming in English poetry (Sestiad II. 181–90):

> He clapped his plump cheeks, with his tresses played,
> And smiling wantonly his love bewrayed.
> He watched his arms, and as they opened wide
> At every stroke, betwixt them would he slide
> And steal a kiss, and then run out and dance,
> And as he turned, cast many a lustful glance,
> And threw him gaudy toys to please his eye,
> And dive into the water, and there pry
> Upon his breast, his thighs, and every limb,
> And up again, and close beside him swim . . .

Again, when Shakespeare sports lyrically with the play of white on white in *Venus and Adonis*:

> Full gently now she takes him by the hand,
> A lily prisoned in a gaol of snow,
> Or ivory in an alabaster band;
> So white a friend engirts so white a foe     (361–4)

he 'Englishes' an Ovidian effect: the white body of Hermaphroditus in the water is like ivory or lilies seen through translucent glass (*Met.* IV. 354–5).

## Ovidian Stories in Milton

### Narcissus

Each of these ways of reading Ovid left its mark on Milton. As one would expect he sometimes uses a classical myth as an example. We have already seen how in the invocation to Book VII Bellerophon illustrates the perils of aspiring too high. A more extended instance, and one based on Ovid, occurs in IV. 449ff. Here Eve describes how on first waking she saw herself in a pool, but was then warned by a divine voice to shun her reflection and seek Adam. The phrase 'unexperienced thought' (457) could be taken as the keynote of the whole sequence: to Eve's innocent, enquiring mind water is like sky, and her ignorance requires education. Her turning from shadow to substance makes her story balance Adam's account in VIII. 452ff of how he dreamed of Eve and then, in Keats's famous phrase, 'awoke and found it truth'.[23] Eve's story is explicitly moralised in that the voice warns against self-love, and at the end she professes herself convinced that wisdom is indeed better than physical beauty. In *Metamorphoses* III the lovely Narcissus, having scorned the love of Echo and many others, falls in love with his own reflection in a pool; eventually realising his mistake he wastes away and dies. There can be no doubt that Milton is recalling this story, and indeed specifically Ovid's version of it, as a number of verbal echoes show. For example, when in Milton the voice warns Eve that she is looking at a reflection of herself (467–9):

> What thou seest,
> What there thou seest, fair creature, is thyself;
> With thee it came and goes

the slight awkwardness in the tenses of 'With thee it came and goes' (469), which gives the words a curious Miltonic power, is due to exact imitation of the tenses of the Ovidian original (434–6):

> ista repercussae quam cernis imaginis umbra est.
> nil habet ista sui; tecum venitque manetque,
> tecum discedet, si tu discedere possis.

(What you see is a shadow, and a reflected image, and has no substance of its own; with you it came and stays, with you will go away, should you be able to go away.)

Milton is perhaps tacitly correcting, with a kind of passionate pedantry not untypical of him, the translation of Sandys which renders *vēnit* by a present tense.[24]

Ovid's interest in Narcissus is not essentially moralistic; his concern is rather with the psychology of such abnormal sexuality, and with the conceits and verbal paradoxes that entangle the self-lover. However, the story lends itself to moralising, and the temptation was not resisted.[25] In the simplest version Narcissus represents self-love and Echo boastfulness: boastfulness naturally loves self-love. The name Narcissus, according to the commentators including Sandys, 'signifies stupid or heavy'. Best known of more

elaborate moralisations is the version of the Florentine Neoplaton-
ist Marsilio Ficino (1433–99) in his commentary on Plato's
*Symposium* (VI. 17). Narcissus here is the anti-type of the Platonic
lover. In the *Symposium* the wise woman Diotima teaches Socrates
to avoid death by leading him from body to soul and thence upwards
to God. By contrast Narcissus is ensnared by the world of
appearances and the beauty of the body, mistaking this for true
beauty. As a result, in Sandys's words (his rambling comments on
Narcissus are much influenced by Ficino), 'Narcissus . . . ignorantly
affecting one thing, pursues another, nor can ever satisfy his
longings.'

Both the simple and complex versions seem relevant to Milton's
purposes. In Book IV Eve behaves in accordance with Diotima's
instructions; she is not caught by the beauty of appearances, and
recognises the true beauty of Adam, even though he initially
appears 'Less winning soft . . . / Than that smooth watery image'
(479–80). But it is also possible to see an ominous prolepsis in the
allusion to Narcissus: Eve will eventually fall through exactly the
self-love of the simple version. Sandys connects the story of
Narcissus with the fall of the angels: 'a fearful example we have of
the danger of self-love in the fall of the angels, who, intermitting the
beatifical vision, by reflecting upon themselves and admiration of
their own excellency, forgot their dependence upon their creator.'
Milton thus makes subtle and allusive use of a familiar story pattern.
However it is worth observing that he does not directly refer to the
'fable' in a simile, and the episode does not prove that he normally
read Ovid 'morally'.

### Beginnings

In the account of the Creation and Flood in *Metamorphoses* I the
correspondences with Scripture almost force themselves upon the
Christian reader, and won widespread acceptance in the Middle
Ages and Renaissance, enabling Milton in *Paradise Lost* to use
Ovid as a quarry to supplement the briefer accounts in Genesis.
Harding has shown in detail how extensive are his borrowings. For
example the description of Chaos in *Paradise Lost* II. 891–916 owes
much to *Metamorphoses* I. 5–20, while many details in Uriel's
account of the ordering of Chaos at the Creation (III. 708–21)
derive from Ovid (I. 21–31), as does Raphael's rather different
version in VII. 232–42. Several details in Milton's exuberant
elaboration of the narrative in Genesis of the six days of Creation

have an Ovidian basis (e.g. for *PL* VII. 267–71, cf. *Met.* I. 30–1; for VII. 276–82, *Met.* I. 417–21; for VII. 288–9, *Met.* I. 43–4). In particular both poets stress the special status of man as God's masterwork and the significance of his upright carriage. It might be objected that this idea is commonplace, and Milton is as likely to be thinking of the early church father Lactantius (fourth century AD), who had developed the standard Christian interpretation of man's uprightness.[26] But Ovid's version is the *locus classicus* of this idea in poetry, and similarities in phrasing confirm Milton's indebtedness:

> There wanted yet the master work, the end
> Of all yet done, a creature who, not prone
> And brute as other creatures, but endued
> With sanctity of reason, might erect
> His stature, and upright with front serene
> Govern the rest, self-knowing, and from thence
> Magnanimous to correspond with heaven
> But grateful to acknowledge whence his good
> Descends, thither with heart and voice and eyes
> Directed in devotion to adore
> And worship God supreme, who made him chief
> Of all his works. (*PL* VII. 505–16)

A creature more holy than these and more capable of lofty thought and suitable to have dominion over the rest was still lacking; then man was born . . . and although all other creatures look down prone on the ground, to man he gave a face uplifted and bade him see the sky and lift his erected face to the stars. (*Met.* I. 76–86)

In the main Milton is content to follow the standard analogies between the Bible and *Metamorphoses* I. There is, however, one surprise. The virtuous Deucalion who, with his wife Pyrrha, was allowed to survive the Flood, was normally associated with Noah (although some, including Golding, argued that Deucalion's flood was a second deluge, later than Noah's). Milton, however, links Deucalion and Pyrrha with Adam and Eve (XI. 8–14):

> yet their port
> Not of mean suitors nor important less
> Seemed their petition than when the ancient pair

In fables old, less ancient yet than these,
Deucalion and chaste Pyrrha to restore
The race of mankind drowned before the shrine
Of Themis stood devout.

The comparison is a curious one, and was censured by the great classical scholar Richard Bentley (1662–1742) as 'rubbish and rags': 'It was very instructive to tell us that the Flood was not as ancient and early as the Creation. But was the man bewitched with his "old fables but not so old as these"? Is Adam and Eve's history an old fable too, by this editor's own insinuation?' Bentley, who will stand as my main example of a neoclassical and anti-Ovidian sensibility, in his notorious edition of *Paradise Lost* (1732) argues, or pretends to argue, that the poem is full of errors and interpolations introduced by an ignorant editor. 'Sense' is restored by massive deletion and emendation.[27] Bentley is right to alert us to the oddity of the simile but wrong to condemn it on that account. In fact the effect of the simile is to introduce a flavour of ancientness which only rarely surrounds Milton's voluble and far from primitive Adam and Eve. The simile also stresses, at precisely the point where it becomes significant, the intense isolation of the pair, a strong feature of Ovid's story. This shift in perspective matters as much as the ostensible point of comparison (the dignity and importance of the prayer), and is comparable with the impact of the more evocative simile in which the partly clothed Adam and Eve are related to the American Indians seen by Columbus (IX. 1115ff):

such of late
Columbus found the American so girt
With feathered cincture, naked else and wild
Among the trees on isles and woody shores.

I have already commented briefly on Milton's use of Ovid's description of the Flood. Not only does he moderate Ovid's flamboyance, but he employs a greater economy, in this too more like Virgil than Ovid, who was notorious for never knowing when to stop. Thus Ovid's neatly witty but repetitive

iamque mare et tellus nullum discrimen habebant;
omnia pontus erat, deerant quoque litora ponto    (I. 291–2)

well rendered by Sandys

> Now land and sea no different visage bore;
> For all was sea, nor had the sea a shore

becomes the more compressed 'sea covered sea / Sea without shore'
(XI. 749–50). The classicising Addison was duly impressed:

> If our poet has imitated that verse in which Ovid tells us that
> there was nothing but sea, and that this sea had no shore to it, he
> has not set the thought in such a light as to incur the censure
> which critics have passed upon it. The latter part of that verse in
> Ovid is idle and superfluous, but just and beautiful in Milton.[28]

Likewise the personification of the south wind as a winged creature:

> Meanwhile the south wind rose, and with black wings
> Wide hovering all the clouds together drove
> From under heaven   (XI. 738–40)

is less of a set piece than Ovid's more extended and particularised
description from which it derives (I. 264–9, Dryden):

> The South he loosed who night and horror brings,
> And fogs are shaken from his flaggy wings;
> From his divided beard two streams he pours,
> His head and rheumy eyes distil in showers;
> With rain his robe and heavy mantle flow,
> And lazy mists are louring on his brow;
> Still as he swept along with his clenched fist
> He squeezed the clouds, the imprisoned clouds resist.

Thus, while Harding is certainly right to draw our attention to the
extent of Milton's indebtedness, the sensibility revealed in these
imitations is not altogether Ovidian, and I believe that we must look
elsewhere in *Paradise Lost* for a more profound and significant
Ovidianism.[29]

### Proserpina

The allegorical tradition glimmers behind one of the most famous
passages in *Paradise Lost* (IV. 268–86):

## Ovid

Not that fair field
Of Enna, where Proserpine gathering flowers
Herself a fairer flower by gloomy Dis
Was gathered, which cost Ceres all that pain
To seek her through the world; nor that sweet grove
Of Daphne by Orontes and the inspired
Castalian spring might with this Paradise
Of Eden strive; nor that Nyseian isle
Girt with the river Triton, where old Cham,
Whom Gentiles Ammon call and Lybian Jove,
Hid Amalthea and her florid son
Young Bacchus from his stepdame Rhea's eye;
Nor where Abassin kings their issue guard,
Mount Amara, though this by some supposed
True Paradise under the Ethiop line
By Nilus' head, enclosed with shining rock,
A whole day's journey high, but wide remote
From this Assyrian garden, where the fiend
Saw undelighted all delight . . .

Ovid treats the story of Proserpina twice, once in the *Metamorphoses* (V. 385ff), and again in the *Fasti* (IV. 417ff). Milton obviously knew both accounts, and presumably too *De Raptu Proserpinae*, an unfinished epic on the rape by Claudian (*c.* 370 to *c.* 404), the last truly classical poet of antiquity. Though the writing is compact in a not quite Ovidian way, both the wit — the play on 'flower' — and the careful rhetorical patterning owe something to Ovid. Milton also shows how well he understands the Ovidian conventions. Frequently in the *Metamorphoses* the beautiful, idealised landscape settings, examples of what scholars call the *locus amoenus*, are the prelude to acts of sexual violence, while the plucking of flowers has an obvious sexual implication.[30] Milton too is preparing for the irruption of violence in the person of Satan and for the 'rape' of Eve; throughout Book IX there is a strong hint that Satan is seducing Eve, while the Fall includes the corruption of innocent sexuality.

The Proserpina image comes close to the medieval allegorical Ovid, for Milton is using the myth typologically to prefigure the Fall. In Book IX, when Satan sees Eve, she is picking flowers, 'mindless the while / Herself, though fairest unsupported flower' (431–2), and earlier she is compared to Ceres 'Yet virgin of Proserpina from Jove' (396), still unravished. In the traditional allegorisation Proserpina represents the Human Soul, Pluto the Devil, Ceres the Church or sometimes Christ, and the flowers worldly goods; nowhere that I have found does the story seem to be read as a type of Eve's fall. Sandys does come close, but even he is tentative: 'Proserpina having eaten seven grains of a pomegranate, a fatal liquorishness which retains her in hell; as the apple thrust Evah out of Paradise, whereunto it is held to have a relation . . .' Milton almost certainly was inspired, not by Ovid commentaries, but by one of his favourite poets, Dante. In *Purgatorio* XXVIII Dante sees the lovely Matelda (a mysterious figure, who appears to be a representative both of the Active Life and the unfallen Eve) picking flowers at the top of Mount Purgatory in a beautiful springtime landscape. It is always spring in the Earthly Paradise, and one phrase in Ovid's description of the fair field of Enna seems to link it with his Golden Age, widely regarded as the pagan equivaient of the Earthly Paradise (I. 107 'ver erat aeternum' — there was eternal spring = V. 391 'perpetuum ver est'; cf. *PL* IV. 268 'the eternal spring', just before the Proserpina passage). It was perhaps this self-echo in Ovid that led Dante to associate the rape of Proserpina with the loss of the Earthly Paradise. At all events in lines 49–51 Dante explicitly compares Matelda with Proserpina, thereby associating her with the prelapsarian Eve:

Tu mi fai rimembrar dove e qual era
Proserpina nel tempo che perdette
la madre lei, ed ella primavera.

(You make me recall where and what was Proserpina at the time when her mother lost her, and she the spring)

Shelley in his translation of this canto combines Dante and Milton:

like Proserpine
Thou seemest to my fancy, singing here
And gathering flowers, at that time when
She lost the spring and Ceres her . . . more dear.

The conjunction shows that Shelley understood the point of the comparison, even if, as Dorothy Sayers observes, in Shelley the human and allegorical levels are not as perfectly fused as they are in Dante. In Dante the twofold loss *is* the loss of Paradise; Shelley's additional point that a mother's love for her daughter matters more than the loss of the spring only distracts.[31] That Dante's application of the myth was unusual is suggested by the failure of Benvenuto da Imola, one of the best of the early commentators on the *Divine Comedy*, to explain the allusion correctly. He mentions two allegorical interpretations of the myth, both 'physical', that is allegories of processes in the natural world, and neither in the least relevant. Milton at any rate was not deceived.

Behind Proserpina and Dis (Pluto) we may thus discern Eve and Satan. The typology indeed matters more than the ostensible point of comparison. Some would go further and understand Ceres as a type of Christ. Nothing in the poem encourages the connection, and, as we have seen, it is wrong to treat Milton's similes as diagrams in which tenor and vehicle must correspond exactly. After the glittering language of the opening there is some change of style for the final phrase 'which cost Ceres all that pain / To seek her through the world'. Most critics find pathos here, although K.W. Gransden suggests that 'all that pain' may rather be dismissive of the mythological *longueurs* of Ovid's narrative of Ceres' search.[32] (An objection to his view is that even the most cursory glance at a concordance will show that 'all' is a powerful word in Milton.) However on either interpretation there seems some extra pressure of reality, so that rape and loss can no longer simply be concealed behind an elegant conceit about the gathering of flowers.

Bentley disliked the whole passage IV. 268–86, arguing for deletion:

> How could the editor find in his heart to part these clauses so lovingly united with an insertion of seventeen lines? With a silly thought in the whole, and as sillily conducted in its several parts. 'Not Enna,' says he, 'not Daphne, nor *fons Castalius*, nor Nysa nor mount Amara could compare with paradise.' Why who, sir, would suspect they could, though you had never told us it? And then . . . you give us their bare names, with some fabulous story to them, not denoting at all any beauty . . . Where your woman-flower is but fit for a madrigal and the rest has a meanness of style contemptible.

Though crass, this criticism is marked by a perverse intelligence. Bentley has noticed that the lines on Proserpina herself are stylistically remote both from anything approaching an epic norm, and from the other comparisons in the series. He has also observed the odd effect of the use of negative comparisons. It is possible to find analogies in classical poetry. Ovid and Lucan are both fond of what might be termed negative description, the description of something in terms of what it is not. The ironic Horace delights in all sorts of negativities, including poems refusing the demands of importunate patrons for celebration in a grand work (scholars call such a poem of refusal a *recusatio*). In *Odes* I. 38. 3–4 he tells his slave 'mitte sectari, rosa quo locorum / sera moretur' (don't hunt for where the late rose lingers). It is wrong to complain (as I have seen done) of Horace's puritanism in dismissing his great baroque image; the simultaneous evocation and rejection of the lingering rose creates a complex mood of checked sensuality which is of indubitable power. The effect in Milton is comparable. Ostensibly Milton's lines constitute an example of what is called 'outdoing': the fair field of Enna was not so fair as Paradise. Spenser handles the figure in the orthodox way when he compares the Bower of Bliss with other famous beauty spots including Tempe and Parnassus ('More sweet and wholesome than the pleasant hill / Of Rhodope . . .', etc.) in *Faerie Queene* II. 12.52. However in Milton it is possible to hear, as a subaudition, a suggestion that such things as the rape of Proserpina never happened. The length of the sentence, the delay before the main verb and the firm thump of the initial 'not' create a sense of disorientation in which the Proserpina comparison becomes momentarily distanced from the immediate point of reference (the comparative splendours of various gardens), and is presented with a strong negative emphasis. The effect of the characteristic Miltonic modulation, from lyricism to scorn, in the description of Paradise under discussion is somewhat analogous to the rhetorical movement of the Mulciber passage analysed in Chapter 2. The precarious lyric beauty of the opening gives way to drier comparisons, and finally to the scornful, mocking pedantry of the close. The pagan house of cards has been laboriously constructed for the purposes of demolition; beauty is evoked, then undermined.

Since Milton is often though of as our prime classicist, it is worth insisting that his evocation of the Proserpina story is not quite 'classical' in feeling (in the normal stylistic sense of the word). A comparison with some lines in *The Winter's Tale*, which Milton may well have had in mind, should make this clear (IV. iv. 113–24):

I would I had some flowers o' th' spring, that might
Become your time of day, and yours, and yours,
That wear upon your virgin branches yet
Your maidenheads growing; O Proserpina,
For the flowers now, that, frighted, thou let'st fall
From Dis's waggon! daffodils,
That come before the swallow dares, and take
The winds of March with beauty; violets, dim,
But sweeter than the lids of Juno's eyes
Or Cytherea's breath; pale primroses,
That die unmarried, ere they can behold
Bright Phoebus in his strength.

For all the lyricism Shakespeare's classicism is a sturdy thing ('Dis's waggon' brings the allusion into an English present as firmly as happens to classical stories in Golding, or in *Venus and Adonis*).[33] By contrast Milton as it were sees the myth through a romantic, shimmering haze, and recreates it with a desperate sweetness which proclaims its precariousness.

In *Paradise Regained* II. 292ff Milton describes 'a pleasant grove', which 'to a superstitious eye' would seem 'the haunt / Of wood-gods and wood-nymphs'. (The whole description is interestingly Ovidian: 'nature taught art' briefly echoes a characteristic Ovidian antithesis, e.g. *Met*. III. 158f 'simulaverat artem / ingenio natura suo,' nature had feigned art by her own cunning; XI. 235f). One wonders what superstitious eyes, likely to peruse learned poetry, were left in seventeenth-century England to be misled by such pagan feigning. One possible answer is Milton himself, or at any rate a part of Milton himself. In the 'Nativity Ode', in the description of the pagan deities routed at the Incarnation, he had shown considerable imaginative insight into the power of rival religious systems. One verse (stanza 20) is especially striking:

The lonely mountains o'er,
And the resounding shore,
    A voice of weeping heard and loud lament;
From haunted spring and dale
Edged with poplar pale
    The parting genius is with sighing sent;
With flower-inwoven tresses torn
The nymphs in twilight shade of tangled thickets mourn.

There is a lack here of any pejorative adjectives, or of anything to run counter to the prevailing note of pathos and even tragedy. This is the more remarkable if those scholars are right who see an allusion to the slaughter of the Innocents in Matthew 2: 18, where Jeremiah is quoted: 'In Rama there was a voice heard, lamentation, and weeping, and great mourning.' Toward the close the ode lurches oddly away from Christianity with the evocative lines on 'the yellow-skirted fays'. Milton's feeling for the power of 'fables' seems to have been of unusual proportions.

In 'The Grail Mass' David Jones criticises Milton for his dismissal of paganism in the ode; in Catholic worship, he argues, Ceres, Bacchus and the Naiads find their proper fulfilment in bread, wine and water:

Inclined in the midst of the instruments
and invoking the life-giving persons
and in honour of the former witnesses
*et istorum*, dusty in the cist
he kisses the place of sepulture.

He turns to ask of the living.
Those round about answer him.
He turns again and immediately
            toward the tokens.

He continues and in silence
inclined over the waiting creatures
of tillage and of shower.

Ceres and Liber and
the dancing naiad
have heard his: Come who makes holy
and now and so still
            between the horns of the *mensa*
they wait awhile
his: ratify, accept, approve.

You are his special signs
and you'll be doubly *signa*
before he's at the *Unde et memores*.

177

O no, not flee away
but wait his word
not to th'infernal jail
(as blind makers
in harmonic numbers tell)
not troop off, not you, nor
Peor's baalim
but wait on him.
Yes, brutish you
but you his forerunners
each of you, his *figura*.
Need peculiar powers forgo their stalls?
He's no douser of dim tapers
and why should Anubis hasten
except to glast the freeing of the waters.
So stay
but when they sing
QUI VENIT
here all of you
kneel
every Lar of you
numen or tutelar
from *terra, pontus* and the air
or from the strait bathysphere.[34]

It would indeed be easy to contrast Milton's Protestant rejection
unfavourably with Jones's Catholic openness to universal experi-
ence, whereby paganism can be redeemed as well as transcended.
Certainly a long and noble tradition of accommodation lies behind
Jones's poem, an accommodation which seeks to answer the
familiar stern question 'What has Athens to do with Jerusalem?' by
arguing that Christ perfects the world into which he came, a world
that was Greco-Roman as much as Jewish. This is none other than
the old doctrine of the *praeparatio evangelii*, the gradual making
ready of the world for the Incarnation. Yet Milton's austerity also
has a noble ancestry, going back at least to St Jerome who once
dreamed that God accused him of being a Ciceronian not a
Christian, and it could be argued that there is something
sentimental, even cosy in Jones's all too easy assimilations. Milton,
with his far greater knowledge of the classical world, could see more
clearly the difficulty of reconciling Athens and Jerusalem. In the

stanza on the nymphs in the ode, and elsewhere in Milton's poetry, paganism is valued with a special intensity precisely because, ultimately, it must be surrendered. To understand Milton's attitude one could compare the end of Evelyn Waugh's *Brideshead Revisited*, where Julia gives up her adulterous relationship with Charles Ryder because she takes it so seriously. Choices have sometimes to be made, nor is Milton necessarily to be criticised for thinking so.

For Milton classical story is untrue and belongs to a vanished world, but such false surmise may offer a little ease to the dreaming poet. While it is doubtless right to claim that Eliot's famous doctrine of 'the dissociation of sensibility' is in essence a Symbolist myth,[35] nevertheless some dissociation does seem characteristic of Milton. Keats puts the point brilliantly:

> The genius of Milton, more particularly in respect to its span in immensity, calculated him, by a sort of birthright, for such an 'argument' as the Paradise Lost: he had an exquisite passion for what is properly, in the sense of ease and pleasure, poetical luxury; and with that it appears to me he would fain have been content, if he could, so doing, have preserved his self-respect and feel of duty performed; but there was working in him as it were that same sort of thing as operates in the great world to the end of a prophecy's being accomplished; therefore he devoted himself rather to the ardours than the pleasures of song, solacing himself at intervals with cups of old wine; and those are with some exceptions the finest parts of the poem. With some exceptions — for the spirit of mounting and adventure can never be unfruitful or unrewarded; had he not broken through the clouds which envelop so deliciously the Elysian field of verse, and committed himself to the extreme, we should never have seen Satan as described —
> 'But his face
> Deep scars of thunder had entrenched', &c.[36]

As a result of this doubleness in his attitude to paganism Milton anticipates certain aspects of Romantic sensibility. We are not so far from Wordsworth's feelings about 'old Triton', and we can see why Keats was enthralled by the Proserpina image. It is interesting that Milton should have helped to pioneer this response to classical myth, since he contributed to a similar sensibility about the Middle

Ages, neo-Gothic rather than Gothic as we might put it, witness the famous lines in 'Il Penseroso' (155–60):

But let my due feet never fail,
To walk the studious cloister's pale,
And love the high embowed roof,
With antique pillars' massy proof,
And storied windows richly dight,
Casting a dim religious light.

Here we have a feeling for vague numinousness that is a feature of the Romantic response to the Gothic and which still affects us today (as was illustrated by the opposition to the cleaning of King's College Chapel in Cambridge), a response alien to the precision and elaboration with which the buildings were originally conceived. Milton's response to church architecture and to religion itself seems in this passage curiously aesthetic. In particular, the phrase 'dim religious light' (whether 'religious' means 'appropriate to religion', as OED and the commentators suppose, or rather 'connected with a religious order') oddly suggests an almost post-Christian sensibility, or at least a strange aesthetic detachment. At all events, it goes beyond the feeling for Gothic ruins (partly a reaction to the effects of the dissolutions at the Reformation) which is characteristic of the period.

Ovid is evidently an important source for Milton's response to classical 'fable'. In his early Latin poem Elegy V, 'In Adventum Veris' (On the Coming of Spring) Milton had recreated, without apology, the sensuous world of Ovidian myth, and indeed increased its lushness. In *Paradise Lost*, the same impulse can be felt, though now no longer wholly unashamed. For example in XI. 126ff Milton alludes to the Ovidian story of Argus. (In the tale of Io, who is transformed into a heifer by her lover Jupiter to evade the jealous Juno, the hundred-eyed Argus is set as guardian by Juno to watch the heifer, but is lulled to sleep and beheaded by Mercury, *Met.* I. 583ff):

the archangelic power prepared
For swift descent, with him the cohort bright
Of watchful cherubim; four faces each
Had, like a double Janus, all their shape
Spangled with eyes more numerous than those

Of Argus, and more wakeful than to drowse,
Charmed with Arcadian pipe, the pastoral reed
Of Hermes, or his opiate rod. Meanwhile
To resalute the world with sacred light
Leucothea waked, and with fresh dews embalmed
The earth . . .

In his comment on Milton's lines Bentley again senses his quarry:
'But our editor had such an itching to mix fable with the most serious
matter that he could not but insert Janus' faces and Argus' eyes and
Mercury's pipe. A great character indeed of the cherubim that they
were more wakeful than a country cow-herd Argus. And note the
fine expression: "more wakeful than to drowse", more vocal than to
be mute, more white than to be black.' Milton's point is presumably
precisely that the Biblical cherubim were free of the shortcomings of
the pagan Argus who was eventually cheated into sleep; but Bentley
certainly alerts us to the oddly relaxed quality of the writing—this is
the closest that we shall come to the Milton of the anti-Miltonists, in
love with sound at the expense of sense — and the combination of
syntactic looseness with the vocabulary ('spangled', 'drowse',
'charmed', 'opiate', 'embalmed') brings us curiously close to Keats
or Shelley.[37] The effect is both like and unlike Ovid, but it does
suggest that Ovid contributed something vital to the structure of
Milton's imagination.

## Orpheus

The story of Proserpina may have had a special significance for
Milton, since, in a letter to his close friend Charles Diodati, he uses
Ceres' search for her daughter as an image of the poet's pursuit of
the idea of the beautiful.[38] Elsewhere Milton uses an Ovidian myth
in an even more obviously personal way. The story of Orpheus had
always appealed to him,[39] and in 'Lycidas' (58ff) he uses it as a focus
for his fears about the poet's insecurity. Some critics, wrongly in my
view, read the passage 'allegorically', finding in it a glimmering of
Christ's redemptive suffering. That the Orpheus-Christ equation
would indeed have been familiar to Milton and his readers is shown
by, for example, this passage from Alexander Ross:

> Christ is the true Orpheus, who by the sweetness and force of his
> evangelical music caused the gentiles, who before were stocks
> and stones in knowledge, and no better than beasts in religion, to

follow after him; it was he only who went down to hell to recover the church his spouse, who had lost herself . . . What was in vain attempted by Orpheus was truly performed by our saviour, for he alone hath delivered our souls from the nethermost hell; and at last was he torn with whips and thorns, and pierced with nails and a spear, upon the cross, for our transgressions.

However nothing in Milton's lines convincingly suggests the Passion. This section of 'Lycidas' is concerned with the powerlessness of the poet, and the particular quality of the lines with their intense personal anguish tells against the allegorisers. Moreover Christ's earthly sufferings do not appear to have moved Milton very deeply at any stage of his poetic career. He sensibly abandoned his early poem on the Passion which conveys only ersatz emotion, while the life of Christ in *Paradise Lost* XII is one of the driest passages in the entire work, the lines on the Crucifixion are almost brutally insensitive ('But to the cross he nails thy enemies', 415), and it is only the Resurrection which seems to fire Milton's imagination: 'ere the third dawning light / Return, the stars of morn shall see him rise / Out of his grave, fresh as the dawning light' (421–3).

The prologue to Book VII lends further support to the view that Orpheus had a personal rather than religious significance for Milton. For 39 lines, like a dog worrying a bone, Milton explains how the Muse he invokes is not one of the pagan nine, but the true Heavenly Muse. The climax is reached when Milton uses the story of Orpheus *against* paganism (32–9):

> But drive far off the barbarous dissonance
> Of Bacchus and his revellers, the race
> Of that wild rout that tore the Thracian bard
> In Rhodope, where woods and rocks had ears
> To rapture, till the savage clamour drowned
> Both harp and voice; nor could the Muse defend
> Her son. So fail not thou, who thee implores —
> For thou art heavenly, she an empty dream.

The tortuous illogic of the lines is almost as remarkable as their extraordinary emotional power. The argument would make strict logical sense only if Orpheus' death were in some sense true, which Milton denies.

The story of Orpheus was so well known that we cannot be sure that Ovid was the source, particularly since Virgil gives an incomparable account of the myth in *Georgics* IV. Nevertheless it is significant that what moves Milton is not so much Orpheus' loss of his wife Eurydice, the focus of Virgil's account — though Milton makes graceful, relaxed use of this in 'L'Allegro' 145–50 — as his death and dismemberment at the hands of the Maenads, which is described in detail in *Metamorphoses* XI. 1ff. In Ovid's version Orpheus cannot be killed until the clamour drowns the music of his lyre (before that the weapons merely fall beguiled at his feet), and this detail seems to lie behind lines 35–7. Milton probably wrote the passage shortly after the Restoration at a time when some of his former colleagues were being dismembered by the restored Royalists, and he himself was potentially in grave danger as one who had endorsed regicide; his old fears that the blind Fury might pre-empt his great task must have returned to him with peculiar strength. Traditional moral and allegorical readings of the myth are thus irrelevant. Golding thought the death of Orpheus a punishment for sexual incontinence (Epistle, 224–5), while to Sandys Orpheus represented 'the life of philosophy' and the Bacchants 'the heady rage of mutiny and sedition'. For Milton, however, Orpheus is simply the inspired bard who could not save himself and who in the world of paganism could not be saved, a figure for Milton as he might have been without grace.

Not surprisingly, in view of their Romantic quality, Keats selected these lines as one of the two finest poetic moments in *Paradise Lost*, the other being the Proserpina comparison:

There are two specimens of a very extraordinary beauty in the Paradise Lost; they are of a nature, as far as I have read, unexampled elsewhere — they are entirely distinct from the brief pathos of Dante — and they are not to be found even in Shakespeare — these are according to the great prerogative of poetry better described in themselves than by a volume. The one is in the fol [lowing] — 'which cost Ceres all that pain' — the other is that ending 'Nor could the Muse defend her son' — they appear exclusively Miltonic without the shadow of another mind ancient or modern.

Furthermore in the lines that conclude the Orpheus passage 'dream' is an almost Keatsian touch, and significantly the stalwart Bentley proposed emending to the more logical 'name'. The passage shows how deeply Milton engaged with classical mythology, and the word 'dream' points to the source of its power and its ultimate dissatisfactions. The Miltonic poet was in part a dreamer, as two beautiful lines from 'L'Allegro' show (129–30): 'Such sights as youthful poets dream / On summer eves by haunted stream' (cf. 'II Penseroso' 147–8). Yet what he dreams could be elusive and unsatisfying, as much an escape from, as a release into, reality. The clash between Milton's Platonism and his Hebraism is strongly felt at such moments; in *Paradise Regained* it is largely resolved, but at tremendous poetic cost.

## Baucis and Philemon

As I have already observed, the loss of a deep natural familiarity with classical texts has often resulted in a preoccupation with supposed verbal allusions, at the expense of more widely diffused influence in matters of style and decorum. Two scenes in *Paradise Lost* are marked by a potent Ovidian presence, without signalling the debt by way either of close imitation or specific reference to a myth, and neither as it happens has won the whole-hearted acceptance of the critics. In Book V Raphael is entertained by Adam and Eve to a vegetarian meal that might remind gourmets of the *nouvelle cuisine* — Eve does not believe in adulterating flavours (334–5). The episode has embarrassed some of the poet's friends, and one infamous detail aroused snorts of derision from Bentley. The scene is what is called a *theoxenia*, the entertainment of a god by a mortal, and the Old Testament provides important models, particularly Abraham's reception of the three angels (Genesis 18), which Milton calls to our mind when Adam sits at the door of his bower sheltering from the sun (299–300 = verse 1). But the Biblical account is somewhat lacking in fullness of detail, and Milton did not so much want a feeling of numinously mysterious visitation as to show man and angel on a familiar footing.

The *locus classicus* (if the mild pun may be forgiven) for a poetic *theoxenia* is Ovid's story of Philemon and Baucis in *Metamorphoses* VIII. 611ff. In Ovid's story, set in Phrygia, Jupiter and Mercury decide to test the piety of mortals by visiting them in disguise. Rejected by all other men they are properly entertained only by the aged Baucis and Philemon, who prepare as lavish a meal as they can from their modest resources. The gods reveal themselves, destroy the other men in the area by drowning them in a flood and reward the old couple by granting them their wish that they may eventually die together. The story was popular in the seventeenth century, and there are splendid versions of scenes from it by Adam Elsheimer and Rembrandt, the latter employing a similar iconography to that in his painting of Christ's revelation of himself to his disciples at Emmaus. Rubens not only produced a painting of the scene in the cottage, now lost, but also painted a different episode, the flight of Baucis and Philemon with the two gods to the mountain top; this flamboyant composition is a variant of traditional scenes of the Flood.[40] In Ovid the story is given a moral framework and a clear moral direction, but it is also a fairy story with an exotic eastern setting, touched with magic at its close when the two old people are turned into trees simultaneously. Much of the tale is given over to 'genre' description and to bourgeois comedy in the manner of Callimachus, which helps to explain its popularity with north-European artists. Renaissance commentators spell out the morality: hospitality is pleasing to God. Philemon and Baucis represent, according to Sandys, 'the patterns of chaste and constant conjugal affections, as of content in poverty . . . A condition as full of innocency as security'. Biblical analogues are also cited: Paul and Barnabas at Lystra mistaken for gods (Acts 14: 8ff), Lot and the angels in Genesis 19 (Sandys speculates that Ovid's story might have been taken from there), and the famous verse from the Epistle to the Hebrews 13: 2: 'Be not forgetful to entertain strangers, for thereby some have entertained angels unawares.' But, unusually, Ovid's wit also aroused comment. Sabinus notes that the tale is told humorously, and even speculates that Philemon may have been modelled by Ovid on his own bailiff; according to Sandys the story is 'most conceitedly expressed by our wittiest of authors', a rare observation of this kind in his commentary. Ovid lovingly describes the preparation of a simple meal in the couple's humble hut, and a comic climax is reached when Philemon and Baucis attempt to catch their goose to sacrifice it to Jupiter. As Dryden gives it in his version (scarcely inferior to the original):

> One goose they had — 'twas all they could allow —
> A wakeful sentry and on duty now,
> Whom to the gods for sacrifice they vow.
> Her with malicious zeal the couple viewed;
> She ran for life and limping they pursued.
> Full well the fowl perceived their bad intent
> And would not make her masters compliment,

But persecuted to the powers she flies
And close between the legs of Jove she lies.

('Baucis and Philemon', 130–8)

In one respect, perhaps deliberately to be remarked on by the sophisticated reader, Milton alters the Ovidian (and Biblical) pattern. Raphael comes undisguised and is not entertained unawares. The unfallen Adam and Eve neither need nor receive a testing, and meet their angel guest on equal terms; hence almost a casualness in the encounter, a lack of awe and mystery, however richly described the visitant may be. In the details of the scene Milton shows his perfect understanding of the Ovidian conventions, while adapting the various motifs to the vegetarian conditions of Paradise, and making the humour less broad. He combines the exotic, the angel — 'another morn / Risen on mid-noon', as Adam puts it, 310–11 — and the spicy forest where 'nature . . . wantoned as in her prime . . . enormous bliss' (294–7) with the homely and domestic as Eve busies herself preparing dinner. Adam and Eve behave as beseems a good bourgeois couple, and have an amusing exchange about stores (308ff); Adam assumes that Eve as a good housewife keeps food ready, while Eve not unreasonably points out that there is little need for stores in Paradise. It would be idle to suppose that Milton himself missed the humour of this conversation, any more than in the case of his splendid if notorious comment on the picnic, 'No fear lest dinner cool' (396), with its jab of social satire, where the heavy Miltonic wit unjustly aroused from Bentley wit yet heavier: 'If the devils want feeding, our author made poor provision for them in his second book, where they have nothing to eat but hell-fire, and no danger of their dinner cooling' (note on V. 415). Even the normally sober Fowler is moved to wit at this point: 'Thyer thought *superfluous moist* too philosophical for Eve, but it seems quite appropriate for an intelligent woman to have technical knowledge about food storage. Eve was in no position to leave such things to the servants.'

In the account of the meal Milton balances simplicity, good housekeeping — for example the moralised vessels (348) — and frugality ('frugal storing', 324), as required by certain aspects of his puritan philosophy and suggested by the Ovidian story, with the sheer abundance of Paradise and with a feast of great richness. Fruits may be frugal fare, but the fruits of Paradise are fit for a feast; the equivocation (if it is such) perfectly suits the in one sense unimaginable unfallen condition which Milton points to so skilfully (337–44):

> . . . and from each tender stalk
> Whatever Earth all-bearing mother yields
> In India east or west or middle shore,
> In Pontus or the Punic coast, or where
> Alcinous reigned, fruit of all kinds, in coat,
> Rough or smooth rined, or bearded husk, or shell
> She gathers, tribute large, and on the board
> Heaps with unsparing hand . . .

The primitivism of the alfresco dinner arrangements with a table of 'grassy turf' (391–2) and 'mossy seats' (392) is offset by the fullness and glamour of 'And on her ample square from side to side / All autumn piled, though spring and autumn here / Danced hand in hand' (393–5). The story of Philemon and Baucis, at once exotic and humorously homely, is found unusually agreeable by most readers of Ovid, but Milton's analogous combination has not proved so popular.[41] It can, however, be defended. Paradise is at once ordinary and wondrous, and if that is not our imagining, then the poet might complain of our moral attitudes as much as of our literary tastes.

Here, as elsewhere, Milton affronts the fastidious by his extreme physicalism and his refusal to retreat into vagueness. An example is the way that he insists, provocatively, on Eve's nakedness throughout the scene. After a witticism about Eve's being undecked save with her own beauty and the comparison with the naked goddesses at the Judgement of Paris (379ff), we have the angelic salutation prefiguring the Annunciation 'Hail mother of mankind', startling, even incongruous, in such a context; the resulting iconographic clash produces a kind of *frisson*. Later Milton observes, dangerously, that Raphael might well have been (though he was not) enamoured by the naked Eve as the sons of God later were by the daughters of men (443ff). Equally marked is the concreteness of the description of Raphael descending and of the dinner arrangements, and the insistence on the actuality of angelic appetite and digestion: 'what redounds, transpires / Through spirits with ease' (438–9). The combination of grandeur and theatricality with a kind of hyper-realism (linked, in Milton's case, with the sheer intellectual obstinacy that leads him to pursue such matters as angelic digestion, a habit of mind everywhere revealed in *De Doctrina Christiana*) is an important aspect of the baroque sensibility, and a further link between the imaginations of Ovid and Milton. Admittedly Ovid's concreteness tends to be used for more frivolous ends. For example in the Phaethon story Apollo wears a crown of rays which he has to take off to allow his son to approach (*Met.* II. 40–2; Milton's imitation, III. 625–6, is far more sober). The zodiac through which the chariot passes is alive with actualised beasts; the poison of the normally torpid Serpent is warmed and thus activated by the proximity of the fiery chariot (*Met* II. 173ff).

What is sometimes found offensive in Milton is admired if we turn to the sister art of painting. In the Galleria Doria-Pamphili is a painting by Caravaggio of 'The Rest on the Flight into Egypt'.[42] An elegant and sexually provocative (if androgynous) angel stands with his back to us. He has immensely solid bird-like wings, and plays a precisely rendered violin, as Joseph holds out some sheet music with a lullaby, which can in fact be transcribed. The picture is not quite a masterpiece, but the concreteness points clearly forward to the great triumphs ahead. Milton's Italian visit doubtless helped to foster this aspect of his sensibility, but Ovid as the most 'baroque' of the great Latin poets will also have played his part.

Furthermore, parallels for the vividly concrete cosmic imaginings of *Paradise Lost* are provided both by baroque painting and by Ovid, especially the Phaethon story, with which Milton was evidently deeply involved. In the description of the fall of Mulciber the comparison with a falling star, although referred by one editor to Theocritus, *Idyll* XIII. 50–1, was surely partly suggested by some lines in *Metamorphoses* II (321–2):

fertur ut interdum de caelo stella sereno
etsi non cecidit, potuit cecidisse videri.

([Phaethon] is carried along, as sometimes a star from a clear sky, even if it has not fallen, still gives the appearance of having fallen.)

Ovid's Phaethon was often linked with Lucifer so that he would naturally come to Milton's mind. Imitation of Homer here fuses with memory of Ovid and of the famous verse from Isaiah, 'How art thou fallen from heaven, o Lucifer, son of the morning!' The style, too, is richer than Homer's, so that we may say that Milton Ovidianises Homer.

## Metamorphosis

Whatever is thought of it as an ensemble, Milton's *theoxenia* undoubtedly contains some of his finest writing. A second episode that would have been seen as Ovidian in overall character is deliberately one-dimensional. In Book X. 504ff Milton turns to the metamorphosis theme itself, to describe how Satan and the fallen angels are changed to snakes and forced to eat bitter ashes. The scene, as Waldock observed, is characterised by a grand-style version of a 'comic cartoon' technique.[43] It might be possible to complain that Milton's most glamorous creation is given his come-uppance with too great ease. However, the ludicrous discomfiture of the villain at the very moment of his apparent triumph has been carefully calculated. In Book IX, to seduce Eve, Satan makes his supreme effort, recovering, in his serpent form, much of his original glamour. The lovely description of his progress towards her 'With burnished neck of verdant gold, erect / Amidst his circling spires' (501–2) perfectly expresses his self-satisfaction and vanity. But, like Iago and other Renaissance literary villains, the deed done he is necessarily deflated ('Back to the thicket slunk / The guilty serpent', 783–4), and his speech on his return is the emptiest of bombast. The style of the peripeteia that follows is thus in accordance with the demands of decorum, the grand masterpiece to observe.

Milton successfully catches the grotesqueness and humour of many Ovidian transformations, but his response to the actual process of change in this episode is less poetically urgent than his master's. As we have seen, classical scholars sometimes suggest that the theme of metamorphosis is to Ovid only a pretext to afford a semblance of unity to his poem, not at the true centre of his concerns; yet the virtuoso descriptions of change are almost always beautifully handled, like the lines on Daphne changing into a laurel which Dryden gives thus (I. 742–53):

> Scarce had she finished, when her feet she found
> Benumbed with cold and fastened to the ground;
> A filmy rind about her body grows,
> Her hair to leaves, her arms extend to boughs.
> The nymph is all into a laurel gone,
> The smoothness of her skin remains alone.

Yet Phoebus loves her still, and, casting round
Her bole his arms, some little warmth he found.
The tree still panted in the unfinished part,
Not wholly vegetive, and heaved her heart.
He fixed his lips upon the trembling rind;
It swerved aside and his embrace declined.

Apollo promises that Daphne will be his tree, and in response 'the
laurel waved her new-made branches and seemed to move her
head-like top in full consent' ('factis modo laurea ramis / adnuit,
utque caput visa est agitasse cacumen', I. 566–7). The moving
equivocation — is this a genuine human gesture of assent, or just a
tree waving in the wind? — is at once delicate and slightly wistful,
and such delicacies are certainly irrelevant to Milton's concerns in
*Paradise Lost* X.

The snake passage is rather designed primarily for scornful comic
effect, with its various learned puns (often a sign of stylistic
lowering) — 'supplanted', 'reluctant', 'sublime', 'exploding' — and
the joke whereby the expected applause is metamorphosed into 'a
universal hiss' (508). Low diction marks the vigorously sensuous
description of the chewing of bitter ashes, 'which the offended taste
/ With spattering noise rejected' (566–7). For the transformation
Milton obviously had in mind the passage in *Metamorphoses* IV
(576ff) in which the Theban king Cadmus and his wife Harmonia are
changed into snakes to the horror of the onlookers. Curiously this is
not specifically alluded to here, though it has been mentioned
earlier, in Book IX (505–6), presumably proleptically, in a way that
can be regarded as typical of Milton. In a notable fit of outdoing in
*Inferno* XXV (94ff), where he describes the horrible transformation
into serpents of some Florentine thieves, Dante claims to surpass
comparable moments in Ovid and Lucan: in the face of what he saw
in hell and now describes with such vivid virtuosity he bids the
classical masters of metamorphosis be silent. In his own treatment
of change Dante showed Milton, who takes hints from all three
poets, how a Christian writer could use Ovidian metamorphosis for
the grotesque cruelties of hell.

Milton's episode is heavily moralised, and it may thus be relevant
to recall that Ovid's transformations were regularly given moral
significance by medieval and Renaissance commentators. In reality
metamorphosis occurs in Ovid for various reasons, as punishment
both merited and unmerited, as confirmation of a changed

psychological state, or else for no perceivable reason at all, as something arbitrary and mysterious. However, Golding treats metamorphosis as something essentially moral. One Italian allegoriser even states (quite falsely) that 'there is not a single transformation which did not result from a disregard of God or from sin'.[44] It is against this background that Milton's fashioning of Satan into the great shape-changer must be seen. This may take various forms, from actual metamorphosis to comparison with delusive shapes (for example the whale-island of the simile in I. 200ff), or descriptions that seem to dissolve Satan's solidity, like the passage about his spear (I. 292–4) already analysed. Keats particularly admired IX. 179–91, the moment when Satan enters the sleeping serpent: 'Whose spirit does not ache at the smothering and confinement — the unwilling stillness — the "waiting close"? Whose head is not dizzy at the possible speculations of Satan in the serpent prison? No passage of poetry ever can give a greater pain of suffocation.' In the splendid completion of this pattern the self-changer is changed at the very moment when he most wants to be himself. The comparison (530ff) of Satan to the Python who was slain by Apollo (*Met.* I. 438ff) creates an appropriate quasi-typology, since Satan is 'the great dragon' as well as 'that old serpent' in Revelation 12: 9. In the final lines of the episode (578–84) Milton returns to classical mythology, identifying the devils with the heathen gods; the pedantic learning has been taken as genuinely speculative, but the dry tone and some details ('fabled' and 'perhaps') rather suggest mockery:

And fabled how the serpent, whom they called
Ophion, with Eurynome, the wide —
Encroaching Eve perhaps, had first the rule
Of high Olympus . . .

Milton probably shared the common humanist suspicion of such perverse ingenuities.

## Conclusion

Ovidian feeling is diffused throughout large parts of *Paradise Lost*, and is perhaps particularly evident whenever Eve is on the scene (an example is the Circe simile at IX. 521–2).[45] Ovid thus becomes the focus not only for ambiguities about classical mythology which at one level meant so much to Milton, but also for ambiguities about women and about sensuality in general, the tensions evident throughout Milton's poetry between his love of beauty and his puritan disdain for it. In Ovid's story of Salmacis and Hermaphroditus there is a finely imagined moment when the amorous nymph watches the naked boy swimming in her pool, unobserved by him (*Met*. IV. 340ff); there is a special quality of voyeuristic sensuality about such unseen watching. The scene is given thus in a poem entitled *Salmacis and Hermaphroditus* (1602) attributed to Francis Beaumont, which contains, amid much embellishment and digression, an almost complete free translation of Ovid's tale:

> So turning back she feigned to be gone,
> But from his sight she had no power to pass;
> Therefore she turned and hid her in the grass . . .
> He, then, supposing he was all alone,
> Like a young boy that is espied of none,
> Runs here and there, then on the banks doth look,
> Then on the crystal current of the brook; . . .
> Whose pleasant coolness when the boy did feel,
> He thrust his foot down lower to the heel;
> O'ercome with whose sweet noise he did begin
> To strip his soft clothes from his tender skin . . .
> When beauteous Salmacis a while had gazed
> Upon his naked corpse, she stood amazed,
> And both her sparkling eyes burned in her face,
> Like the bright sun reflected in a glass . . .
> When young Hermaphroditus as he stands,
> Clapping his white side with his hollow hands,
> Leapt lively from the land whereon he stood,
> Into the main part of the crystal flood.
> Like ivory then his snowy body was,
> Or a white lily in a crystal glass.[46]

A similar atmosphere, increased by the even greater verbal opulence, characterises the scene in *Paradise Lost* IX when an unseen Satan watches Eve moving among the flowers, though the eroticism is more conventional than in Ovid in view of the masculine sex of the watcher. The reminiscence of Proserpina brings into focus the familiar Ovidian theme of rape in a beautiful landscape. Indeed this whole section of Book IX is full of Ovidian allusions,[47] in particular the simile cluster 386–96, where the comparison of Eve with Pomona creates a mood of sweet fruitfulness (there is little attempt here to deny a value in classical stories). At such moments the austere puritan becomes the most sensuous of English poets (421ff):

> He sought them both, but wished his hap might find
> Eve separate, he wished, but not with hope
> Of what so seldom chanced, when to his wish,
> Beyond his hope, Eve separate he spies,
> Veiled in a cloud of fragrance, where she stood,
> Half spied — so thick the roses bushing round
> About her glowed — oft stooping to support
> Each flower of slender stalk, whose head though gay
> Carnation, purple, azure or specked with gold,
> Hung drooping unsustained; them she upstays
> Gently with myrtle band, mindless the while,
> Herself, though fairest unsupported flower,
> From her best prop so far, and storm so nigh.
> Nearer he drew, and many a walk traversed
> Of stateliest covert, cedar, pine or palm,
> Then voluble and bold, now hid, now seen
> Among thick-woven arborets and flowers
> Embordered on each bank, the hand of Eve . . .

In this chapter I have attempted to show how various aspects of the Renaissance Ovid influenced Milton's deployment of Ovidian material in *Paradise Lost*. Familiarity with the text of the *Metamorphoses*, and the traditional ways of reading it, run deeper with Milton than with any other English poet, even Shakespeare. But in the last resort Milton used the *Metamorphoses*, as the Romantics later used the *Faerie Queene*, as a door into 'faery lands forlorn'. In this way Ovid became part, and not an unimportant part, of Milton's sensibility, and thus of the delicate balance of opposed feelings that created the greatest of English narrative poems.

# Ovid

## Notes

1. For this exordium see E.J.Kenney in E.J.Kenney and W.V.Clausen (eds), *The Cambridge History of Classical Literature: II Latin Literature* (Cambridge University Press, 1982) pp. 432–4. Kenney believes that Ovid wrote 'et illa' in line 2, and is referring to his own change from elegy to hexameter poetry.

2. Gilbert Murray, 'Poiesis and Mimesis' in *Humanist Essays* (repr. Allen & Unwin, London, 1964), pp. 78–92 (pp. 85–6).

3. 'The Life of Milton' in Samuel Johnson, *Lives of the English Poets*, ed. G.B. Hill (3 vols, Clarendon Press, Oxford, 1905), vol. 1, p. 154.

4. Francis Meres, *Palladis Tamia* (London, 1598), pp. 281–2.

5. John Dryden, *Of Dramatic Poesy and Other Critical Essays*, ed. George Watson (2 vols, Dent, London and New York, 1962): in order, vol. 1, pp. 98–9; vol. 2, pp. 22 and 279; vol. 1, p. 277. See further Rachel Trickett, *The Honest Muse: A Study in Augustan Verse* (Clarendon Press, Oxford, 1967), pp. 68, 73–4, 77, and for Dryden's translations of Ovid see William Frost, 'Dryden's Versions of Ovid', *Comparative Literature*, vol. 26 (1974), pp. 193–202.

6. Charles Tomlinson, *Poetry and Metamorphosis* (Cambridge University Press, 1983) p. 7.

7. Davis P. Harding, 'Milton and the Renaissance Ovid' *Illinois Studies in Language and Literature*, vol. 30 (1946), p. 90.

8. Louis L. Martz, *Poet of Exile: A Study of Milton's Poetry* (Yale University Press, New Haven and London, 1980), part 3 ('Figurations of Ovid', pp. 203–44).

9. See S. Lee, 'Ovid and Shakespeare's Sonnets', *Quarterly Review*, vol. 210 (1909), pp. 455–76. For Shakespeare and Ovid in general see T.W. Baldwin, *William Shakspere's small Latine and less Greeke* (2 vols, University of Illinois Press, Urbana, 1944), vol. 2, pp. 417–55.

10. For the sources of the simile see Charles Grosvenor Osgood, *The Classical Mythology of Milton's English Poems*, Yale Studies in English 8 (Henry Holt, New York, 1900), p. 41; Ricks ably defends the syntax against the criticisms of Donald Davie in Christopher Ricks, *Milton's Grand Style* (Oxford University Press, London, Oxford, New York, 1963), pp. 43–5.

11. For a bibliography of studies of Ovid's reception and influence see *Aufstieg und Niedergang der Römischen Welt*, II. 31. 4 (de Gruyter, Berlin, 1981), pp. 2214–45 and 2254–63. See also, in addition to works mentioned elsewhere, Madeleine Doran, 'Some Renaissance "Ovids" ' in Bernice Slote (ed.), *Literature and Society* (University of Nebraska Press, Lincoln, 1964), pp. 42–62; Caroline Jameson, 'Ovid in the Sixteenth Century' in J.W. Binns (ed.), *Ovid* (Routledge & Kegan Paul, London and Boston, 1973), pp. 210–42; Albert C. Labrida, 'The Titans and the Giants: *Paradise Lost* and the Tradition of the Renaissance Ovid', *Milton Quarterly*, vol. 12 (1978), pp. 9–16; Ann Moss, *Poetry and Fable: Studies in Mythological Narrative in Sixteenth-Century France* (Cambridge University Press, 1984); John Wain, 'Ovid in English' in *Preliminary Essays* (Macmillan, London and New York, 1957), pp. 36–77.

12. George Sandys, *Ovid's Metamorphoses, Englished, Mythologized and Represented in Figures* (Oxford, 1632; photographic reprint, ed. Stephen Orgel, Garland Publishing, New York and London, 1976), p. 66. Other citations from Sandys's notes will be found on the following pages: in order, unnumbered page 'Ovid Defended', 7, 105–6, 195, 387, 295 (wrongly numbered 265). There is another edition by Karl K. Hulley and Stanley T. Vandersall (University of Nebraska Press, Lincoln, 1970), with a useful introduction by Douglas Bush. For this translation see Lee T. Pearcy, *The Mediated Muse: English Translations of Ovid 1560–1700* (Archon Books, Hamden, Conn., 1984), chs 3 and 4.

13. Thomas Elyot, *The Book named the Governor* (London, 1531), ed. S.E. Lehmberg (Dent, London, 1962), p. 32.

14. For this translation see the edition of J.F. Nims (Macmillan, New York, 1965), and Gordon Braden, *The Classics and English Renaissance Poetry: Three Case Studies* (Yale University Press, New Haven, 1978), pp. 1–54.

15. See Rosemond Tuve, *Allegorical Imagery: Some Medieval Books and their Posterity* (Princeton University Press, 1966), p. 304.

16. *Mystagogus Poeticus*, (enlarged edn, London 1675) p. 69. The other quotation in this chapter will be found on pp. 338–9. See also George Wither, *A Preparation to the Psalter* (London, 1619), pp. 77–8.

17. Addison, 'Notes on Ovid's *Metamorphoses*', in *Works*, ed. Richard Hurd (6 vols, George Bell & Sons, London and New York, 1893–1902), vol. 1, pp. 141–2.

18. *The Works of John Milton*, ed. F.A. Patterson *et al.* (18 vols and 2 vols index, Columbia University Press, New York, 1931–40), vol. 12, p. 144. (Hereafter *Columbia Milton*.)

19. Ann Moss, *Ovid in Renaissance France: A Survey of the Latin Editions of Ovid and Commentaries Printed in France before 1600*, Warburg Institute Surveys 8 (London, 1982).

20. Addison, 'Notes upon the Twelve Books of Paradise Lost' (*The Spectator*, 1712): in John T. Shawcross (ed.), *Milton: The Critical Heritage* (Routledge & Kegan Paul, London, 1970), p. 215, and Donald F. Bond (ed.), *The Spectator* (5 vols, Clarendon Press, Oxford, 1965), vol. 3, pp. 363–4. Cf. L.P. Wilkinson, *Ovid Recalled* (Cambridge University Press, 1955), pp. 432–4.

21. See William Keach, *Elizabethan Erotic Narratives: Irony and Pathos in the Ovidian Poetry of Shakespeare, Marlowe and their Contemporaries* (Harvester Press, Hassocks, 1977).

22. See Erwin Panofsky, 'Titian and Ovid' in *Problems in Titian Mostly Iconographic* (Phaidon, London, 1969), pp. 139–71.

23. Letter to Bailey, 22 Nov. 1817 (see H.E. Rollins (ed.), *The Letters of John Keats 1814–1821* (2 vols, Cambridge University Press, 1958), vol. 1, p. 185).

24. So K.W. Gransden in Charles Martindale (ed), *Virgil and his Influence: Bimillennial Studies* (Bristol Classical Press, 1984), p. 101.

25. See Louise Vinge, *The Narcissus Theme in Western European Literature up to the Early Nineteenth Century* (Gleerups, Lund, 1967), especially pp. 123–7, 224–6; C.R. Edwards, 'The Narcissus Myth in Spenser's Poetry', *Studies in Philology*, vol. 74 (1977), pp. 63–88. Satan's love for sin is specifically narcissistic (*PL* II. 764–5); see J.H. Collett, 'Milton's Use of Classical Mythology in *Paradise Lost*', *PMLA*, vol. 85 (1970), p. 91.

26. See C.A. Patrides, *Premises and Motifs in Renaissance Thought and Literature* (Princeton University Press, 1982), ch. 5, pp. 83–9.

27. Richard Bentley (ed.), *Milton's Paradise Lost: A New Edition* (London, 1732). Bentley's criticisms of *Paradise Lost* are reminiscent of Johnson's attack on 'Lycidas'. For Neoclassical hostility to myth see Richard F. Hardin, 'Ovid in Seventeenth-Century England', *Comparative Literature*, vol. 24 (1972), pp. 44–62.

28. Addison, 'Notes': in Shawcross (ed.), *Milton*, p. 215, and Bond (ed.), *Spectator*, vol. 3, p. 364.

29. Harding, *Milton and the Renaissance Ovid*, pp. 95–8, gives another example of Milton's use of the allegorised Ovid. Scylla, whose metamorphosis into a monster, woman above, baying dogs below, is described in *Met.* XIV. 1ff, was taken as an allegory of concupiscence, an interpretation found in Sandys and elsewhere. Milton appropriately uses Ovid's description for his own personified figure of Sin, acknowledging his debt in a simile (II. 650–61). Douglas Bush, *Mythology and the Renaissance Tradition in English Poetry* (University of Minnesota Press and Oxford University Press, Minneapolis and London, 1932), p. 270 note 56, suggests that in *PR* IV. 563–8 Milton may be glancing at the traditional allegorisation of the contest

195

between Hercules and Antaeus; see also Carey's note *ad loc* in John Carey and Alastair Fowler (eds), *The Poems of John Milton* (Longman, London, 1968).

30. See Charles Paul Segal, *Landscape in Ovid's Metamorphoses: A Study in the Transformations of a Literary Symbol* (Franz Steiner Verlag, Wiesbaden, 1969), pp. 6–19, 33–8.

31. Dorothy Sayers, 'Dante and Milton' in *Further Papers on Dante* (Methuen, London, 1957), pp. 178–82; see also Timothy Webb, *The Violet in the Crucible: Shelley and Translation* (Clarendon Press Oxford, 1976), pp. 313–26.

32. Gransden in Martindale (ed.), *Virgil and his Influence*, p. 97.

33. See A.D. Nuttall, *William Shakespeare: The Winter's Tale*, Studies in English Literature 26 (Edward Arnold, London, 1966), pp. 40–2.

34. David Jones, *The Roman Quarry and Other Sequences*, ed. Harman Grisewood and René Hague (Agenda Editions, London, 1981), pp. 106–7.

35. See Frank Kermode, *Romantic Image* (Routledge & Kegan Paul, London, 1957), pp. 138–61.

36. John Keats, 'Notes on Milton's "Paradise Lost" ' in H. Buxton Forman (ed.), *The Complete Works of John Keats*, (5 vols, Gowans & Grey, Glasgow, 1900–1), vol. 3, pp. 256–7 (the other quotations in this chapter will be found on pp. 264–5); Joseph A. Wittreich, Jr (ed.), *The Romantics on Milton: Formal Essays and Critical Asides* (Case Western Reserve University Press, Cleveland and London, 1970), pp. 553, 559–60. Cf. Murray, 'Poeisis and Mimesis', p. 84: 'my own feeling is that, in the main, his [Milton's] imagined world is almost nothing to him but a place of beauty, a sanctuary and an escape'.

37. See Collett, 'Milton's Use of Classical Mythology', pp. 95–6, for a very different reading, one that seems to me to ignore the character of the poetry.

38. *Columbia Milton*, vol. 12, pp. 26–7.

39. See Osgood, *Classical Mythology*, pp. 66–7.

40. See Wolfgang Stechow, 'The Myth of Philemon and Baucis in Art', *Journal of the Warburg and Courtauld Institutes*, vol. 4 (1941), pp. 103–13. For Elsheimer's and Rembrandt's paintings see Keith Andrews, *Adam Elsheimer: Paintings, Drawings, Prints* (Phaidon, London, 1977), plate 87, and Henri Focillon and Ludwig Goldscheider, *Rembrandt: Paintings, Drawings and Etchings* (Phaidon, London, 1960), plate 96. For Rubens see Lisa Vergara, *Rubens and the Poetics of Landscape* (Yale University Press, New Haven and London, 1982), pp. 179–83. For Dryden's version see D.W. Hopkins, 'Dryden's "Baucis and Philemon" ', *Comparative Literature*, vol. 28 (1976), pp. 135–43.

41. See A.D. Nuttall, *Overheard by God: Fiction and Prayer in Herbert, Milton, Dante and St John* (Methuen, London, 1980), pp. 85–93.

42. See Howard Hibbard, *Caravaggio* (Thames & Hudson, London, 1983), pp. 53–5.

43. A.J.A. Waldock, *Paradise Lost and its Critics* (Cambridge University Press, 1947), pp. 91–2.

44. Quoted by Don Cameron Allen, *Mysteriously Meant: The Rediscovery of Pagan Symbolism and Allegorical Interpretation in the Renaissance* (Johns Hopkins, University Press, Baltimore and London, 1970), p. 177.

45. For Milton and Circe see Harding, *Milton and the Renaissance Ovid*, pp. 58–66; L.L. Brodwin, 'Milton and the Renaissance Circe', *Milton Studies*, vol. 6 (1974), pp. 21–83.

46. Text in Elizabeth Story Donno,, *Elizabethan Minor Epics* (Routledge & Kegan Paul, London, 1963), pp. 281ff. I give lines 822–64 with many omissions.

47. For *PL* IX. 386, cf. *Met.* VI. 452–4; *PL* IX. 393–5 alludes to *Met.* XIV. 623ff; the lush description of Satan in snake form owes something to *Met.* III. 32ff.

# 5

# LUCAN

## The Reputation of the *Pharsalia*

Lucan's *Bellum Civile* or *De Bello Civili* — the exact title is uncertain, and in the seventeenth century the poem was known as the *Pharsalia* after the battle which forms its climax — is the most original post-Augustan Latin epic. It describes the civil war between Julius Caesar and Pompey and the decline and fall of the Republican system of government which the poet admired. Properly speaking it is an historical epic, but we might prefer to think of it as a political poem, since it is an impassioned attack on the unchecked rule of the state by a single individual. Lucan writes to commend *libertas*, freedom, conceived of both politically as the Republic overthrown by the Caesars and spiritually as the inner freedom of mind that can be obtained in any circumstance by the Stoic sage. Political liberty died at Pharsalia, where Caesar defeated Pompey and the senate (though Lucan implies in VII. 645–6 that a new civil war would be justified to regain it), whereas the second kind of freedom often in practice meant, under a tyrant, resort to suicide. The defender of liberty in the poem is the Stoic saint and martyr, Cato the younger, who struggles for the dying Republic and — although Lucan never reached this point of the story — himself dies heroically by his own hand rather than become a slave of Caesar. Whether because of the ideological nature of the poem or for other reasons Lucan was forbidden to recite or publish; he joined a conspiracy to overthrow Nero which was discovered, and on the Emperor's orders he committed suicide in AD 65, his poem still unfinished.[1]

The work is highly declamatory, and it is usual to emphasise the satiric quality of some of the best writing, which anticipates the manner of the satirist Juvenal. Since the subject was comparatively recent history, Lucan spurned flowery poetic embellishment, preferring a drier, deliberately modernist approach which affronted conventional classicising critics in antiquity and thereafter. In the stuffy judgement of Quintilian (X. i. 90) Lucan was a model for the orator more than the poet; as Johnson puts it, 'Lucan is distinguished by a kind of dictatorial or philosophic dignity, rather, as Quintilian observes, declamatory than poetical.'[2]

The Columbia index to Milton's works contains only seventeen references to Lucan, so that, when one considers that it has six and a half columns under Virgil, more than four each under Homer and Ovid, and two under Horace, one might be tempted to conclude that Lucan was not a major influence on Milton. Nevertheless there is no reason to doubt that Milton was thoroughly familiar with the *Bellum Civile*, since he alludes to lines from five of Lucan's ten books and not just to more famous passages. More significantly there are certain broad similarities of poetic strategy in *Paradise Lost* and the *Bellum Civile* which in some important respects differentiate the poems from the mainstream epic tradition, and which will be the subject of this chapter.

First, however, it will be useful to give, by way of context, a sketch of Lucan's reputation and influence in this period.[3] Lucan was, at least until the end of the eighteenth century, widely held in some esteem. Some even preferred him to Virgil, including Horace Walpole, as we learn from a letter that he wrote to the Rev. H. Zouch, dated 9 December 1758:

I am just undertaking an edition of Lucan, my friend Mr Bentley [son of the famous scholar] having in his possession his father's notes and emendations on the first seven books. Perhaps a partiality for the original author concurs a little with this circumstance of the notes to make me fond of printing at Strawberry Hill the works of a man who alone of all the classics was thought to breathe too brave and honest a spirit for the perusal of the Dauphin and the French. I don't think that a good or bad taste in poetry is of so serious a nature that I should be afraid of owning too, that with that great judge Corneille and with that perhaps no judge Heinsius, I prefer Lucan to Virgil. To speak fairly, I prefer great sense to poetry with little sense — There are hemistichs in Lucan that go to one's soul and to one's heart — for a mere epic poem, a fabulous tissue of uninteresting battles, that don't teach one even to fight, I know nothing more tedious. The poetic images, the versification and language of the *Aeneid* are delightful, but take the story by itself, and can anything be more silly and unaffecting? There are gods without power, heroes without character, heaven-directed wars without justice, inventions without probability, and a hero who betrays one woman with a kingdom that he might have had, to force himself upon another woman and another kingdom to which he had no pretensions, and all this to show his obedience to the gods! In short I have always admired his numbers so much and his meaning so little, that I think I should like Virgil better if I understood him less.[4]

Yet, despite his enthusiasm for the good sense of the *Bellum Civile*, Walpole here does less than justice to Lucan as a poet. Certainly Lucan always had his critics, particularly after the Restoration. For example Dryden is generally tepid,[5] while in *An Essay upon Unnatural Flights in Poetry* (1701) George Granville Lord Lansdowne criticises, for frigid ingenuity, the poem's most famous line 'victrix causa deis placuit sed victa Catoni' (the conquering cause pleased the gods, the conquered pleased Cato, I. 127).[6] These criticisms increased in the nineteenth century, when, at least in this country, false distinctions between poetry and rhetoric led to a great decline in Lucan's reputation, despite the initial enthusiasm of Shelley. Lucan's poetry, as Robert Graves saw,[7] might have been expected to appeal to modern sensibilities, but the decline in the prestige of classical studies, together with the conservatism of classical scholarship, have until recently prevented the revaluation that one might have thought probable. At all events in the late sixteenth and early seventeenth centuries the *Bellum Civile* was widely read, and was imitated by poets including Daniel, Drayton, Chapman and Jonson. For example Drayton's *The Barons' Wars* (1603) employs a rhetorical manner which derives from Lucan, including the flamboyant use of apostrophe.[8] Verse translations appeared by Marlowe (first book only), Sir Arthur Gorges and Thomas May, the last later a staunch parliamentarian who wrote *The History of the Parliament of England* (1647). May's popular translation was first published in 1627, with the title *Lucan's Pharsalia or the Civil Wars of Rome*. Milton knew this version and took from it the phrase 'adamantine chains' in the first book of *Paradise Lost* (48). In a poem 'To My Chosen Friend, the Learned Translator of Lucan, Thomas May, Esquire' Ben Jonson pours lavish praise on both the translater and on Lucan's poem. That was in a panegyric; William Drummond of Hawthornden reports his true opinion: 'Lucan taken in parts excellent, altogether nought.'[9]

There is no positive evidence, so far as I know, that Milton knew Marlowe's fine translation into blank verse of *Lucan's First Book*, but it seems likely enough. In his discussion of this rendering A.L. Rowse goes so far as to say that 'it would seem obvious that if we are to look for the origin of Milton's blank verse style, we shall find it in Marlowe'.[10]

During the Civil War period the *Bellum Civile* must have assumed an unusual relevance, and poets turned to it for inspiration. Aubrey interestingly reports that May, originally a Royalist, was first attracted to republicanism through his study of Lucan (the cynical attributed this volte-face to his failure to gain the laureateship).[11] A recent study suggests, without mentioning Lucan, that there was a group of parliamentarians who might be called the 'classical republicans', and who derived part of their notion of liberty from Latin writers like Livy and, it should be added, Lucan; the group would have included both May and Milton.[12] Nor was an interest in Lucan confined to Republicans. Cowley's unfinished epic on the English Civil War, published in full for the first time by Allan Pritchard, owes a great deal to Lucan.[13] The work is competent, rather than inspired, but certain passages would give a Latinless reader quite a good idea of Lucan's style, particularly the grisly description of the effects of disease on Essex's army (II. 159ff), or the account of the battle on the Thames near Brentforth (I. 325ff), with its fire and water conceits, for example:

> Witness those men blown high into the air,
> All elements their ruin joyed to share.
> In the wide air quick flames their bodies tore,
> Then drowned in waves they're tost by waves to shore.   (325–8)

Cowley ends his account of the siege of Lichfield with a paradox of the sort with which the *Bellum Civile* abounds. Of the brave parliamentary defenders Cowley writes (II. 135–6):

> Unhappy men! Who can your curses tell?
> Damned and infamed for fighting ill [i.e. on the wrong side] so
> well!

We may compare this comment of Lucan's on the mutiny of Caesar's troops at Placentia (May's translation of *BC*. V. 297–9):

So let it go, ye gods, since piety
Forsakes us, and our hopes on vice rely,
Let discord make an end of civil war.[14]

Marvell's 'An Horatian Ode upon Cromwell's Return from
Ireland' is formally modelled on Horace's political lyrics, especially
the Cleopatra Ode (1. 37), whose imagery and movement Marvell's
poem to some extent reproduces; even the metre is apparently
designed to represent Horatian Alcaics. But Marvell also alludes to
passages in the first book of the *Bellum Civile*, which he apparently
knew in May's translation. In particular, in his account of
Cromwell's irresistible rise to power, he adapts into his own tersely
paradoxical manner the lightning simile which Lucan uses to convey
Caesar's ruthless velocity:

And, like the three-forked lightning, first
Breaking the clouds where it was nursed,
   Did thorough his own side
   His fiery way divide.  (13–16)

As lightning by the wind forced from a cloud
Breaks through the wounded air with thunder loud,
Disturbs the day, the people terrifies,
And by a light oblique dazzles our eyes,
Not Jove's own temple spares it; when no force,
No bar can hinder his prevailing course,
Great waste, as forth it sallies and retires,
It makes, and gathers his dispersed fires.
(May's translation of *BC*. I. 151–7)

The dual background — part Horace, part Lucan — contributes to
the ode's much admired poise, whereby to a degree Marvell holds
an even balance between Cromwell and Charles, and is surprisingly
objective in his assessment of the former. The useful suggestion has
been made that Marvell uses Horace to reflect his hopes and Lucan
his fears about Cromwell.[15] This is perhaps an over-simplification,
since Cromwell's abnormal energy, which is the main quality he
shares with Lucan's Caesar, is seen by Marvell as an essential part of
his effectiveness. Nevertheless we may say that in broad terms
Cromwell is welcomed as a modern Augustus, feared as the heir of
Lucan's Caesar. The *Bellum Civile* was in fact difficult to claim

directly for either king or parliament, since, although Lucan's Republican sympathies were not in doubt, it was difficult to avoid casting Cromwell as Caesar, clearly the villain of Lucan's poem as the subverter of the Republic. That Marvell in his ode on the English Revolution should have thought of Lucan is no surprise. The *Bellum Civile* plots a crucial stage in the revolutionary process by which the Roman Republic was transformed into an autocracy, and Caesar like Cromwell was the great breaker of the mould. Clearly, however, the parallelism is inexact, since the 'ancient rights' that Caesar overturned were republican, not monarchical. Hence it is not surprising that in the ode at one moment it is Charles who is Caesar, at another Cromwell (23, 101).

## The Epic of Ideas

### Theme

In the *Iliad* and *Odyssey* interest is centred on plot and to a lesser extent on character, as Aristotle saw. Since so much recent criticism has concentrated on the many distinctions between the epics of Homer and Virgil, it is worthwhile emphasising a basic similarity. Virgil, like Homer, has a story to tell. It is a story of considerable ethical and other consequence, but any meaning or significance it may have is left largely to the reader (or listener) to determine. W.A. Camps describes the *Aeneid* thus: 'In essence it is a story consisting of splendid and moving episodes, organized in a strongly shaped architectural pattern, and told in language of great expressive and emotive power. This story is centred on examples of intense and important human experience.'[16] This may not seem a particularly exciting formulation, but it is surely a reasonable one. *Paradise Lost* and the *Bellum Civile* fall into a rather different category, which may be termed, if largely for convenience, the 'epic of ideas'. This is not of course to imply that there are no ideas in the *Iliad*, let alone the *Aeneid*. Indeed some might argue that one of Virgil's main achievements lay precisely in recreating Homeric epic along more obviously thematic lines. But Virgil maintains, on the whole, the traditional anonymity of the epic bard, and his attitude to his characters and their actions is often hard or impossible to determine. In the 'epic of ideas', theme has overtaken the creation of character for its own sake, and sheer storytelling, as the poet's dominant concern. It has become explicit: the poet is more open about his ideas and the reader is simply not allowed to escape the meaning of the story. Most readers would probably agree that this is true of *Paradise Lost*. Milton gives an account of the Fall and its significance, which constitutes the poem's 'great argument'. The actual narrative content of the poem is in fact rather slight, a point emphasised by Waldock, but the implications of the narrative are immense. Nor is Milton slow to make his own viewpoint plain. The poet has become in other words not merely the storyteller but also the interpreter of the story, a point to which we shall return.

The description of the *Bellum Civile* as an 'epic of ideas' will need justifying at rather greater length. This will involve looking at the view, which has had some adherents in modern times, that Lucan was engaged in writing a verse chronicle, and is hardly to be accounted a poet at all. It might seem that this view can claim the support of some of Lucan's ancient critics.[17] Thus Servius in a note on *Aeneid* I. 382 remarks that 'Lucan did not deserve to be numbered among the poets, because he seems to have composed a history, not a poem', 'quia videtur historiam composuisse, non poema'. It is important to be aware of the limited scope of such an observation. As with so much ancient literary criticism the point is essentially stylistic, and concerns decorum. We can see this from Petronius's novel the *Satyricon*, written like the *Bellum Civile* during the rule of Nero, where the poetaster Eumolpus launches what is almost certainly a thinly veiled attack on the *Bellum Civile* (ch. 118).[18] Eumolpus implies that Lucan treats his subject-matter like a historian; the true poet ought rather to immerse himself in the Greco-Roman literary tradition, and in particular should employ 'deorum ministeria', the traditional 'divine machinery' which Lucan had wisely omitted. Eumolpus then declaims a poem on the Civil War, which is intended by him to show the correct way to write historical epic, and in which the gods play an important part. Servius too accuses Lucan of ignorance of the law of poetry, 'lex artis poeticae'. Lucan in other words did not approach the subject in the correct way: it was Virgil who for Servius and the traditionalists supplied the model and the norm. These ancient criticisms were often revived. For example Sir William Davenant in the Preface to *Gondibert* (1650) argued that Lucan's 'enterprise rather beseemed an historian than a poet':

 . . . for wise poets think it more worthy to seek out truth in the passions than to record the truth of actions; and to practise to describe mankind just as we are persuaded or guided by instinct, not particular persons, as they are lifted or levelled by the force of fate, it being nobler to contemplate the general history of nature than a selected diary of fortune.

Davenant compares the historical poet to the portrait painter who merely records likenesses; Lucan is thus drawn into the perennial battle between realism and idealism in art.[19]

One line of defence of Lucan would run like this. Aristotle in *Poetics* 1451[a] 36ff says that poetry is more philosophical than history, since history deals with things that have been, brute fact, while poetry is concerned with the kind of things that might be, universally observable truths. In Aristotle's terms Lucan could be said to belong with the poets rather than the historians.[20] Historical facts may provide the raw material — or most of it — for the poem, but Lucan, who was not writing versified history, seeks the universal in the particular. One might say that civil war is as much his concern as the Civil War. Moreover the war is regarded as a paradigm of the incessant struggle between freedom and tyranny. As Lucan himself puts it, 'it was the never-ending struggle between Freedom and Caesarism', 'par quod semper habemus, libertas et Caesar . . . erit' (VII. 695–6). An historical event has become part of a cosmic struggle with Caesar and Liberty as perpetual combatants (the image is of a gladiatorial match). In consequence Lucan felt no more qualms than Shakespeare in his histories about inventing some incidents and embroidering others almost out of recognition. It is almost certain that Lucan simply invented the splendid episode in which Sextus Pompey consults the witch Erictho about the outcome of the battle of Pharsalus, in a grisly séance that is a sort of parody of Aeneas' visit to the Underworld (*BC*. VI. 413ff). Other apparently equally unlikely episodes are in fact derived from the historical tradition. For example the attempt by Caesar to sail across the Adriatic in a fisherman's boat during a violent storm was recorded by historians, but Lucan uses the storm to symbolise the tyrant's superhuman pride (V. 497ff).[21] On this view the poet wanted not so much to give an historically accurate account of the war between Caesar and Pompey as to say some important things about the eternal human condition.

All this is persuasive as far as it goes. However it is also important that the historical poet, however much he may embroider his subject with additional fictions, generally employs material of a factual nature. The other obvious rejoinder to the complaints of Servius and the rest is to argue for the superiority of historical truth to mythological fable. This point is often made by Lucan's defenders, including Dr James Welwood in the preface attached to the translation of the *Bellum Civile* by the poet and playwright Nicolas Rowe (1674–1718), first published immediately after his death and praised by Johnson as 'one of the greatest productions of English poetry':[22]

> The *Pharsalia* is properly an historical heroic poem, because the subject is a known true story. Now with our late critics truth is an unnecessary trifle for an epic poem, and ought to be thrown aside as a curb to invention. To have every part a mere web of their own brain is with them a distinguishing mark of a mighty genius in the epic way. Hence it is, these critics observe, that their favourite poems of that kind do always produce in the mind of the reader the highest wonder and surprise; and the more improbable the story is, still the more wonderful and surprising. Much good may this notion of theirs do them; but to my taste a fact very extraordinary in its kind that is attended with surprising circumstances, big with the highest events, and conducted with all the arts of the most consummate wisdom, does not strike the less strong, but leaves a more lasting impression on my mind, for being true.[23]

This defence would certainly have pleased Lucan, in view of the attitude which he takes, in the *Bellum Civile*, towards mythological narrative.[24] The poem purports to tell the truth about what Lucan regards as the most important event in Roman history, the loss of liberty. The subject is not myth but fact. Consistency — and even decorum properly understood — demanded the controversial omission of the traditional mythological trappings of epic, including the divine machinery. Thus Lucan refuses to invoke the Muse or Apollo (I. 66), while in a number of passages he is openly cynical about *fabulae*, mythological stories (e.g. III. 211–3). In describing Caesar's massive earthworks at Dyrrachium he writes, employing a version of the 'outdoing' *topos* (VI. 48–9): 'nunc vetus Iliacos attollat fabula muros / ascribatque deis' (now let the old fable praise the walls of Troy and ascribe them to the gods). History here 'outdoes' myth; truth is literally stranger than fiction. The story of the origin of the Libyan snakes is told because none better is available, but its falsity is stressed (IX. 619ff). Myth is abandoned and truth found in history.

In this respect there is a link between Lucan and Milton, the historical and the Biblical poet. Both tell a story that, despite some fictional additions, is in essence held to be true (I have already examined Milton's hostility, at one level, to pagan fable, and the deliberateness of his choice of a Biblical and non-heroic subject for his epic). A second link is that each poet believes that his story is directly relevant to the reader, and wants to make the nature of that relevance explicit, by constantly intervening in his narrative. In the *Poetics* (1460ª 7) Aristotle laid down that the epic poet should not give his point of view *in propria persona*. This prescription, based on Homeric practice, was in the main observed by Virgil, and became part of neoclassical epic theory.[25] Milton, however, had no qualms about transgressing the Aristotelian canon, most notably in the prologues of Books III, VII and IX. Johnson was too much of a classiciser not to feel some theoretical misgivings about these passages, although he was too honest a critic to allow dogma to override his more immediate response. 'The short digressions at the beginning of the third, seventh and ninth books might doubtless be spared' he avers, continuing disarmingly,

> but superfluities so beautiful who would take away? Or who does not wish that the author of the *Iliad* had gratified succeeding ages with a little knowledge of himself? Perhaps no passages are more frequently or more attentively read than those extrinsic paragraphs; and, since the end of poetry is pleasure, that cannot be unpoetical with which all are pleased.[26]

A number of critics have shown that the autobiographical passages should not be regarded as 'extrinsic paragraphs' at all. For example Martz writes: 'These personal touches are no mere self-indulgence: they have a function — to remind us, intimately, that this poem is an action of thoughts within a central, controlling intelligence that moves with inward eyes toward a recovery of Paradise.'[27] In particular the images of light and darkness and the contrast between external blindness and inner illumination are, as we have seen, central to the poem.

More importantly, in the 'epic of ideas' the poet, as already noted, serves as both narrator and interpreter, and thus his personality and views are not peripheral, but central. The ideas have become too important to be left merely implicit. To some this seems like manipulation. Waldock complains of what he calls 'the running fire of belittling commentary'[28] in Books I and II of *Paradise Lost*, where the speeches of the fallen angels are continually undercut by explicit authorial comment. In fact, as Martz observes, the 'voice of the bard' is to be heard throughout 'advising, exhorting, warning, praising, denouncing, lamenting, promising, judging, in all ways guiding us'.[29] In addition to the invocations we have numerous passages of a satiric, didactic or moralising character. Such moralising may be extended, or it may be restricted to a brief stab, as in the lines that describe Satan's entry into paradise (IV. 183–96):

> As when a prowling wolf,
> Whom hunger drives to seek new haunt for prey,
> Watching where shepherds pen their flocks at eve
> In hurdled cotes amid the field secure,
> Leaps o'er the fence with ease into the fold;
> Or as a thief bent to unhoard the cash
> Of some rich burgher, whose substantial doors,
> Cross-barred and bolted fast, fear no assault,
> In at the window climbs, or o'er the tiles;
> So clomb this first grand thief into God's fold —
> So since into his church lewd hirelings climb.
> Thence up he flew, and on the tree of life
> The middle tree and highest there that grew,
> Sat like a cormorant.

Here the leisurely epic narrative is interrupted by a single line of invective, even if this has been prepared for by the traditional allegorical image of the wolf and sheep and by the 'low' language of the second simile. Milton also puts into Raphael's mouth the sort of material, for example the discussion of angelic sex and digestion, that Aristotle would probably have regarded as inappropriate in an epic (and Aristotle is not without his modern followers, in the twentieth as in the eighteenth century).

Milton's technique had, to an extent, been anticipated by Lucan in the *Bellum Civile*. Addison draws our attention to the similarity:

If the poet, even in the ordinary course of his narration, should speak as little as possible, he should certainly never let his

narration sleep for the sake of any reflections of his own . . .
Lucan, who was an injudicious poet, lets drop his story very
frequently for the sake of his unnecessary digressions . . .
Milton's complaint of his blindness, his panegyric on marriage,
his reflections on Adam and Eve's going naked, of the angels
eating, and several other passages in his poem, are liable to the
same exception, though I must confess there is so great a beauty
in these very digressions that I would not wish them out of his
poem.[30]

W.E. Heitland, in an essay published in 1887 which until recently
was the fullest discussion of the *Bellum Civile* available in English,
regards the presence of moralising passages as one of the 'four
characteristic defects' of the poem:

> The poet's business is surely to develope his moral by the simple
> interaction of characters and circumstances. The reader should
> be left to judge: half the pleasure and most of the profit of poetry
> lies in the discovery of the moral significance of the characters
> and the meaning of the story, not by direct statement, but from
> the story and characters themselves. Now Lucan is always
> thrusting himself forward to tell us what it all means: and,
> whatever Roman audiences may have thought of the practice, on
> us the effect is simply to destroy the illusion of poetry and bring
> us face to face with an orator.[31]

The shadow cast by the *Poetics* is, it seems, a long one.
    Lucan's interventions fall into the same general categories as
Milton's. There are personal passages, as when the poet prays that
he may be allowed to bring back Pompey's headless corpse to Italy
for proper burial (VIII. 843–5, May):

> O too too happy I, if Rome would choose
> My hand to open that base sepulchre,
> And his dear ashes hither to transfer.

There are satiric and moralising observations. For example, when
Caesar knocks at the hut of the poor fisherman Amyclas to ask him
to take him across the Adriatic in his boat, Lucan comments
ironically on the peace of mind that poverty brings (V. 527–31,
May):

O safe blest poor man's life, o gift of all
The gods, not yet well known; what city wall,
What temple had not feared at Caesar's stroke?

Several times he breaks off his description of the battle of Pharsalus
to reflect on its crucial significance (VII. 185ff, 385ff, 638ff, 847ff).
We are never allowed to forget the presence of an individual voice,
with a particular point of view, and it is the presence of this voice
which gives the poem much of its distinctive character and what
unity it has. One of the effects of the authorial interventions is to
involve the reader more closely in the issues. Welwood rightly
observed that, in the seventh book, the battle of Pharsalus is so
related that 'the reader may rather think himself a spectator of, or
even engaged in the battle than so remote from the age in which it
was fought'.[32] This is important because Lucan believed that his
readers were indeed experiencing the consequences of the loss of
liberty that was the fruit of the Civil War. Similarly Milton's readers
share in Adam's fall, a point which the poet will not long allow them
to forget.

Even Raphael's didacticism has its parallel. At a feast of
extravagant luxury given by Cleopatra in Alexandria, Caesar asks
about the causes of the Nile flood and the secret of the river's
source, and is answered at length by the Egyptian priest Acoreus
(X. 172ff). This exchange is usually regarded as irrelevant padding,
but Lucan may have had good reasons for including it. The
description of the feast and its setting is designed to contrast with the
account given earlier in the poem of Cato's austere home and frugal
life-style (II. 380ff). Caesar's disgraceful liaison with Cleopatra is
opposed to Cato's chaste and unconsummated re-marriage to
Marcia. I think it probable that the poet is also inviting us to
compare Caesar's intellectual curiosity (which Caesar himself calls
'virtus' and 'amor veri', 'virtue' and 'love of truth', 188–9) with
Cato's genuine concern with moral virtue, the only true virtue.

### Characterisation

In the 'epic of ideas' as described above it is natural that
characterisation should to some extent be tailored to theme. It is an
assumption of much modern criticism that the freer characterisation
that we associate above all with Shakespeare and certain novelists is
superior to such 'controlled' characterisation. But restrictive
dogmas of any sort are undesirable, and it is reasonable to argue

that different types of characterisation suit different types of work. It has already been observed that Lucan treats the Civil War as a struggle of cosmic significance. Milton, of course, is dealing directly with a cosmic event. This is reflected in the characterisation. In both poems there is a triad of principal characters, two of them representing the polarities of good and evil, God and Satan, Cato and Caesar, and caught between them, much more ordinary and recognisable, 'like us' as Aristotle says, Adam and Pompey. Lucan's Pompey is in fact a plausible enough portrait of the historical figure. The same can hardly be said of his Cato or Caesar.[33] Cato is the perfect Stoic saint, whose every word has an almost oracular quality. To him is assigned the task of embodying and enunciating the sacred truths of Stoicism, to which Lucan, like his uncle Seneca, subscribed. For example, in Book IX Cato instructs one of his lieutenants on the omnipresence of deity, a tenet of Stoicism (578–80):

> estque dei sedes nisi terra et pontus et aer
> et caelum et virtus? superos quid quaerimus ultra?
> Iuppiter est quodcumque vides, quodcumque moveris.

> Is there a seat of god, save earth and sea,
> Air, heaven and virtue? Why for gods should we
> Seek further? What ere moves, what ere is seen
> Is Jove.   (May)

Rowe's note on this passage is worth quoting, since it would have been applauded by Milton:

> I cannot but observe here how finely our author in this passage reprehends the folly of those who are fond of and believe in a local sanctity, as if one part of the world were holier than another, and the ubiquity of the divine nature were confined to a particular place; but, thank God, the foppery of pilgrimages is out of fashion in England . . .

Milton imitated these impressive lines in *Paradise Lost* XI, but hardly improved on them (Milton's 'virtual' was presumably suggested by Lucan's 'virtus'):

210

Adam, thou know'st heaven his, and all the earth,
Not this rock only; his omnipresence fills
Land, sea and air, and every kind that lives,
Fomented by his virtual power and warmed.    (335–8)


Caesar is Cato's complete antithesis, a tyrant in the sway of his
every passion, the perfectly bad man. This is in accordance with
Stoic theory: 'a wicked man does not lack any vice', Seneca observes
(*De Beneficiis* IV. 27.2), 'dicimus . . . malum ac stultum nullo vitio
vacare'. Caesar rejoices in every act of violence and political
chicanery. He has no religious scruples: after the battle of
Pharsalus he forbids the burial of the senatorial dead, electing to
feast in a place where he can view the piles of already putrefying
corpses (VII. 792–4). He is a hypocrite who weeps crocodile tears
over the head of the decapitated Pompey (IX. 1035ff). Though so
totally evil, Caesar nevertheless has a kind of perverted greatness.
A man of huge vigour, he is prompt in action, restless, energetic,
'thinking nought done, whilst ought undone remained' (II. 657), in
contrast to Pompey who is content to rest on his laurels:


          but in Caesar now
Remains not only a great general's name,
But restless valour, and in war a shame
Not to be conqueror; fierce, not curbed at all,
Ready to fight, where hope or anger call
His forward sword; confident of success
And bold the favour of the gods to press;
O'erthrowing all that his ambition stay,
And loves that ruin should enforce his way.
    (May's translation of I. 143–50)

He has qualities which, if his purposes were not depraved, might be
considered virtues. In particular he is in a sense courageous, though
Lucan clearly regards such misdirected courage as mere reckless-
ness (this was the usual Stoic view).

William Blissett in an article entitled 'Caesar and Satan'[34] argues
convincingly that Lucan's Caesar is one of Milton's sources of
inspiration for his characterisation of Satan. Blissett describes the
similarity thus:

The Satanic in Lucan's Caesar is plain to see: the continual restlessness and demonic impatience are stressed over and over again; the unhesitating leadership in evil, the impulse of the gambler and allied to that the fascination of the idea of total ruin; the moments of hesitation, remorse and magnanimity which serve only to make more horrifying the defiant impenitence. The Caesarian in Milton's Satan is as plain. Satan is the enemy, as Caesar had been, of quiet and custom and accepted right: he is a tyrant, a sultan, more than a king.

Both Caesar and Satan, it should be added, are tyrants who pose as democrats, exerting an almost hypnotic control over their followers. Thus both obtain silent attention with a mere gesture of the hand: 'who with hand / Silence, and with these words attention won' (X. 458–9) is another of Milton's reminiscences of Lucan (*BC.* I. 298). More particularly Blissett shows how Satan's journey through the abyss owes something to the episode in the *Bellum Civile* where Caesar by night and alone but for a single companion, the fisherman Amyclas, tries to cross the stormy Adriatic in a little boat, an episode which illustrates, as we have seen, Caesar's superhuman arrogance. In each case we have 'a lone heroic voyage through chaos by the antagonist', and this general resemblance is reinforced by verbal echoes. It may be (a point not observed by Blissett) that the simile with which Milton ends his account of Satan's journey, comparing Satan to 'a weather-beaten vessel', is meant to indicate the debt (II. 1037–44):

> here nature first begins
> Her farthest verge, and Chaos to retire
> As from her outmost works a broken foe
> With tumult less and with less hostile din,
> That Satan with less toil, and now with ease,
> Wafts on the calmer wave by dubious light
> And like a weather-beaten vessel holds
> Gladly the port, though shrouds and tackle torn.

The protagonists of both episodes display a grotesque heroism. Like Satan, Caesar remains outwardly unbowed, scorning the storm which threatens to destroy him (V. 654–60, May):

Are the gods troubled so to ruin me,
Whom sitting here in a small barque, quoth he,
They have assaulted with a storm so loud?
If on the seas, not wars, they have bestowed
The glory of my death, fearless I come,
Ye gods, to any death that ye can doom;
Though this too hasty fate great acts break off,
I have already done things great enough.

His bravado has a heroic ring, until we remember the wickedness of his overall ambitions. In both respects the analogy with Satan is exact.

The similarity between Milton's Satan and Lucan's Caesar is interesting when we recall the parallelism between Cromwell and Caesar implied in Marvell's 'Horatian Ode'. The point may even be of some relevance to the long-standing debate about Satan. It is a familiar paradox that Milton, a Republican on earth, should be a Royalist in heaven. A Satan who poses as a democrat and has the energy of Lucan's Caesar may have made some readers think of contemporary politics. Milton's attitude to his earthly chief can hardly have been free from ambiguity, and mixed feelings about his Republican colleagues may well be reflected in his portrayal of Satan and the fallen angels. Or to put the point another way, when Milton puts Republican sentiments into Satan's mouth, that is because he wants the reader to have sympathy with the arguments, if not their proponent: Satan should be plausible.

Lucan's Caesar, like Milton's Satan, has aroused admiration, so that we encounter, in some discussions of the *Bellum Civile*, something not unlike a version of the Satanist heresy. Such admiration is not merely the result of a depraved romantic or post-romantic sensibility, but rather reflects a perennial human fascination with heroic glamour and power. Even the sober Welwood thinks that Lucan does Caesar justice despite himself:

His greatness of mind, his intrepid courage, his indefatigable activity, his magnanimity, his generosity, his consummate knowledge in the art of war, and the power and grace of his eloquence are all set forth in the best light upon every proper occasion. He never makes him speak but it's with all the strength of argument and all the flowers of rhetoric.[35]

Certainly both Caesar and Satan are marked by a tremendous energy which is to some extent denied their opponents, a fact that has seduced some critics into regarding them as the 'true' heroes of the poems. In fact the search for a hero has in both cases led to much bad criticism. In the case of the *Bellum Civile* a surprising number of candidates has been fielded over the years, including Pompey, Cato, Caesar, the Senate, the Roman People, Lucan himself.[36] Likewise disagreement about who is really the hero of *Paradise Lost* began early with the Neoclassical critics. Addison shows awareness of the true nature of the problem, but just fails to have the courage of his convictions:

> There is another objection against Milton's fable . . . namely that the hero in the *Paradise Lost* is unsuccessful and by no means a match for his enemies. This gave occasion to Mr Dryden's reflection that the Devil was in reality Milton's hero. I think I have obviated this objection in my first paper. The *Paradise Lost* is an epic, or a narrative poem, and he that looks for an hero in it searches for that which Milton never intended; but if he will needs fix the name of an hero upon any person in it, 'tis certainly the Messiah who is the hero, both in the principal action and in the chief episodes.[37]

In fact Addison could have pointed out that Aristotle, whose 'rules' were so often invoked, was opposed to the idea that real organic unity could be achieved in an epic merely by having a single hero, and that the much admired *Iliad* has in fact not one principal character but two. At all events we have here another important difference between the *Bellum Civile* and *Paradise Lost* on the one hand and on the other Virgil's *Aeneid*, which, like Homer's *Odyssey*, owes part of its unity to the presence throughout of a single hero.

### Style

It is a truth that cannot be too often stated that style should not be considered *in vacuo*: style is not an absolute, it is relative to the job to be done. As we have seen, in the 'epic of ideas' the job to be done is in part an intellectual one. Jonathan Richardson's judgement on Milton's language is well known: 'A reader of Milton must be always upon duty; he is surrounded with sense, it rises in every line, every word is to the purpose; there are no lazy intervals; all has been considered and demands and merits observation.'[38] The *Bellum Civile* too makes heavy demands on the reader. Both poets make extensive use of puns, paradoxes, word plays, pointed collocations of words. In each case the style helps to create that tremendous 'argumentative drive' which Carey has noted as 'a factor which activates the whole framework of *Paradise Lost*'.[39] Phrases like 'darkness visible', 'this windy sea of land', 'the fiend / Saw undelighted all delight', 'kindly rupture', 'stupidly good' can be related to such Horatian oxymorons as 'lene tormentum', 'gentle torture' or 'splendide mendax', 'magnificently false' (I. 63; III. 440; IV. 285–6; VII. 419; IX. 465; Horace *Odes* III. 11. 35; 21. 13). It was Lucan, however, who most clearly demonstrated the effectiveness of such stylistic devices in epic (as we have seen, Virgil does not often write in this way). Of course this element in Milton's style is not due to one model alone. For example the conceited manner of Metaphysical verse is in some ways analogous, as is the use of word play by various Italian poets whom Milton admired.[40] The clever Ovid, with his fondness for wit out of season, is to a degree the father of the pointed style of the Silver Age. Nevertheless the *Bellum Civile* is the most extreme example of this kind of writing in antiquity; moreover, unlike Ovid but like Milton, Lucan uses it in a work that is sombre and profound, not light-hearted and humorous.

It will be helpful to give a few instances of 'pointed' writing of various kinds in the *Bellum Civile*. A typical example occurs near the beginning of the poem. Of the first triumvirate, the political compact between Caesar, Pompey and Crassus, Lucan writes (I. 84–6):

> tu causa malorum
> facta tribus dominis communis, Roma, nec umquam
> in turbam missi feralia foedera regni.

> (you, Rome, are the cause of woe, made common to three masters, and the fatal compact of power never before sent among a crowd)

'In turbam' (among a crowd) applied to three men is a touch of wit. One might say that for Lucan two consuls are company, three triumvirs a crowd.[41] Often Lucan's verbal paradoxes draw attention to the paradoxical nature of the events. For example, when Caesar's lieutenant Curio is defeated by the Moors in Africa, his troops are so closely packed that the dead bodies cannot fall to the ground (IV. 787): 'compressum turba stetit omne cadaver' (pressed by the numbers every corpse stood upright). 'Cadaver' (corpse) is connected etymologically with 'cado' (I fall), so that the abnormal situation is verbally indicated by the piquant notion of something that falls standing. Three further examples of this style of writing all come from the sixth book. In 513 Lucan tells us how the witch Erictho was able 'to listen to the assemblies of the silent dead': 'coetus audire silentum'. 'Silentes' is regularly used to mean no more than 'the dead', but Lucan glances at its literal meaning, 'the silent'. The idea of 'hearing the silent' is characteristically ingenious. Later (640–1) we learn of the cave which 'grim Erictho had damned to witness her sacred rites': 'quem tristis Erictho / damnarat sacris'. There is a deliberate clash here between the verb 'damnare' ('to doom') and the noun 'sacra' (literally 'sacred rites' and hence any rites). Again the witch talks about Hades 'hearing her magic herbs': 'licet has exaudiat herbas' (715). To translate 'exaudire' as 'obey' glosses over the tension in the words: strictly speaking one cannot 'hear' herbs, only spells, but Lucan would be rightly hurt by one editor's uncomprehending comment, 'an absurd collocation'.[42]

Milton too required a style that appealed to the mind, forcing the reader to think, as well as to the emotions. He too frequently exploits the tensions obtainable by pointed collocations of words, as Ricks has shown at length. For example the splendidly ponderous pun in the lines describing the bridge-building activities of Sin and Death may not be to the taste of some of Milton's modern critics, but would have undoubtedly delighted Lucan (X. 312–15):

> Now had they brought the work by wondrous art
> Pontifical, a ridge of pendent rock
> Over the vexed abyss, following the track
> Of Satan . . .

Such writing, it must be insisted, is not confined to the devil and his works, nor should we regard as deliberately 'bad' puns such Satanic plays as 'build their ruin' (Landor's sally is well known: 'the first overt crime of the refractory angels was *punning*'[43]). For Satan shares this fondness for verbal wit with both his creators, human and divine. For example in XI. 28 the Son makes a translingual pun in which 'manuring' gestures towards the Latin word for hand, *manus* (26–30):

Fruits of more pleasing savour from thy seed
Sown with contrition in his heart than those
Which his own hand manuring all the trees
Of Paradise could have produced, ere fallen
From innocence.

Hands are of considerable emblematic significance in *Paradise Lost*
— appropriately and touchingly so in view of Milton's blindness —
but the Son's verbal dexterity at this point might still be felt tasteless
by austere judges.[44] Addison, who claims that Milton generally
avoids the stylistic faults of Ovid and Lucan, has to concede that
Milton's 'sentiments' are sometimes 'too much pointed', and
occasionally 'degenerate even into puns'; he instances 'that small
infantry / Warred on by cranes' (I. 575–6).[45] Some have denied that
Milton is punning here, but at the cost of suggesting that the poet
was nodding. It is better to grant Milton's alertness to verbal
meaning, and robust unwillingness to conform to the blander
aspects of neoclassical taste. Addison also notes Milton's fondness
for verbal jingles like 'beseeching or besieging' (V. 869).

It is interesting to observe in this respect how both Milton and
Lucan suffered from the attentions of Bentley, who, as we have
seen, had a brilliant but somewhat prosaic mind. His 'emendations'
of *Paradise Lost* are to an extent an attempt to remove some of the
'faults' that offended classic taste in Milton's 'Babylonish dialect'.
One of the most valuable features of Ricks's book is the way that he
shows how the twentieth-century battles about Milton's style had to
a large extent already been fought in the eighteenth. Housman, in
the preface to his edition of the *Bellum Civile*, makes the following
observations on Bentley's work on the text of Lucan:

> The characteristic which Napoleon so much admired in Turenne,
> that he grew bolder as he grew older, was not for Bentley a
> fortunate endowment. His judgment ripened early and reached
> perfection before he was forty: from that time onward the vices
> of his temper began to invade his intellect, and confidence
> usurped the place of consideration . . . by the time he came to
> Lucan he had acquired the worst habits of deity.[46]

One revealing example of this over-confidence concerns another
passage from the sixth book. Erictho is described as being 'weighed
down by pallor': 'pallore gravatur' (517). The metaphor is a striking

217

one in Latin without exact parallel. Bentley proposed emending 'pallore' into the more commonplace 'squalore' ('filth'), commenting 'is there any weight in pallor?' This is, of course, precisely the point: there is a deliberate tension between the noun and the verb. Bentley's procedure here and in many of the emendations of *Paradise Lost* discussed by Ricks is strikingly similar. In both cases he should at least be given the credit of having read the text attentively. With both poets 'a reader must be always upon duty'.

Particularly close to Lucan in spirit and style is Milton's account of the War in Heaven. This is full of passages in which the poet pulls out all the stops, and which have been censured as bombastic or even absurd. The War in Heaven is an obvious target for those who regard Milton's 'grand style' as mere pomposity. Its grandeur is in fact a debased grandeur:

> Part hidden veins digged up (nor hath this earth
> Entrails unlike) of mineral and stone,
> Whereof to found their engines and their balls
> Of missive ruin; part incentive reed
> Provide, pernicious with one touch to fire.   (VI. 516–20)

Lines like these, as Fowler points out in his note, are marked by ponderous wit and the sort of inflated diction that the rhetoricians call bomphiologia. Moreover it is not really only simple bombast that repels many readers of the sixth book, but rather the combination of exaggeration and particularity. It is not bombast but something more disturbing when Satan and Belial exchange schoolboy jokes after first firing their cannon. There is no vague 'grandeur' about the moment when the good angels pick up and hurl hills at their opponents, an episode which derives in part from the mountain-throwing in Claudian's *Gigantomachia*. Instead Milton describes with literal-minded precision the appurtenances of the hills (643–6):

> From their foundations loosening to and fro
> They plucked the seated hills with all their load,
> Rocks, waters, woods, and by the shaggy tops
> Up lifting bore them in their hands.

The result in such cases is hardly 'sublimity' as Pope's *bête noire* the critic John Dennis thought, nor is it simple parody, but a kind of virtuoso extremism which is a form of abstraction and which cannot be judged by the criterion of naturalness.[47] One might describe the result as a species of surrealism. This extremism can be interesting for its own sake (and to that extent is likely to remain a minority taste), but it should be noticed that there is a kind of decorum at work as well. As usual Milton is adapting his style to suit his subject-matter. The unusual stylistic inflation of the War in Heaven is a reflection of the sheer enormity of rebellion against God. In the brilliant passage in which Satan first fires his newly invented cannon (571ff), the incongruous juxtaposition of low language — 'belched', 'entrails', 'glut' and so on — with deliberately inflated diction like 'with hideous orifice' 'portending hollow truce', 'deep-throated engines' is purposely grotesque, mirroring the grotesqueness of Satan's attempt to overthrow God. The War in Heaven is thus part of the process by which the brightest of the angels is gradually stripped of his glamour. One of the remarkable features of the style of *Paradise Lost* is its flexibility; it is not Milton but his critics who want to turn it into a blunt instrument.

Such stylistic extremism is notoriously characteristic of the *Bellum Civile*. A particularly striking example is the description of the storm which prevents Caesar from crossing the Adriatic in Amyclas' boat. Here Lucan pretends to take completely seriously what to other poets had been merely tropes. His treatment of the 'battle of the winds' (conventional in epic storms), in which the four winds struggle for the possession of the sea, is typical. The reader is wittily shown what the necessary consequences would be if such a battle really took place in nature (V. 649, May):

> the barque upright maintains
> Her course, supported by all winds.

The contrary winds simply neutralise each other. No less extreme is Lucan's account of the sea battle at Massilia (III. 509ff). 'The episode of the siege of Massalia,' writes Heitland, 'is one mass of absurd hyperbole: it is meant to be very impressive and grand, but its effect is grotesque and unreal.'[48] *De gustibus non est disputandum*, but it is important to understand exactly what Lucan is doing and why he is doing it. In the description paradoxes abound. Some of these are merely verbal tricks, although they help to enliven the poetic texture. For example the phrase 'sanguis / emicuit lentus' (638–9) is a paradoxical way of saying 'the blood trickled out', since the literal meaning of 'emicare' ('to appear quickly') is contradicted by the adjective 'lentus' ('slow'). More commonly the situations themselves breed paradox. A land battle is fought on the sea (566); it is not the enemy who break up the ships, but rather their own crews in search of weapons (671ff); fire puts out water (680ff). Lucan also lays stress on the horror and abnormality of the fighting. The words 'multaque ponto / praebuit ille dies varii miracula fati' (633–4), 'that day provided many strange forms of varied deaths on the sea', introduce a virtuoso series of grotesque and bizarre deaths. As with Milton's War in Heaven this display of stylistic fireworks is no doubt meant to be enjoyed (if that is the right word) to some extent for its own sake, but we also need to remember Lucan's attitude to his subject. The Civil War to him is something unnatural and monstrous. It has its origin in the superhuman wickedness of Caesar, and leads to the disastrous overthrow of political liberty. It produces every form of bizarre and perverted behaviour. Style then reflects situation. As the war involves the collapse of all moral restraints, so Lucan breaks all stylistic bounds. So decorum is maintained.

Addison censured the use by Milton of 'technical words' which he thought unpoetic.[49] The diction of *Paradise Lost* provides another link with Lucan, who frequently employs technical terms in astronomical passages (e.g. IX. 528ff), and uses certain unpoetic words. Virgil had already pointed the way. It has been shown that the language of the *Aeneid* is a combination of poetic diction (including archaisms and Grecisms), neutral words — that is words that were used in a variety of types of writing — and specifically prosaic or colloquial words, for example the coarse 'praegnas' (pregnant) at VII. 320, the colloquial 'heus' (hi!) at I. 321, or the movingly diminutive 'parvulus' (tiny) at IV. 328.[50] Lucan, however, goes further along the road. For example the ordinary Latin prose word for sword is *gladius*, which is normally replaced in high-flown epic contexts by the poetical *ensis*. Virgil uses *gladius* on five occasions, *ensis* on 64; the statistics for Lucan's usage are very different, *ensis* 54, *gladius* 45. *Cadaver* (corpse) is another prosaic word favoured by Lucan (where *corpus* is normal in epic). Style is not to be allowed to cloak the harsh realities of civil war. Milton too is not averse to such directness. On one occasion he even makes God speak thus of Sin and Death (X. 629–36):

And know not that I called and drew them thither

My hell-hounds, to lick up the draff and filth
Which man's polluting sin with taint hath shed
On what was pure, till crammed and gorged, nigh burst
With sucked and glutted offal, at one sling
Of thy victorious arm, well-pleasing Son,
Both Sin and Death and yawning grave at last
Through chaos hurled obstruct the mouth of hell.

Other low words, or semi-technical terms that might not have been expected to find their way into an epic include: 'scurf', 'spade and pickaxe', 'cast a rampart', 'rifled', 'sound-board', 'every band of squared regiment' (all in I. 670ff) and 'proboscis' (IV. 347). Elsewhere Milton can shatter his own carefully constructed decorum, as when he superbly replaces the grand and Latinate 'serpent', with which the poem has familiarised us, with the ignobly monosyllabic 'snake' (a word not in itself unpoetic, but made to sound shocking) in 'So glistered the dire snake' (IX. 643).

### Conclusion

With Homer, Virgil and Ovid Milton was consorting with his peers. Lucan, even if his present reputation is unduly depressed, is not in the same class. One of the clearest instances of an allusion to the *Bellum Civile* in *Paradise Lost* shows something of the obvious difference between a good poet and a great one. In *Paradise Lost* X Satan, his mission successfully completed, returns to Hell to announce his success, but, before he can enjoy the fruits of his triumph, he and the other fallen angels are changed into snakes and forced to eat bitter ashes (410ff). *Bellum Civile* IX contains the *locus classicus* for snakes in Latin literature. After the defeat at Pharsalus Cato, who commands the senatorial forces in Africa, marches his men through the Sahara, and, as the last of a series of trials, they are attacked by a host of venomous serpents (607ff), an episode much admired by Dante, and also by Shelley who alludes to it more than once, most effectively in some lines from *Prometheus Unbound* (III. i. 39–41):

all my being,
Like him whom the Numidian seps did thaw
Into a dew with poison, is dissolved.

Milton's list of snakes comes from Lucan (among other sources):[51]

dreadful was the din
Of hissing through the hall, thick swarming now
With complicated monsters head and tail,
Scorpion and asp and amphisbaena dire,
Cerastes horned, hydrus and ellops drear,
And dipsas (not so thick swarmed once the soil
Bedropped with blood of Gorgon, or the isle
Ophiusa).   (X. 521–8)

Like Lucan he uses *s* sounds to evoke the hissing of the snakes, although he nowhere attempts to rival the virtuosity of such lines as

    stabant in margine siccae
aspides, in mediis sitiebant dipsades undis.   (IX. 609–10)

(Dry asps stood on the edge, dipsades thirsted in the midst of the waters.)


Here the word-play 'sitiebant dipsades' (from *dipsāo* the Greek word for 'I thirst') is the sort of stylistic trick that, as we have seen, Lucan (like Milton) loves.

The whole episode in *Paradise Lost* X, for all the tremendous actuality of the description, has, of course, allegorical significance. Lucan's snakes too can be seen as part of an extended allegory.[52] Lucan's account of Cato's desert march owes little to the historical tradition. According to Plutarch, for example, Cato made a journey of a week *(Life of Cato the Younger* 56), whereas in Robert Graves's words 'Lucan sends him on a two months' march for thousands of miles in a wide semi-circle through the waterless Sahara; meanwhile the troops battle day and night, apparently without any food but sand, against fantastically unzoological serpents.'[53] In fact Lucan uses the incident to develop his own Stoic ideas. In his hands the desert march becomes a test of virtue, a Stoic obstacle race. Its allegorical significance is made clear in the initial speech of Cato. 'Durum iter ad leges,' he tells his men, 'ours is a hard way to legality' (385). They must prepare their minds 'ad magnum virtutis opus summosque labores', 'for a mighty exercise of virtue and utmost hardships' (381). For the moral sluggard there is always an easier way (390–4, May):

Let only those
My followers be whom dangers do invite,
Who think it brave and Roman in my fight
To endure the worst of ills. He that would have
A surety for his safety and fain save
His loved life, let him be gone from me,
And find an easier way to slavery.

Stoics believed that adversity was a necessary test of a man's virtue. In Cato's words 'gaudet patientia duris', 'endurance rejoices in hardship' (403). Cato, the Stoic sage, guides his men through a series of trials (storms by sea and land, thirst, heat and deadly snakes) in which they prove themselves the true possessors of spiritual freedom.

Both the episodes under consideration, the metamorphosis of Satan and the fallen angels into snakes and the snakes' attack on Cato's army in the desert, combine an overwhelming sense of immediacy with an underlying allegorical significance. There is, however, this important difference. Lucan makes no attempt to harmonise his local rhetorical effects, in particular the virtuoso descriptions of the various deaths by snake bite that fascinated Shelley, with his overall conceptual scheme. In Milton, on the other hand, the surface meaning coheres superbly with the allegorical framework, and the imagery has more than local significance. Satan, first described as 'the infernal serpent' (I. 34), takes the form of a snake to tempt Eve. His undignified exit from the poem is thus magnificently apt: his true nature is laid bare.

The deficiencies of the *Bellum Civile* and the fact that it was not quite as authoritative an epic model as the *Iliad* and *Aeneid* may help to explain why there are relatively few indisputable echoes of Lucan in *Paradise Lost*, although there are enough to show Milton's easy familiarity with the poem. It is worth remembering that *Samson Agonistes* contains few *direct* borrowings from the Greek tragedians, and yet conveys the essential manner and style of Greek tragedy, far better indeed than most translations. It is precisely in manner and to a lesser extent in style that *Paradise Lost* resembles the *Bellum Civile*. The similarities between the two poems that I have been describing would seem to me to suggest direct influence. At any rate both poets faced similar difficulties and found analogous solutions for some of them. During antiquity and in the Renaissance, epic was widely regarded as the 'highest' poetic genre.

The problem, at least for serious poets, was how to write epic, a 'naive' narrative form, in a sophisticated age. The 'epic of ideas' was a natural late development, a development at once post-classical and, in a sense, anti-classical. The classical epic form was retained (as it was not, for example, by Spenser), but personalised and made a vehicle for the explicit expression of, in Lucan's case, Stoic ideas and, in Milton's, Christian ones. Further, both the *Bellum Civile* and *Paradise Lost* could be regarded as much as anti-epics as epics. Lucan parodies Virgilian episodes and polemicises against Virgil in his main theme. Thus, while Virgil praises Augustus as Rome's second founder and restorer of the Golden Age, Lucan castigates the Caesars as the subverters of political liberty and Rome's true greatness. In *Paradise Lost* Milton attacks the traditional subject-matter of epic. He claims to find epic values morally reprehensible and their literary expression, to use his own word, 'tedious' (IX. 30). Both Lucan and Milton make sophisticated 'modernist' use of the tired epic machinery. In *Paradise Lost* episodes like the War in Heaven show how the poet is no longer prepared to use conventional epic ingredients, in particular the fights (which Spenser had still been able to take seriously) in the old way. The heroic endeavours of Satan must be seen to be a mere sham when compared with 'the better fortitude Of patience and heroic martyrdom' (IX. 31–2). Lucan, struck down by Nero in his twenties, was too young and inexperienced, and perhaps insufficiently gifted, to make a complete success of his brave and exciting experiment. But in some important ways he had prepared the ground for a greater talent. Moreover, in following the anti-epic elements in the *Bellum Civile* to their conclusion, Milton took the form to a point from which further developments were difficult if not impossible. In the words of T.J.B. Spencer, 'Never was the death of an art form celebrated with such a magnanimous ceremony, splendid in ashes and pompous in the grave. The death of tragedy was a mere decline into a whine and a whisper. But the death of epic was, in Milton's hands, a glorious and perfectly staged suicide.'[54]

## Notes

1. For the politics of the poem see my article 'The Politician Lucan', *Greece and Rome*, vol. 31 (1984), pp. 64–79.
2. 'The Life of Rowe' in Samuel Johnson, *Lives of the English Poets*, ed. G.B. Hill (3 vols, Clarendon Press, Oxford, 1905), vol. 2, p. 77.
3. For a useful survey see O.A.W. Dilke, 'Lucan and English Literature', in D.R. Dudley (ed.), *Neronians and Flavians: Silver Latin I* (Routledge & Kegan Paul, London and Boston, 1972), pp. 83–112.
4. *Horace Walpole's Correspondence*, ed. W.S. Lewis (39 vols, Oxford University Press and Yale University Press, London and New Haven, 1937–74), vol. 16 (1952), pp. 22–3.
5. John Dryden, *Of Dramatic Poesy and Other Critical Essays*, ed. George Watson (2 vols, Dent, London and New York, 1962), vol. 1, pp. 95, 201; vol. 2, pp. 22, 82, 118–19, 204.
6. J.E. Spingarn (ed.), *Critical Essays of the Seventeenth Century* (3 vols, Clarendon Press, Oxford, 1908–9), vol. 3, pp. 294, 296–7.
7. *Lucan: Pharsalia* (with the subtitle *Dramatic Episodes of the Civil Wars*) trs. Robert Graves (Penguin books, Harmondsworth, 1956), Introduction, pp. 23–4.
8. See Anthony LaBranche, 'Drayton's *The Barons Warres* and the Rhetoric of Historical Poetry', *Journal of English and Germanic Philology*, vol. 62 (1963), pp. 82–95. For Daniel see George M. Logan, 'Daniel's *Civil Wars* and Lucan's *Pharsalia*', *Studies in English Literature*, vol. 11 (1971), pp. 53–68.
9. Ben Jonson, *The Poems, the Prose Works*, ed. C.H. Herford and Percy and Evelyn Simpson (Clarendon Press, Oxford, 1947), p. 395; cf. 'Conversations with William Drummond of Hawthorden' in *Ben Jonson: The Complete Poems*, ed. George Parfitt (Penguin Books, Harmondsworth, 1975), p. 478.
10. A.L. Rowse, *Christopher Marlowe: A Biography* (Macmillan, London, 1964), p. 42.
11. *Aubrey's Brief Lives*, ed. Andrew Clark (2 vols, Clarendon Press, Oxford, 1898), vol. 2, p. 56.
12. See Blair Worden, 'Classical Republicanism and the Puritan Revolution' in *History and Imagination: Essays in Honour of H.R. Trevor Roper*, ed. Hugh Lloyd-Jones, Valerie Pearl and Blair Worden (Duckworth, London, 1981), pp. 182–200.
13. *Abraham Cowley: The Civil War*, ed. Allan Pritchard (University of Toronto Press, 1973). My brief remarks owe much to the Introduction, especially pp. 40ff. To his list of parallels add *PL* I. 181ff which recalls *BC* I. 231ff.
14. All quotations are from the third edition corrected (London, 1635).
15. See R.H. Syfret, 'Marvell's Horatian Ode', *Review of English Studies*, n.s., vol. 12 (1961), pp. 160–72, especially 171–2.
16. See W.A. Camps, *An Introduction to Virgil's Aeneid* (Oxford University Press, London, 1969), p. 110.
17. See E.M. Sanford, 'Lucan and his Roman Critics', *Classical Philology*, vol. 26 (1931), pp. 233–57.
18. Petronius' own attitude is disputed: see J.P. Sullivan, *The Satyricon of Petronius* (Faber & Faber, London, 1968), pp. 165ff; P.G. Walsh, *The Roman Novel* (Cambridge University Press, 1970), pp. 48ff.
19. *Sir William Davenant's Gondibert*, ed. David F. Gladish (Clarendon Press, Oxford, 1971), p. 5. For the controversy about Lucan see Heinz-Dieter Leidig, *Das Historiengedicht in der englischen Literaturtheorie: Die Rezeption von Lucans Pharsalia von der Renaissance bis zum Ausgang des achtzehnten Jahrhundert* (Herbert Lang, Bern; Peter Lang, Frankfurt, 1975).

20. See B. Marti, 'The Meaning of the *Pharsalia*', *American Journal of Philology*, vol. 66 (1945), pp. 352–76 (p. 354).

21. See M.P.O. Morford, *The Poet Lucan: Studies in Rhetorical Epic* (Basil Blackwell, Oxford, 1967), pp. 37ff.

22. 'The Life of Rowe' in Johnson, *Lives of the English Poets*, ed. Hill, vol. 2, p. 77.

23. James Welwood, Preface to Nicolas Rowe, *Lucan's Pharsalia Translated into English Verse* (London, 1720), pp. xv–xvi.

24. See my article 'Lucan's Hercules: Padding or Paradigm? A Note on *De Bello Civili* 4. 589–660', *Symbolae Osloenses*, vol. 56 (1981), pp. 71–80.

25. It would be wrong to exaggerate the anonymity of ancient epic; see, for example, Virgil's promise to Nisus and Euryalus (*Aen.* IX. 446–9). It is simply a matter of degree. For a useful discussion, but without mention of Lucan, see Francis C. Blessington, *Paradise Lost and the Classical Epic*, (Routledge & Kegan Paul, Boston and London, 1979), pp. 90ff.

26. 'The Life of Milton' in Johnson, *Lives of the English Poets*, ed. Hill, vol. 1, p. 175.

27. Louis L. Martz, *The Paradise Within: Studies in Vaughan, Traherne and Milton* (Yale University Press, New Haven and London, 1964), p. 106.

28. A.J.A. Waldock, *Paradise Lost and its Critics* (Cambridge University Press, 1947), p. 83.

29. Martz, *The Paradise Within*, p. 107.

30. Addison, 'Notes upon the Twelve Books of Paradise Lost' (*The Spectator*, 1712): in John T. Shawcross (ed.), *Milton: The Critical Heritage* (Routledge & Kegan Paul, London, 1970), p. 167, and Donald F. Bond (ed.), *The Spectator* (5 vols, Clarendon Press, Oxford, 1965), vol. 3, pp. 60–1.

31. W.E. Heitland, Introduction to C.E. Haskins's edition of Lucan (George Bell & Sons, London, 1887), p. lxxi.

32. Welwood, Preface to Rowe, p. xxviii.

33. My remarks on Lucan's characterisation owe much to Marti, 'The Meaning of the *Pharsalia*', pp. 358ff (Cato); 361ff (Caesar). See also Frederick M. Ahl, *Lucan: An Introduction* (Cornell University Press, Ithaca and London, 1976), chs 5–7.

34. *Journal of the History of Ideas*, vol. 18 (1957), pp. 221–32. The quotations are from p. 231. For the journey see Claes Schaar, *The Full Voic'd Quire Below: Vertical Context Systems in Paradise Lost*, Lund Studies in English 60 (Gleerup, Lund, 1982), pp. 233–51.

35. Welwood, Preface to Rowe, p. xx.

36. See Marti, 'The Meaning of the *Pharsalia*', pp. 352–4.

37. Addison, 'Notes': in Shawcross, (ed.), *Milton*, p. 166, and Bond (ed.), *Spectator*, vol. 3, p. 59.

38. *Explanatory Notes and Remarks on Milton's Paradise Lost* (London, 1734; repr. Garland, New York, 1970), p. cxliv.

39. John Carey, *Milton*, Literature in Perspective Series (Evans Brothers, London, 1969), p. 121.

40. See F.T. Prince, *The Italian Element in Milton's Verse* (Clarendon Press, Oxford, 1954), pp. 123ff.

41. For this and other examples of conscious paradox see my article 'Paradox, Hyperbole and Literary Novelty in Lucan's *De Bello Civili*', *Bulletin of the Institute of Classical Studies*, vol. 23 (1976), pp. 45–54.

42. C.M. Francken in his edition (2 vols, A.W. Sijthoff, Leiden, 1896–7), note *ad loc*.

43. Quoted by Fowler, note on *PL* VI. 566 in John Carey and Alastair Fowler (eds), *The Poems of John Milton* (Longman, London, 1968).

44. See M. Di Cesare in R.D. Emma and J.T. Shawcross (eds), *Language and Style in Milton: A Symposium in Honor of the Tercentenary of Paradise Lost*

(Frederick Ungar Publishing Co., New York, 1967), pp. 20–3.

45. Addison, 'Notes': in Shawcross (ed.), *Milton*, pp. 168–9, and Bond (ed.), *Spectator*, vol. 3, pp. 61–3 (cf. Shawcross, pp. 156–7; Bond, vol. 2, p. 588).

46. A.E. Housman, Preface to his edition of Lucan (Basil Blackwell, Oxford, 1926), p. xxxii.

47. See John T. Shawcross (ed.), *Milton: The Critical Heritage*, (Routledge & Kegan Paul, London, 1970), pp. 237ff; Carey, *Milton*, p. 118.

48. Heitland, Introduction to Haskins's edition, p. lxxvii.

49. Addison, 'Notes': in Shawcross (ed.), *Milton*, p. 169; and Bond (ed.), *Spectator*, vol. 3, p. 63.

50. See R.O.A.M. Lyne, 'Diction and Poetry in Vergil's *Aeneid*', *Atti del convegno mondiale scientifico di studi su Vergilio*, Mantua, Rome, Naples, 1981 (a cura dell' Accademia Nazionale Virgiliana, Milan, 1984), pp. 64–88. For Lucan's diction see also R. Mayer, *Lucan Civil War VIII* (Aris & Phillips, Warminster, 1981), pp. 12–14. For levels of style in Milton see A.J. Gilbert, *Literary Language from Chaucer to Johnson* (Macmillan, London and Basingstoke, 1979), ch. 4; however, Gilbert relies too heavily on the traditional three styles of classical rhetoric — plain, middle and high — and adduces insufficient supporting evidence for the stylistic levels of words and phrases in Milton.

51. For the sources and some analogues see Fowler's note and Schaar, *Full Voic'd Quire*, pp. 106–12. Dante *Inferno* XXV, partly inspired by Lucan as lines 94–6 show, was obviously in Milton's mind. That Lucan was a direct source for Milton's snakes is shown by the reference to the story that snakes were formed from the blood of the Medusa (from *BC*. IX. 619ff).

52. See Ahl, *Lucan*, p. 261; M.P.O. Morford, 'The Purpose of Lucan's Ninth Book', *Latomus*, vol. 26 (1967), pp. 123–9.

53. Graves, *Lucan: Pharsalia*, Introduction, p. 22.

54. T.J.B. Spencer in C.A. Patrides (ed.), *Approaches to Paradise Lost*, The York Centenary Lectures (Edward Arnold, London, 1968), p. 98.

# SELECT BIBLIOGRAPHY
## (With Suggestions for Further Reading)

Addison, Joseph 'Notes Upon the Twelve Books of Paradise Lost', *The Spectator*, 1712. References are to John T. Shawcross (ed.), *Milton: The Critical Heritage* (Routledge & Kegan Paul, London, 1970) and Donald F. Bond (ed.), *The Spectator* (5 vols, Clarendon Press, Oxford, 1965).

Allen, Don Cameron *Mysteriously Meant: The Rediscovery of Pagan Symbolism and Allegorical Interpretation in the Renaissance* (Johns Hopkins University Press, Baltimore and London, 1970).

Blessington, Francis C. *Paradise Lost and the Classical Epic* (Routledge & Kegan Paul, Boston and London, 1979).

Bowra, C.M. *From Virgil to Milton* (Macmillan and St Martin's Press, London and New York, 1945).

Bush, Douglas 'Notes on Milton's Classical Mythology', *Studies in Philology*, vol. 28 (1931), pp. 259–72.

——*Mythology and the Renaissance Tradition in English Poetry* (University of Minnesota Press and Oxford University Press, Minneapolis and London, 1932); ch. 14 on Milton.

——*Paradise Lost in Our Time: Some Comments* (Peter Smith, Gloucester, Mass., 1957), ch. 4.

——(ed.) 'The Latin and Greek Poems' in vol. 1 of *A Variorum Commentary on the Poems of John Milton* (Columbia University Press, New York, 1970).

Carey, John *Milton*, Literature in Perspective Series (Evans Brothers, London, 1969).

Clark, Donald Lemen *John Milton at St Paul's School: A Study of Ancient Rhetoric in English Renaissance Education* (Columbia University Press, New York, 1948).

Clarke, Howard *Homer's Readers: A Historical Introduction to the Iliad and the Odyssey* (Associated University Presses, London and Toronto, 1981).

Collett, J.H. 'Milton's Use of Classical Mythology in *Paradise Lost*', *PMLA*, vol. 85 (1970), pp. 88–96.

*Columbia Milton = The Works of John Milton*, ed. Frank Allen Patterson *et al.* (18 vols and 2 vols index, Columbia University Press, New York, 1931–40).

Commager, Steele (ed.), *Virgil: A Collection of Critical Essays*, Twentieth Century Views Series, (Prentice-Hall, Englewood Cliffs, N.J., 1966).

Emma, Ronald David and Shawcross, John T. (eds) *Language and Style in Milton: A Symposium in Honor of the Tercentenary of Paradise Lost* (Frederick Ungar Publishing Co., New York, 1967).

Fish, Stanley Eugene *Surprised by Sin: The Reader in Paradise Lost* (Macmillan, London and New York, 1967).

Fletcher, Harris Francis *The Intellectual Development of John Milton* (2 vols, University of Illinois Press, Urbana, 1956–61).

Fowler, Alastair *Paradise Lost* in *The Poems of John Milton*, ed. John Carey and Alastair Fowler (Longman, London, 1968).

Freeman, James A. *Milton and the Martial Muse: Paradise Lost and European Traditions of War* (Princeton University Press, 1980).

Frye, Roland Mushat *Milton's Imagery and the Visual Arts: Iconographic Tradition in the Epic Poems* (Princeton University Press, 1978).

# Select Bibliography

Greene, Thomas *The Descent from Heaven: A Study in Epic Continuity* (Yale University Press, New Haven and London, 1963); ch. 12 on Milton.

Griffin, Jasper *Homer on Life and Death* (Clarendon Press, Oxford, 1980).

———*Homer* Past Masters Series (Oxford University Press, Oxford, Toronto, Melbourne, 1980).

Harding, Davis P. 'Milton and the Renaissance Ovid', *Illinois Studies in Language and Literature*, vol. 30 (1946).

———*The Club of Hercules: Studies in the Classical Background of Paradise Lost* (University of Illinois Press, Urbana, 1962).

Hunter, William B., Jr (ed.) *A Milton Encyclopedia*, (8 vols, Bucknell University Press and Associated University Presses, Lewisburg and London, 1978–80), including entries on dictionaries, epic, Homer, Horace, humanism, iconography, inspiration, muse(s), myth, Orpheus, Ovid, *Paradise Lost*, Urania, Vida, Virgil, etc.

Johnson, Samuel *Lives of the English Poets*, 1779–81, References are to the edition of G.B. Hill (3 vols, Clarendon Press, Oxford, 1905).

Johnson, W.R. *Darkness Visible: A Study of Vergil's Aeneid* (University of California Press, Berkeley and London, 1976).

Kirk, G.S. *Homer and the Oral Tradition* (Cambridge University Press, 1976).

Lewis, C.S. *A Preface to Paradise Lost* (Oxford University Press, London, Oxford, New York, 1942).

Martz, Louis L. *The Paradise Within: Studies in Vaughan, Traherne, and Milton* (Yale University Press, New Haven and London, 1964).

Martindale, Charles (ed.) *Virgil and his Influence: Bimillennial Studies* (Bristol Classical Press, 1984).

Martindale, Joanna (ed.) *English Humanism: Wyatt to Cowley*, World and Word Series, (Croom Helm, Beckenham, 1985).

Nuttall, A.D. Introduction to *John Milton: The Minor Poems in English*, with notes by Douglas Bush (Macmillan, London, 1972).

Ogilvie, R.M. *Latin and Greek: A History of the Influence of the Classics on English Life from 1600 to 1918* (Routledge & Kegan Paul, London, 1964).

Osgood, Charles Grosvenor *The Classical Mythology of Milton's English Poems*, Yale Studies in English 8 (Henry Holt, New York, 1900).

Prince, F.T. *The Italian Element in Milton's Verse* (Oxford, Clarendon Press, 1954).

Revard, Stella Purce *The War in Heaven: Paradise Lost and the Tradition of Satan's Rebellion* (Cornell University Press, Ithaca and London, 1980).

Ricks, Christopher *Milton's Grand Style* (Oxford University Press, London, Oxford, New York, 1963).

Schaar, Claes *The Full Voic'd Quire Below: Vertical Context Systems in Paradise Lost*, Lund Studies in English 60 (Gleerup, Lund, 1982).

Starnes, Dewitt T. and Talbert, Ernest William *Classical Myth and Legend in Renaissance Dictionaries: A Study of Renaissance Dictionaries in their Relation to the Classical Learning of Contemporary English Writers* (University of North Carolina Press, Chapel Hill, 1955); ch. 8 on Milton.

Wilkinson, L.P. *Ovid Recalled* (Cambridge University Press, 1955).

Willcock, Malcolm M. *A Companion to the Iliad* (Based on the Translation by Richmond Lattimore) (University of Chicago Press, Chicago and London, 1976).

Wittreich, Joseph A., Jr (ed.) *The Romantics on Milton: Formal Essays and Critical Asides* (Case Western Reserve University Press, Cleveland and London, 1970).

# INDEX OF PASSAGES

Note: This index includes the major passages quoted from Milton, Homer, Lucan, Ovid, and Virgil. Other authors are to be found in the general Index.

**Milton, John**

*Paradise Lost*

233

# GENERAL INDEX

# Bristol Classical Paperbacks

*The Satires of Persius,* Cynthia Dessen
*Science, Folklore and Ideology,* G.E.R. Lloyd
*The Stoics,* F.H. Sandbach
*The Story of the Iliad,* E.T. Owen
*Suetonius,* A.Wallace-Hadrill
*Tacitus,* R.H. Martin
*Themes in Roman Satire,* Niall Rudd
*Three Archaic Poets: Archilochus, Alcaeus, Sappho,*
    Ann Pippin Burnett
*Virgil's Epic Technique,* Richard Heinze
*Wild Justice,* Judith Mossman
*Women in Greek Myth,* Mary Lefkowitz
*Xenophon,* J. Anderson

*Bristol Classical Paperbacks on the classical heritage:*

*Johnson's Juvenal,* Niall Rudd
*John Milton and the Transformation of Ancient Epic,*
    Charles Martindale
*Pope's Iliad,* Felicity Rosslyn
*Shakespeare's Plutarch,* T.J.B. Spencer
*To Homer Through Pope,* H.A. Mason